D0172409

SWALLOW THIS

Copyright 2009 by Mark Phillips
All rights reserved. Except for brief passages quoted in newspaper, magazine,
radio, television, or online reviews, no part of this book may be reproduced in
any form or by any means, electronic or mechanical, including photocopying,
recording, or information storage or retrieval system, without
permission in writing from the publisher.

Published in the United States by
20 Sips, LLC
4101 W Eddy St, Suite 200
Chicago, IL 60641

Cover and layout design by 📖 theBookDesigners

Cover photography by Charles Osgood

First Edition

10 9 8 7 6 5 4 3 2 1

Printed in U.S.A.

SWALLOW THIS

The Progressive Approach to Wine

Mark Phillips

AS SEEN ON PUBLIC TELEVISION

CONTENTS

Acknowledgments

THE FOLLOWING ARE PEOPLE that have a special place in my heart. Elizabeth Cox, for instance, I only met once, but during that five minute conversation, she said something that made a huge difference on how this book turned out. On the flip side, others I've known all my life, like my parents and siblings. Because of their support, I was able to pursue my dreams. My family is the best. In fact, my family can take your family.

This book came about because I questioned the wine establishment. My inquisitive, nonconformist spirit was nurtured along by many folks who allowed me to be me. Below are a mix of family, friends and others who made an impact on me, somehow, some way, that kept me moving forward and encouraged me to stick to my guns.

Carl and Margaret Waldschmidt, My great aunt Edith Luecke, Kathy Bowdring and her sister Elizabethm, Barb Mcdermott, Elizabeth Cox, Julie Schmidt, Janet Ricksen, Chasity Mosher, Kelley Donovan, Jeanne Grewe, Suzannah Martin, Natalie Lord, Kate Lord, Kimberley Freeman, Alida Graham, Donna Mcdowell and Eric Waldschmidt.

Last but not least is my best bud, Jon Steimen, The Flower Guy, who will join me on the picnic bench when we're both broke and homeless.

Introduction

IN THE LATE '80S, I was living in Dallas, Texas running a company that I had founded. Kind of a wacky
company; one part of the business was doing shuttle bus
systems and spouse tours for conventions. The spouse
tours were the worst. If I went to Southfork one more
time, I thought I would shoot myself. The other part
was taking care of celebrities and/or folks who were
silly rich. That was certainly the most interesting part:
interacting with David Lee Roth, Cher, Rob Lowe, Elton
John, Diana Ross, the Royal Family of Saudi Arabia, etc.
(Talk about stories; I think I should be writing about
that vs. wine. Maybe next time.)

The business was doing well, so it was time to take it
up a notch. Since many of my clients were headquartered

in the Washington, D.C. area, I moved there to make it easier to make sales/service visits. Once I got there and away from the day-to-day operations, I began to lose interest and felt I should try something else in life. So I flew back to Dallas to sell the company in May, 1990.

Just prior to flying to Dallas, the Mansion at Turtle Creek invited me and a guest to have dinner, on them, for all the business I had sent their way. For those of you not familiar with the Mansion, it is a very nice hotel and restaurant and at that time, probably the most expensive one in Dallas. I had been away from Dallas long enough that I didn't have anyone to accompany me. Luckily, when I arrived in Dallas, I went to a party and met this beautiful gal named Nancy. I asked her to go to dinner with me at the Mansion and she said yes — clearly because it was the nicest and most expensive restaurant in Dallas, not because of me, but no matter; I had a date.

Nancy and I arrived at the restaurant and it was time for a drink. Up until this moment, I had never had wine in my life. Okay, I did have Boone's Farm in grade school on church youth retreats, but that was it. From grade school on, I was a beer-drinking, pool playing, dart throwing kind of guy. Wine? You've gotta be kidding.

However, sitting at this nice restaurant with a beautiful gal, I just didn't think it was right to order a beer. The sommelier came to the table and presented the wine list. I don't recall the guy's name but I think it was

Jacques or Pierre. Either way, he seemed very formal and snobby. But, since I didn't even know what Chardonnay was, I had to rely on his advice to pick a wine.

I decided to get a bottle of white wine first. Jacques (let's call him that for now) pointed at a fairly inexpensive wine. Jacques didn't know that my whole dinner was being paid for....or maybe he did, and didn't want me ordering expensive wines for the sake of the restaurant. I asked Jacques if there was a white wine that was better than the one he had selected, and he picked another one. I asked him the same question, and this went on, back and forth going up the price ladder until I noticed a change in his expression. When he selected this particular wine, his face lit up and I knew this was the one. It was $125 a bottle, which is high these days but was crazy high back in 1990. But hey, I wasn't paying for it.

Jacques brought the wine out and poured it. When I tasted it, I couldn't believe how good it was. I realized I had been missing out on so much just drinking beer. The two of us finished the white and the accompanying appetizers and were feeling good. Nancy was great fun. The food and atmosphere were wonderful. Just perfect.

We needed another bottle, and I thought a red wine was in order. Jacques came over and started low with the suggestion, but back and forth we went again as I watched his expression. On about the fifth suggestion, he got that expression again and a glimmer in his eye. This was the one. It was $250 per bottle!

When he brought it out, he carried it very carefully through the restaurant. Everyone was watching. After opening it, he poured a little bit for both Nancy and me and instructed us to let it breathe for 15 minutes.

When the time was up, I tasted it. At that moment, I think my life changed. The white wine was good, but this red was unbelievable! In fact, it was orgasmic. It was the first time in my life that something other than sex made my body feel so good. Holy cow!

Nancy had quit drinking. (Lightweight.) I could have finished the red on my own, but it was so good I had to share it. I asked Jacques to offer a sample of the wine to diners around me. He said he couldn't do that. The restaurant wasn't that type of place. So I got up myself and walked around to the adjacent tables with the bottle of wine, explaining to each table that this was a fantastic wine and they should try it.

Well, the dinner ended and I'm not even sure if I kissed Nancy goodnight. I was so infatuated with the wine, I lost track of her.

The next day, having sold my company, I flew back to Washington with the idea of starting another company there. In the meantime, I looked for a wine group to join to learn more about this outstanding beverage. But there was really none in existence. A couple of groups had sporadic events, maybe once every month or two, but even then, the folks were older and seemed kind of snobby for me. I thought there must be many people like me who knew little about wine, but wanted to learn.

Being the entrepreneurial type, I decided to start a wine group and learn along with everyone else. In June 1990, I started the Wine Tasting Association (WTA). The mission of WTA was to educate people about wine through tastings, classes, dinners, etc. I know it was kind of crazy to start a wine group knowing nothing about wine, but what better way to learn?

I went on a crash course to learn about wine before I started putting on events. I read every book I could get my hands on. I flew to France and visited the different wine regions. I bought expensive wine to see what it tasted like. I attended wine tastings, and when one wasn't happening, I would taste wine at home. I subscribed to *Wine Spectator* and *The Wine Advocate*. Wine. Wine. Wine.

About a month after I started my crash course, I was invited to attend an Italian wine tasting for the wine trade only, hosted by the Italian Trade Commission (ITC). They flew in a bunch of Italian winemakers and wine writers to Washington to present seminars on Italian wine.

I arrived, checked in and went into the tasting. I had already had my business cards printed, making me the Executive Director of the Wine Tasting Association. I felt so cool.

There was a cute gal across the room; I struck up a conversation with her and whipped out my card. She was impressed. She worked for the PR company running the event. We kind of hit it off, so she invited me

to a dinner that evening hosted by the ITC with a half
dozen or so wine writers and winemakers. This would
be my first interaction with "real" wine people.

We went to a nice restaurant and sat down, and
I thought I could just sit in obscurity and learn from
these experts. Some goofball at the table reasoned that
since we were at a Washington restaurant and I was
the only one at the table from Washington, that I
should order the wine for the table. After all, my date
had told them I was the Executive Director of the
Wine Tasting Association. My card was coming back
to haunt me.

I was screwed. I had only started reading about
wine one month before this, and barely knew that
Chardonnay was a grape. White grape, wasn't it? How
was I going to pick out a wine for these experts?

I was in a state of sheer panic. So many things
were racing through my mind as the sommelier was
presenting me with the wine list. I didn't know the
names of the winemakers at my table. If I did, would
I have to order their wine? Should I even order Italian
wine? How expensive should the bottle be? Should it be
white or red?

The experts were no help. So many French and
Italian wines on the list, none of which I knew anything about, let alone could pronounce.

But then I saw a Chassagne-Montrachet. I had just
read about that wine the day before, but I didn't know how
to pronounce it. Of course, I didn't recognize the producer

and I wasn't sure if the vintage was good, but the hell with it; it was the only one I knew anything about, so I had to go for it. I pointed to it on the list and the waiter left to get the bottle. Luckily the experts were talking amongst themselves, so I didn't have to pronounce it.

Whew! Out of the woods, I thought, but I was wrong. The nightmare was about to begin.

The waiter brought out the bottle and poured the taste into my glass. I tasted it and gave my approval and the rest of the guests were poured.

After tasting the wine again, I realized the wine wasn't right. Not that I would really know, since I had not yet been exposed to a faulty wine. I had never had a Chassagne-Montrachet, so I didn't know what it was supposed to be like. But something inside told me this wine wasn't right.

Although I had panicked when I had to order the wine, I was really in a jam now. If the wine was bad and I had approved it, I would look like an idiot. If the wine wasn't bad and I called the waiter over to say it was, I would be an idiot. The guests had all tasted their wine and hadn't made funny faces or anything, so it must have been okay. But I was convinced the wine wasn't right.

In a moment like this, you have to go with your gut. I knew I might crash and burn, but I went forward. I raised my hand to call the waiter to the table. When he arrived, I said that I didn't think the wine was right. Everyone stopped talking and looked at the waiter. He tasted the wine and then apologized. He said it was indeed bad, and he would bring another bottle.

YES! What a score for me. But wait. Why hadn't the experts picked up on that? I realized at that moment I might have been in an "Emperor has no clothes" moment, and that the waiter had agreed with me just to be polite and not embarrass me in front of the others. Was I really a moron?

He brought a new bottle to the table, and it tasted the same as the first. Oh no! My worst fear was realized. I was a moron. Maybe that was how the wine was supposed to taste.

I had about two seconds to decide what to do. In that period of time, I raced through the options.

1. Could I have gotten two bad bottles in a row? Doubtful. But how could I accept this one when it tasted the same as the first, which I had sent back?

2. The experts hadn't given any indication that the first one was bad, so I probably had made a mistake about sending the first bottle back. I guessed I should minimize my loss, be smart, and just accept this wine. They would all think I was an idiot, but at least it wouldn't have to be said to my face.

But I didn't want to be an idiot. The only hope I had to come out okay was if I sent this second bottle back too, saying that it was bad, and hoping that the third bottle would be good. I was already an imbecile for misjudging the first bottle, so what difference would it make to be an idiot another time over? Of course, I would be sending two perfectly good bottles of $60 wine back if I was wrong. Boy, it would be a gutsy move to send the second one back, a long shot at best; but it was my only chance to redeem myself.

So I went for it and told the waiter that I didn't think this one was good either. The waiter looked at me for about three seconds, telling me with his eyes, "Listen buddy, I let you slide on the first one and you're pushing your luck. I'll bring you one more bottle, you moron, but then I'm going to hang you out to dry if you don't accept it." He brought out the third bottle and everyone waited for my verdict.

Praise Bacchus and all of his descendants! The third bottle was completely different from the first two and tasted great. I approved the wine. The waiter poured the wine for the experts.

A few experts had held on to the first wine and when they had a chance to compare the two, they commented how the first one was truly not good. They all complimented me on my discerning palate, and I just wanted to cry with relief.

One thing that I thought about a few days later was why none of the experts had said anything about the first bottle being bad. Sure, maybe they weren't trying to embarrass me for accepting the first bottle, but I don't think that was it. I have learned since that time that so many people in the wine world, even experts, often can't tell if a bottle of wine is bad.

A few weeks later, I was attending a wine tasting class as a guest just to learn more about wine. I had met

Ron, the teacher, at a trade tasting, so he knew I had just started WTA. The first day of the class he introduced me as the Executive Director of WTA, so the other classmates thought I knew all about wine.

Ron did a good job teaching the sessions, and the final exam was a blind tasting of just one wine. All we had to do was identify the grape variety. There were about 60 people in the class. He poured the wine to everyone, and then started at the front and asked each person for his or her answer. I was about two-thirds of the way from the front.

I thought the wine was a Sauvignon Blanc. Now, I had had only one taste of Sauvignon Blanc in my life at this point, in the first session of this class a couple of weeks before. No one had guessed Sauvignon Blanc by the time it got to me, so I was doubting myself, thinking that if it really were Sauvignon Blanc, someone would have said it. Of course, all eyes were on me as the "expert," so I was quite nervous.

I went with my gut again and said Sauvignon Blanc. Ron congratulated me and didn't bother asking the remaining students what their guesses were. I was so happy I got it right.

Those two experiences, just a few weeks apart and under pressure in my first months of tasting wine, made me think that I was made to be a wine guy — and the journey began.

1

Not Another
Wine Book!

OH BOY! ANOTHER WINE BOOK. Does the world need
another book on wine? No and yes. No, in that
nearly every book that I've seen has the same philo-
sophical approach to wine, which I call the Traditional
Approach. The Approach's origin was in England and
probably because wine, at that time, was a beverage of
the aristocracy, there was an elitist tone to the Approach.
To know and adopt the Traditional Approach set one
apart from the "commoners" who didn't drink wine, or
drank swill. The elite wanted to bond together to enjoy
wine properly, separately, kind of like a private club.

In fact, I think they actually formed a club: The
Club. Oh, it wasn't done consciously. No one started
it. It didn't have a building or membership. It was an

understanding that evolved among wine aficionados, the sophisticates, that there was a proper way to enjoy wine that separated them from the masses. All one had to do to join the Club was to adopt the teachings of the Traditional Approach and drink the wines that were worthy of the elite.

As interest in wine spread to America, the only guides to learn about wine were the books written by the British. Americans read the books, adopted the Traditional Approach and became members of the Club. As the American wine scene grew, it was the Club members in America who authored new books, wrote for the newspapers and taught folks about wine. Club members begat Club members, and that has continued to this day. One approach — the Traditional Approach.

The Traditional Approach is based on two key tenets:

KNOWLEDGE - I love knowledge. In fact, nothing thrills me more than learning new things. But if the information is impractical, I don't see the point. The Traditional Approach puts a heavy emphasis on learning about wine, which would be good if it was practical information that helped you enjoy wine better and buy wine you like. I don't see the practical need to know the composition of the soil in Burgundy or all about the state-run system in Scandinavia (examples of things one needs to know to pass the Master of Wine exam). The Master of Wine and the Master Sommelier certifications are the two biggies for Club members. Of course they were created by the British, based on the Traditional Approach. The tests require the memorization of a massive amount of knowledge, years of study and thousands of dollars. And after one gets a certification, are the certificate holders any better at buying a bottle of good wine than you? No. But they're revered by fellow Club members. because it means they know a lot. And they do know a lot....of useless information.

Since Club members write most wine books, they want to make sure they include as much information as possible. That's why so many books are encyclopedic. Who can read those? Some give lip service to making wine simple by including "Simple" in the title, yet those books run more than 300 pages. What?! How simple could that be? I'm bugged that my book is as long as it is. I wanted to write a two-sentence book. It would have said something like this: "It doesn't make any difference what wine someone else likes. Good wine is one that you like." Done. Now that's simple. What's all the other info for? To make money, I guess. No one is going to buy a two-sentence book.

Club members are consumed with the idea of knowing stuff: soil composition, what kind of oak is used, the yield of the vineyard, etc. They can't help themselves. They've been indoctrinated by their Club member mentors that knowledge is necessary. Knowledge for knowledge's sake. The more the better.

AUTHORITY - When a person seeks to learn something, they seek out an authority. Nothing wrong with that. In wine, the authorities are the many Club members who have adopted the Traditional Approach and have gone on to write books, teach classes, become sommeliers, etc. But one Club member stands out from all the rest: Robert Parker.

Robert Parker is the author of the newsletter *The Wine Advocate*. A lawyer by training, Parker was concerned that the wine reviewers of old might not be completely honest, as many writers also sold wine and that might be a conflict of interest. He started a wine newsletter in the mid '70s, now called *The Wine Advocate*. His big break came when he declared the 1982 vintage of Bordeaux one of the best, while other writers said it wasn't. Over time, most agreed that he was right. Thus he was vaulted to be a dominant voice on wine, and is now the most influential wine critic in the world. He started using the 100-point scale to rate wines that now has become the standard.

A second authority is *Wine Spectator* magazine. Its annual "Top 100 wines of the year" issue sets off a frenzy among Club members to race out and buy them before they're gone. The *Spectator* has a broader reach than *The Wine Advocate*, but it is still not as influential as Parker. He's the man.

Robert Parker doesn't write about many of the specifics of the Traditional Approach like matching wine and food, proper serving temperature, how to taste wine, how to buy wine, etc. He just focuses on tasting, rating and describing wine. His ratings and opinions are revered by Club members and wield great influence in the world of wine. Sure, there are some detractors, but even they would agree that Parker has enormous influence, good or bad.

Parker does deal with three aspects of the Traditional Approach. Because of his influence, everyone has accepted his opinions as gospel. That some guy's opinions can shape the whole world of wine is nuts to me.

I want to be clear here that Parker doesn't say his opinions should be the gospel truth, but Club members take it that way. So I don't blame Parker for being so powerful. Good for him. It's made him rich, and he gets to drink great wine. I *do* disagree with the following three ideas that are ingrained in Club members' minds as a result of his opinions:

1. GOOD WINE IS ABSOLUTE, NOT SUBJECTIVE. A few sources dictate what good wine is, and it's wine rated highly by Robert Parker ... and to a lesser degree, *Wine Spectator*. Oh, many Club members might mouth things like, "Everyone should drink what they like," which seems to be an all inclusive philosophy — but in their mind, only the unsophisticated drink oaky Chardonnay, jug wine, box wine, white Zinfandel, Beaujolais Nouveau and Merlot (remember Miles in the movie *Sideways* stating outside the restaurant that he WILL NOT drink any f******* Merlot).

The Club members follow the ratings like sheep. They rely on them to legitimize their collections. They don't buy wine because *they* like it. They buy it because it's been rated highly. And then they can boast about their collection to other Club members.

Speaking of sheep, I was hired by an insurance company regarding a claim by a homeowner whose basement wine cellar's refrigeration unit malfunctioned. He had to move the wine out of the cellar into a non-temperature controlled part of the basement. He was claiming that because the wine went from 55 degrees in the cellar to 65 degrees in the other part of the basement, that it was ruined. I was called in to give an expert's opinion. The insurance agent and I went to the man's home and I had to smile as we pulled up. Clearly new money. Over-the-top everything. All the toys and ostentation money could buy. The agent told me he was a construction guy who hit it big.

We went inside and met Jerry. Big guy. Arms the size of Popeye and a rough, unrefined demeanor. Gaudy decor. Oh, but he was proud of it. He was rich! And he was equally proud of his wine collection. He took us down to his cellar, a simply-built room in the corner of the basement with an air conditioner in it. No decor, racks or seats. Just a place to store his wine. He was giddy about the wines and started reciting them to me. Mostly Bordeaux and California Cabernet Sauvignon. As he named each one, he stated the rating that was given by Robert Parker. All in the 90s, of course.

I asked him how long he had been drinking wine. He said since he'd hit it big and bought his house in the neighborhood. All of his neighbors drank wine, and he wanted to fit in. He said his collection rivaled any of his neighbors. After talking with him further, it was clear he didn't know a thing about wine. But he knew what it took to impress his neighbors: highly-rated wine.

I can go on and on with similar stories of people not really knowing about wine but buying the highly-rated wines to impress others. One wouldn't think of trying to impress someone with a wine they liked but that wasn't rated. Heaven forbid. People need an authority to validate a wine, and Parker is the top dog.

2. **WINES NEED SPECIAL WINEGLASSES.** Robert Parker said, "The finest glasses for both technical and hedonistic purposes are those made by Riedel. The effect of these glasses on fine wine is profound. I cannot emphasize enough what a difference they make." Wow. What a boost for Riedel. (Of course, Parker hasn't tried the Mark Phillips Wine Glass that I created.) As a result of that endorsement, whatever the folks at Riedel preach is considered indisputable. For instance, Riedel has been able to convince people that it is necessary to use a glass that is specifically designed for the wine. When you're drinking a Chardonnay, you need the proper glass for Chardonnay. A Cabernet, another. A Pinot Noir, another. And so on. Everyone has accepted that to be true despite the stack of evidence to the contrary.

3. THE MORE ADJECTIVES YOU USE TO DESCRIBE A WINE, THE BETTER. The Traditional Approach encourages one to use a whole slew of adjectives to describe wine, and the more adjectives, the better. Other wine raters have probably used more adjectives and more obscure adjectives than Parker, but the fact that he uses a bunch of adjectives solidifies in Club members' minds that describing wine that way is important.

That doesn't seem so bad, does it? I didn't think so either, for a long time.

When I first learned about wine, I was way into the Club. I bought all the different Riedel glasses. I sought out the highly-rated wines. I bought and read every wine book I could get my hands on. I competed in blind tasting competitions. I subscribed to *The Wine Advocate* and *Wine Spectator.* I attended wine dinners. I started judging wine on panels. I was on fire!

The more I learned and got "into" wine, the less I wanted to be around unsophisticated wine drinkers. I didn't want to go to restaurants that didn't have a good wine list, or the right stemware. One day I remember thinking that I didn't even want to be around my old friends any more because they all drank crap. That's what happens to a person when they're in the Club. They get exclusionary. And that's not me. So that got me thinking about my view of wine.

When I started thinking about it, I began to notice things I didn't see before. It helped that I ran a wine group to educate people about wine. I hired wine experts to come and teach the classes, and I heard each one of them speak. If you have heard one or two wine experts speak, you probably didn't pick up on the common phrases they use. But I heard so many speak that it became clear that each of them was using the same phrases and illustrations as the others. I recognized that they were pulling stuff from the books I had read. These experts were just regurgitating concepts from books — word for word, in some cases.

In addition, there was a huge disconnect between the teachers and the students. The teachers were talking in their sophisticated, elitist Club way ... and the students complained.

I started looking at the Traditional Approach with a more critical eye and I noticed a lot of things didn't add up. I did some research into the process of rating wine, the differences between wine glasses, the advice being given on matching wine and food, how books were written, and so much more. The further I got in my research, the more it seemed the Traditional Approach wasn't the way to go. In fact, I thought a lot of what the Approach espoused was wrong.

It didn't seem right that some authority should dictate what I could and could not do and then criticize me if I didn't do it their way. I didn't want to feel intimidated because I didn't know enough, chose the wrong wine to pair with a dish, used an improper wine glass or didn't drink the right wines. The focus on knowledge and authority didn't seem to mesh with how I felt when I drank wine: friendly and social. One of my favorite quotes is, "With every glass of wine, I double the number of friends I have in the room." Wine was about a carefree attitude, sharing and inclusion. The Traditional Approach, and Club members, seemed to be about rules, formality and the exclusion of unsophisticated people and wines.

I looked for an alternative approach, but I couldn't find one. So I went out on my own. I started over. I "resigned" from the Club. I had to re-teach myself about wine — to learn about wine by doing it myself, not just from listening to Club members. And I had to do it in a radical way.

The first thing I did was to drink white Zinfandel. Boy, that got my attention. Then I bought every box and jug wine and compared them to more expensive wines to see if I could tell the difference in blind tastings. I drank wine from a variety of glasses: highball, plastic, crystal, different shapes, etc., to see if it *really* made a difference in my enjoyment of wine.

I froze wine. I microwaved wine. I kept opened bottles in my refrigerator for months to see if they would change. I talked to people who liked wine and listened to their concerns and needs. I paired every possible wine with every possible food to see about wine and food matching. I drank white wine warm and red wine cold. I bought wine that *wasn't* highly rated to see if it could be good. I even canceled my subscriptions to

The Wine Advocate and *Wine Spectator.* (Ouch, that was like throwing away the Holy Bible.)

The result? It's a lot more relaxing to be out of the Club. I'm free to enjoy wine *my* way. I learned that so much of what is taught about wine is baloney, and it hinders one from having fun with wine.

I came up with a different way to approach wine, the Progressive Approach, an alternative to the Traditional Approach. The Progressive Approach can be summed up in two words: "Who Cares?" Who cares what the wine experts say is a good wine? Who cares that some supposed know-it-all says you should use a certain shaped wine glass for a particular wine? Who cares about describing wine with a slew of adjectives that makes no sense? Who cares about all the rules and affectations that have been passed down for decades to keep wine an elitist beverage?

Enjoying wine isn't about following rules, memorizing bunches of useless information about soil types, oak barrels, etc., and looking to others to tell you what's good. Ugh! Enjoying wine is about finding wine you like and enjoying it anyway you want, whether that's putting ice cubes in your wine, mixing different wines together in the same glass, having wine spritzers, drinking wine out of a highball glass or plastic cup, having Chardonnay with steak — whatever strikes your fancy.

The Progressive Approach seeks to empower the wine consumer, to give them the authority and confidence to explore the world of wine. It gives practical, useful tips on how to enjoy wine. And it offers easy-to-understand systems and explanations to take the intimidation factor out of wine.

In this book, I'll start off by contrasting the basic tenets of the Traditional Approach with the Progressive Approach. Then we'll leave the Traditional Approach behind and dive in to the full-blown Progressive Approach so you can reach wine nirvana.

Throughout the book, I'll give you Club Jargon Alerts (CJA). Club Jargon is how Club members talk because it was told to them as they were being taught the Traditional Approach, cloned from other Club members. Take the word "plonk," the British slang word for cheap, uninspiring wine. Only Club members use that word. There are many other words and illustrations that I'll point out. If anyone uses even one of them, you'll know they're a member of the Club. If anyone uses even one of the words or analogies, you'll know they're a member of the Club.

So do we need another wine book? I think so. I think it's important to offer wine consumers a choice in wine education and approaches. After reading this book, you can choose the approach that fits you best.

2

There is No Such Thing as Bad Wine

WHAT IS A GOOD WINE? Everyone, no matter how much they know about wine, can taste a wine and can decide if they like it or not. It would make sense that if the wine tastes good, that's a good wine. But Club members don't accept that. Just because the wine tastes good, doesn't mean it's good wine. They want to judge wine on a more objective standard.

What is the standard for good wine? Balance? But then, what is balanced? Low or high acidity? Tastes good? Complex? Aged? Who decides? Club members look to Parker or *Wine Spectator* to tell them what's good.

A winery wants to prove to buyers that its wine is good. It wants a score over 90 points, and it wants it from a reputable source. A 90+ point score from Robert

Parker is the most coveted. *Wine Spectator's* score is next in line in prestige. A 90+ score from Parker or *Spectator* will guarantee that a wine will fly off the shelf or be bought by restaurants or collectors.

But the tasters at *Wine Spectator* and Robert Parker can taste only so many wines. Those two sources don't even taste most of the wine on the market. If those two don't taste a winery's wine OR give the wine a sub-par rating, the winery looks to other sources for proof its wine is good. Other publications give scores to wines, some magazines, but mostly online rating services or newsletters; none carry the clout of the above two. But a good score for a second tier publication is better than nothing. If a winery is aggressive enough, it usually can get its wine tasted by *someone* who will give it a good score.

An alternative to the scores are medals. Medals are much less prestigious than a good score, but if the winery can't get its wine in front of one of the major scoring publications, or if it does and gets a lousy score, the winery will submit its wines to medal competitions — and there are a ton of them. A winery can enter as many competitions as it wants, but will probably publicize a medal only if the competition is at least as prestigious as its wine. For instance, if a wine is distributed internationally, then a winery will only want to publicize a medal won in an international competition. To publicize a gold won at some county fair would be embarrassing. Yet, for a local winery who only distributes in a small area, that county fair gold may be just the ticket. Walk

into any small winery and you'll typically see all kinds
of medals won. There are enough competitions that a
wine is bound to get a medal from one of them.

The average wine drinkers, when they see a rating
or a medal won, associate that with an objective level of
quality. But the ratings rarely hold up in actual tastings.
I've done hundreds of tastings with thousands of people,
just like you. For the tastings, I selected highly-rated
wines by the *Wine Spectator*, Robert Parker of *The Wine
Advocate* or even the lesser sources that rate wines or
award medals.

When the people tasted the wines, over 90% of the
time they didn't like the highly rated wines. Over 90%
of the time! The wines wine writers like, over 90% of
the time, the common wine drinker doesn't like. You
can see that the odds are not in your favor if you buy
wines by the ratings or by an expert's recommendation,
but more on that later.

Why is it that folks usually won't agree with the
ratings? A wine writer's palate is coming from a completely different perspective. First, wine writers taste
so many wines that they want a wine that is different,
one that breaks the monotony or sameness of so many
of the wines out there. So while you think an $8 easy-
drinking Merlot is a good thing, to the writer it's a
bad thing because it doesn't have any uniqueness to
it. Second, wine writers taste a lot of expensive wines
that do have more character, but they also cost more.
I'll talk more about whether or not those expensive

wines are worth it later in the book. More expensive
wines can offer more enjoyment to a wine drinker.
Once one gets used to having better, more complex
wine, it's hard to rate the average wines favorably. So
the wine writer and you are viewing wine from completely different perspectives. One perspective is not
better than the other. They're just different.

The Progressive Approach says, "Who Cares?" You
have to ingrain those words in your brain. Who cares
what anyone else thinks about the wine you like or
don't like? If a wine expert says a certain wine is great
and you taste it and think it's lousy, then it's lousy for
you. Don't apologize for it. If you like a wine that an
expert thinks is trash, the hell with them. You have to
recognize that all wine preferences are subjective.

Good wine can be REALLY subjective. I'm sure
you can recall having some awful wine. I know I can.
In fact, I was at a party where the host had put out a
dozen different wines for folks to graze on. I tasted one
that was great and commented to the host how good it
was. He noticed the bottle was empty, so he got another
bottle and I volunteered to open it so he could go and
do his host duties.

I tasted it and it was terrible. Terribly corked (I'll
explain that term later). I had to spit it out, it was so bad.

Two people were there to witness me spitting out
the wine. They asked me what the deal was, and I told
them that the wine tasted awful. Both explained they
were new wine drinkers and wanted to try it. Luckily

I still had some of the same wine from the first bottle that was tasty. I gave the good version to the two people, then the bad.

Even as beginning wine drinkers, the difference was obvious. They suggested I pour the wine down the sink, but I had a different idea, as a little show and tell. I told them that I'd leave the bad bottle of wine on the counter and let others try it. My belief was that someone would taste the wine and like it. The two said, "No way." It was sooo bad. But I told them that everyone has different tastes.

Up walked Alice, a member of my wine group, a regular wine drinker who had quite a collection of wine at her home. She poured a glass of the bad wine. The three of us cringed, anticipating that as soon as she tasted it, there would be spewage as the wine came out of her mouth involuntarily.

Alice tasted it. Swallowed it. And turned to me, asking about this wine, because she LOVED it. My two "students" looked at me in disbelief. A wine we thought was liquid vomit, Alice loved!

It happens not only to common folks, but even to the experts who are supposed to know better. I remember attending a seminar for the wine trade where the speaker was a nationally recognized wine expert named Doug So And So, a Master of this and that. We were served a wine that was obviously rotten. All the audience knew it, but the speaker didn't recognize it. When the folks in the audience mentioned it, he stuck by his opinion that the wine he had was right, as if it might have come from a different bottle. But a few audience members wouldn't let him off the hook. They smelled blood. They offered him a taste of the wine they were poured, which they knew was rotten. Now he had two options: to admit he was wrong, or try to pull rank among dozens of fellow wine professionals. He did the latter. How embarrassing for him.

I can go on and on with stories of how people in the wine business failed to recognize a rotten wine. And some of these are wine writers who are recommending wine for you to buy. How screwed up is that?

People's habits can be affected by what the experts call good wine or bad wine. Recently, my buddy John at the tennis club came up to me and asked in a dejected way what was wrong with Merlot. He likes Merlot, but saw the movie *Sideways*, where Miles is outside the restaurant yelling that he will NOT drink any f****** Merlot. After seeing the movie, John felt bad about drinking Merlot because he realized that wine snobs think Merlot is trash. I assured him it was okay to drink Merlot or anything else he liked, and to hell with the snobs.

The critical comments made by writers make folks feel bad about what they drink. I know that because every time I meet someone and they find out what I do, they start apologizing to me for what they drink, saying that I probably think it's lousy wine. It's funny (actually it's sad) how people cower when around wine

experts, but it's probably because they've learned somewhere down the line that what they are drinking is
considered unsophisticated by a wine expert.

Folks, don't cower. Rise up and believe in what you
like, whether it's white Zinfandel, Merlot, box wine, jug
wine, Chardonnay that is oaky or any other wine that
snobs and wine writers think is unsophisticated. Even
though a wine is rated highly or wins a gold medal,
that should mean *nothing* to you unless *you* like it.

And don't criticize what other people drink because
you think it's trash. Remember, every wine you like,
someone else thinks is lousy and every wine you think
is lousy, someone else likes. So just enjoy the wine you
like, and "who cares" what others like.

3

Why the Ratings are Silly

O N THE SURFACE, it seems like ratings are a good idea. If you haven't had a wine, how do you know if it's good? One who hasn't had the wine must rely on someone who has had the wine to tell them if the wine is good. Oops. What did we just learn from the last chapter? What is good wine? We know it's subjective. Well, WE know it's subjective, but the folks who follow the Traditional Approach didn't get the memo. So you can probably guess that I think the ratings are useless, since why do I care what someone else likes? It's what I like that's important.

But that's not true. I believe people need advice when buying wine, as the buyer hasn't tasted the wine, so what are the options?

I hope it's obvious to you that wine is totally subjective, and that the ratings are just one person's opinion that probably won't match your taste. But just in case, I want to show how nonsensical the ratings are.

Is a 90-point wine that costs under $10 the same as a 90-point wine that costs $300? Of course not, but they both exist. I just pulled this off the *Wine Spectator* website: Columbia Crest Shiraz Columbia Valley Two Vines 2001, 90 points, $8. Or another 90-point wine you could buy is the Tenuta dell'Ornellaia Toscana Masseto 2000, 90 points, $300. They both got 90 points. Do you think they're the same? Of course not! That's what makes the ratings so stupid. It doesn't make any sense.

Second, the variance of a rating from one tasting to another of the same wine can be five to 10 points. A wine is tasted one day and given 93 points, and the next week the wine can get a score of 88 from the same taster. Most wines are rated between 91 and 86. Since a wine can easily vary 5 points depending on when it is tasted, all the wines are essentially the same. Why even have the ratings in the first place?

There is a reason, and it's mainly for the collectors. They don't care about their own tastes. They just want to buy what Parker and the *Wine Spectator* rates highly. They need the ratings for two reasons:

1. When they show off their collection of highly rated

wine to fellow Club members, it's a stroke to their fragile egos. And if you're not a Club member who appreciates the value of a highly rated wine, they'll announce the rating of a wine when they bring it out just so you know how special that wine is, and how cool they are for having that wine. And they'll enjoy the wine, not because it tastes good, but because it's highly rated.

A little FYI: typically the folks with the big collections can't taste their way out of a paper bag. In blind tastings of highly rated wines compared to not highly rated wines, they are not even close on discerning which ones are which.

2. Ratings also are imperative for folks who collect wine as an investment. At auctions, it's the highly rated wines for which everyone pays top dollar.

Should we just toss out all ratings? Yes; all numerical ratings, or any other scale if it doesn't take price into consideration.

But ratings have a place to help people buy wines. That's why I created the Progressive Approach to rating wines, based on value. A $6 bottle of wine will be judged differently than a $50 bottle. One would expect much more from a bottle that costs $50. So a wine cannot be scored until the rater knows the price, to see if the wine is worth it. This is my scale:

A – The wine is a great value, almost no matter what the price. A must buy!

B = The wine is better than what you would expect to pay for it, so it's worth seeking it out.

C = The wine tastes like what you'd expect for the price.

D = The wine is good, but not worth the price.

F = The wine is no good and/or not at all worth the money.

I will add a "Y" to the score if the wine is too young. For instance, you can taste a wine that doesn't taste up to its expected potential, so it would be unfair to score it a "D" or an "F" when the wine may turn into an "A" or "B" given some aging. In those situations, when I believe the wine will get significantly better with time, I'll add a "Y" to the score.

I go to a ton of tastings and have expensive wines, but very few of them get more than a D, because they aren't worth the money. Once a wine costs more than about $40, it becomes pretty difficult for it to get a C or better because so many wines are equally good for less.

On the flip side of the price scale, I taste bunches of inexpensive wine, as my goal in life is to find the least expensive wine that I love. But if the wine is no good, even if it's under $10, it won't get a C because I know there are other wines that cost the same that are much better. It's all about value.

Now whether it's me or someone else rating a wine using the Progressive Approach, it's still an opinion, and you shouldn't follow hook, line and sinker. Remember, good wine is what YOU like, not necessarily what a rater says.

4

Different Shaped Glasses are a Waste of Money

I DON'T THINK HOW YOU GET the wine into your mouth is a big deal. In Europe, they often drink wine out of a highball-type glass. I like that, because it keeps one from being too pretentious about wine. A variation of the casual highball glass that has come out on the market is the stemless glass. It's selling like hotcakes.

Whatever glass you use is fine. The wine won't taste significantly different coming from different shaped glasses. You're mainly choosing a glass for the mood or setting.

Riedel (ree del) is an Austrian glass company that dominates the market. They bought their biggest competitor, Spiegelau, so now they really have the market locked up. Riedel has convinced people that it is important that they use the "right" glass for whatever type of wine they are drinking. In fact, Riedel makes a different shape/size glass for every type of wine. There's a glass for Chardonnay, Cabernet Sauvignon, Shiraz, Sauvignon Blanc, old Cabernet Sauvignon, etc. It's nuts. But they have done so well on making consumers believe the right glass is important that it's like gospel now. Once Robert Parker stated that Riedel is what he prefers (remember, he's God), that endorsement really got Riedel off the ground. All Club members worship Riedel.

When I was in the Club, I fell for the Riedel message. I bought Riedel glasses and made sure I was using the right wine glass when I had certain types of wine. I even started making dining decisions at restaurants by what stemware they used. It was over the top. But one day I started wondering if that was really necessary. Besides, when I started having people over and suddenly needed 4-8 of each shaped glass, it got to be very expensive.

Frustrated with the whole glass deal, I wanted to know the truth. I took a variety of glasses, all different shapes and sizes, ones made from crystal and some made from regular glass and poured the same wine in all of them. I had people taste the same wine from each glass and rate the following:

A) which glass made the wine taste the best;

B) which glass felt best in their hand.

The results:

A) The glass that was designed to be used for the grape variety that was poured NEVER received the majority of votes. The red Burgundy glass that was designed for Pinot Noir was never chosen by the majority as the glass that made the Pinot Noir taste better. The glass designed for Chardonnay never got the most votes when a Chardonnay was poured in all of the glasses. In fact, the "proper" glass never got the most votes for any of the wines. Yet Riedel claims each glass is designed specifically for a type of wine. Oops!

B) The glass that felt the best to drink from was always a hand-blown crystal glass. Of all the hand-blown glasses in the lineup, more people chose the Sommelier series Hermitage/Syrah glass by Riedel as the one that not only felt the best but made all of the wines taste good.

Conclusion: The glass does make a difference, but the glass designed for a particular wine doesn't seem like the right choice. So the idea of trying to match the glass to the type of wine is just a bunch of baloney and a waste of money. Instead, it seems that one size and shape was what people preferred no matter what the wine was. Second, hand-blown crystal was the favorite, hands down. Drinking a wine from a hand-blown crystal glass makes any wine seem better. A glassmaker can make a lighter glass out of crystal, and lighter translates into more elegant. It's not like a heavy goblet that is unwieldy.

From my research, the idea of trying to match the glass to the type of wine seemed silly, but I was curious to see if anyone else had done a study. Daniel Zwerdling, an NPR reporter, wrote an article about Riedel that was published in *Gourmet* in August 2004. Daniel discovered that the Monell Chemical Senses Center, one of the world's most prestigious laboratories studying taste and smell, had conducted a study. They compared wine poured in Riedel glasses, cheap wine glasses and a water goblet. The subjects were not allowed to see or hold the glasses. The subjects couldn't tell any difference from one glass to another.

Georg Riedel was so bothered by the results, he asked Thomas Hummel, a prominent physician and researcher at the University of Dresden to do a major experiment to prove that Riedel's glasses work the way he claims. This study was much bigger than the one done at the Monell Center, but the results were the same: the subjects couldn't tell the difference between the glasses.

Daniel Zwerdling called Georg Riedel for an explanation. Riedel said, "I don't know the studies in detail that I can really comment on them ... Ask consumers if my glasses make a difference. And the consumers say, 'Wow!'"

Most people who have attended a Riedel seminar walk out convinced that the wine glass makes a difference. The scientists explain this as a combination of great salesmanship and the power of suggestion.

Many other studies have shown the impact of the

power of suggestion. In 1998 Frederic Brochet, a researcher at the University of Bordeaux, fooled wine professionals into thinking that a white wine was a red wine simply by adding food coloring to it. They didn't stop there. The second part of the study was sampling two wines. The wine professionals were told the first one was an inexpensive wine. Then a second wine was brought, and the professionals were told it was very expensive. All the wine professionals preferred the second one. Of course, the first and the second wines were the same.

Brochet stated that all of the information that people have, the label, the cost, the producer, etc. plays a huge role in their opinion of the wine. He supposes the same thing is happening with wine glasses. People prefer the Riedel because they cost more, they look good, they are delicate and wine experts and writers say they make a difference. But all the science says they don't. The idea of a wine glass designed for a specific type of wine is just plain wrong. It's all a marketing gimmick by Riedel, and they've done a great job of it.

But back to the results of my study. The Sommelier series Hermitage/Syrah glass by Riedel came out on top for all types of wine. It has a 575 ml bowl and it is very light, since it is hand-blown crystal. Perfect. One glass that worked for all wines, so I didn't have to fill up my cabinets with glasses and waste all of that money.

So I got one ... for $110 (from www.williamsonoma. com). That's right. That's not a typo. The glasses cost $110 each! The first time I washed it, it broke. I bought another.

It broke too. I bought more, and they broke. I couldn't use the glass more than a few times before the bowl broke.

So that's when I decided to have my own glass made. I found a group of old-world artisans in Slovakia to produce the glass to my specifications. I designed my glass to be 500 ml and a slightly different shape than the Riedel that won the competition. I changed it for aesthetic reasons and for how it made the wine taste. Mine was also hand-blown crystal, but I added a few twists. First, the design of my glass makes it the lightest glass in the world, up to 30% lighter than the Riedel. Light means elegant. The lighter the glass, the more elegant it feels. My glass is so light and delicate, it scares people when they first hold it. They're worried they'll break it, which is understandable if you have ever had hand-blown crystal wine glasses that stay in your cabinet for fear of breakage.

But what makes my glass so special is that it is not only elegant, but durable. It can actually be washed in the dishwasher, a breakthrough for hand-blown crystal. In fact, I recommend you wash them in the dishwasher rather than by hand. (See a video of my glass in action at www.winetasting.org)

Whether you buy my wine glass or not, it's important you support companies that are trying to spread the truth about the nonsense that Riedel is proclaiming. I suggest not buying wine glasses from a company that proclaims a glass is made for a particular grape variety. I could tolerate a company that makes different shaped glasses for different *styles* of wine. The only problem with that is that most folks don't know the style of a wine and thus, which glass to use — but it's a better approach than what Riedel is saying.

Whatever you think or decide, don't worry about getting different shaped glasses for different types of wine. Pick a shape that you think looks good and a weight that feels good in your hand.

5

How to Taste Wine

THE NEXT CHAPTER should be "How to Describe Wine," to keep the momentum going to define the Traditional Approach. But I want to insert this chapter on "How to Taste Wine," as it will help you understand the next chapter better.

The tasting process is so important in understanding wine. But tasting wine is different than drinking wine. When you drink wine, you put it in your mouth and swallow it, unless you're chugging wine (which has some advantages, like before a date or a downhill ski run on a slope that is pushing your ability). But when chugging is not the strategy, what's left is either drinking or tasting.

Drinking wine is meant for casual, non-critical consumption of wine. You're just trying to enjoy the taste, and maybe catch a buzz. You can go through your whole life drinking wine and be happy. But you'll never really understand wine until you learn how to taste it.

The purpose of tasting wine is to understand it, to become one with it (Be the wine Danny), to understand all of the facets of its personality. I'm going to explain the four-step process below, but it would be best to see it done. Visit www.winetasting.org to watch the video on how to taste wine.

In the interim, the four steps in the tasting process are:

Appearance – how the wine looks

Aroma – how the wine smells (probably the most important step). This is usually the step when the orgasm kicks in.

Taste – There are two aspects of taste, feeling and flavor.

Aftertaste

Let me expand on each step.

APPEARANCE

Nothing about the appearance of the wine tells you anything about the quality of the wine. No one looks at a wine and deduces that it must be a great wine. So why bother?

There are two reasons to look at wine. First, you can tell if the wine is flawed (usually only in whites). If the white wine is brown, that's not good. A white wine turns brown when it is WAY too old. But it is next to impossible for you to buy a wine like that. Typically, a white wine that is too old will come out of someone's wine supply at home.

In the past, wine critics would look at a wine to spot other flaws like cloudiness or stuff floating around in it. Cloudiness is still a bad thing (usually it's present in a wine that is still fermenting). But with the technology available to winemakers these days, wine is easily stabilized before leaving the winery, so you will probably never see a cloudy wine. Critics also used to look for stuff floating around in the wine. In the old days, a good wine was one with nothing floating around in it, because it meant it was filtered thoroughly. But nowadays, that floating stuff is actually a good sign because winemakers have learned that filtering strips away the flavor components in wine. So, since flavor is paramount, many winemakers choose to keep the filtering to a minimum or not to filter at all and maintain as much flavor as possible. The stuff floating around in an unfiltered wine is nothing that can hurt you.

The second reason you look at the appearance is to determine what the wine is, like in a blind tasting competition. A person adept at blind tasting can often identify the grape variety, the origin and the vintage just from the appearance.

Do you plan to enter blind tasting competitions? No. I didn't think so. So let's skip that reason. And since wine made today usually doesn't have the flaws that one can tell from looking at the wine, the first reason isn't a factor either. There isn't much reason to worry about the appearance, So the appearance is not a big deal, and nothing to spend a lot of time analyzing.

Oh, before I go on, I guess this is a good time to address the legs (or tears) of a wine. When you swirl a wine in a glass, once you stop, you'll see the wine has coated the glass above the level of the wine, and the sheeting forms into legs or tears that move down into the wine. Some believe you should look at them to learn how much glycerin is in the wine.

First of all, there is no glycerin in wine. It's glycerol that is in alcohol. The legs can give you an idea of how much alcohol is in wine — a seemingly helpful hint if you're competing in a blind tasting. However, the difference in the legs between a low-alcohol wine and a high-alcohol wine is so minute that it really doesn't help much.

AROMA

In the drinking process, you don't even bother to smell the wine. You just go right for your mouth. However, in the tasting process, you would never do that because the aroma is everything in experiencing wine. The taste is also important, but aroma is the aspect of wine that gets the juices flowing. The aroma of wine is the foreplay of the tasting experience. It is like having someone lick your inner thigh, nibble on your ear lobes, softly kiss you on your neck and lightly massage you with his or her hands.

Whenever I have a great wine, it's the aroma that stops me in my tracks. I swirl and smell it over and over again because I just don't want the foreplay to stop. I want to draw it out as long as possible. But if you don't smell the wine the right way, you'll miss out.

Before I go on, make sure you have a glass of wine in front of you so you can participate, white or red. You want to only have about one ounce in your glass (a shot glass worth). If you have too much, drink some. Hopefully your wine glass has the traditional bowl shape to it.

Tilt the glass toward you at a 45-degree angle and smell the wine without swirling. Put your nose all the way into the glass. If the top and bottom of the rim isn't hitting your face, your nose isn't in far enough. You can see why you only want a little wine in the glass; otherwise, you might drown. Think about how much aroma you get from the wine.

I first went to France back in 1990, just a few months after I had my first glass of wine. I traveled to many of the different wine regions just to get an idea about wine. When I was tasting wine with the "big boys," whenever they smelled a wine, they always tilted their head to one side or the other to use just one nostril in smelling the wine. They did it because it was their "better" nostril. I was pretty impressionable at the time, being new to wine, so I thought it was cool to tilt.

From that point on I have always tilted my head to the left when I smell wine. Not that my left nostril is any better than my right, but that is the habit I've gotten into. So if you want to look cool, tilt your head to one side when smelling wine.

Now swirl the wine in the glass. The easiest way to do it is to put the glass down on a surface and make small circles, clockwise or counter-clockwise. (It doesn't make any difference.) Really whip the wine around for about five seconds, and then smell it again. You will notice that you get so much more aroma out of the bowl by swirling. If you're drinking a non-orgasmic wine, it will just have a fruity, hopefully nice smell. I'll talk about how to describe the smell in just a minute.

But if you have an orgasmic wine, the aroma travels up your nose like the tail of a comet. It's got length. It just keeps coming. And when the aroma hits your nasal cavity, it opens up like a firework in the sky. It goes all over, and the aromas are so integrated you can't even really describe them. The length of the aroma going in and the complexity of it once it gets to your nasal cav-ity are what make a great wine. And when you experi-ence that, you want more — more and longer-lasting intensity. So you swirl more vigorously to get even more aroma from the wine. You close your eyes and just let it open up inside of you.

After about 30 seconds or so, you repeat the process and let the wine just toy with you, tease you, seduce you. On one hand, you're getting so excited you want to complete the experience, to taste it; but on the other hand, you don't want the seduction to end. Since you know how much better delayed gratification is, you opt to continue smelling the wine over and over again. Swirl, smell and reflect on the wine. Repeat.

What you'll find is that the wine will reward you for that. The aroma will change over time, giving you a reason to repeat the process. Soon the juices will be flowing so much, you can't hold off any longer from tasting the wine.

I'm going to have to get a bit technical so the geeks don't come after me for excluding stuff. But I'm going to share something with you that even most geeks don't know, so you can stump them.

I use "aroma" and "bouquet" interchangeably for how a wine smells, but technically, "aroma" is a term for the smell of a young wine, while "bouquet" is what develops over time when a wine ages.

Oh, and there isn't just one aroma in a wine. There are primary aromas, secondary aromas and tertiary aromas. This is the part most geeks don't know. The primary aromas come from the grape(s) used. The secondary aromas come from the fermentation and yeast used. The tertiary aromas come from the aging of the wine in the bottle. Ask any geek what each aroma comes from, and I'll bet you they won't know. Anyway, it's not important. The only thing to remember is to swirl the wine and get your nose all the way in the bowl to get as much aroma as possible.

Once you smell the wine, what do you say? I'll address that in the next chapter. This chapter is just on the mechanics of the tasting process.

Before moving on to the third step, I want to talk about how to hold the glass. When you're drinking wine, anything goes: hold it by the bowl, use a straw or do shots. But when you're tasting wine, the geeks would say that you should only hold the glass by the stem. If you hold the glass by the bowl, your hand blocks the appearance of the wine and even though the appearance isn't a big deal, it still counts. Second, your hand will warm up the wine in the bowl, and that's bad if the wine is at the right temperature. So that's why a wine glass is built the way it is, with a stem, so you can keep your hand away from the bowl.

However, geeks often try to hold their glass a different way to communicate to others around that they are in the know. It's like a mating call to other geeks to come and show off to each other how much they know about wine. Geeks hold the glass by the base. Knowing that, you shouldn't hold a glass that way unless you want to attract geeks to you. If someone walks up to you to start a conversation and they're holding their wine glass by the base, turn and run. If you don't, you'll be subjected to the most boring conversation known to mankind.

TASTE

Taste is the third step, but it should have an "a" and a "b" because there are two facets to this step. The two facets correspond to the two components found in all wine: Feeling and Flavor.

The feeling of wine is the tactile sensation left in your mouth after you swallow the wine. There are only two feelings in wine: acidity and tannin. Remember, these are feelings, not flavors.

Acidity is a real tart sensation that you'll feel on the back sides of your tongue. If the wine has a ton of acidity, you'll start salivating in your lower gum area after you swallow. Both red and white wines can have acidity, but it's usually a little more obvious in white wines. But not all wines have acidity and the ones that do may have a little, a medium amount, or a lot. All you're doing is trying to determine if a wine has it and if so, how much it has.

The same goes for the second feeling, tannin. Tannin is only found in red wines because tannin comes from the skins of the grape. Tannin makes your mouth feel like cottonmouth, like you're chewing on cotton balls; it completely dries it out. In fact, after feeling tannin, one usually starts "chewing" to try to get saliva back in their mouth. You feel tannin especially in your upper gum area.

The way to identify the feeling of wine is to put some wine in your mouth and swish it around like it's mouthwash. You want to get it all over the inside of your mouth. Once you swallow, you'll feel the wine. Now it's your turn. (Geez, I wish I was there with you to show you, but this will have to do.)

We're going to do a "before and after" exercise. Take a sip of wine and don't mouthwash. Just swallow it like you're drinking wine. Make a note about the feeling left in your mouth after you swallow.

Now take another sip and mouthwash like crazy, all over your mouth. Swallow, and you should notice a difference. If you're having a white wine and it isn't a Chardonnay from California or Australia, you should feel acidity on the back sides of your tongue. If it's a red, you will feel some tannin, maybe a lot of it, in your upper gum area and dryness all over your mouth. You will never know the feeling of wine unless you mouthwash it.

You might be asking why anyone would want to experience acidity or tannin, as it isn't very pleasant. You're right. It isn't pleasant by itself, but the feeling of wine is a key consideration in matching wine and food. When wines with high acidity or tannin are consumed by themselves, they seem out of balance. But when you have the wines with food, you don't notice the acidity and/or tannin at all because the feelings are being absorbed by the food. The feeling of wine is what cleanses your palate after each bite. So once you know how much feeling a wine has, you'll know when to have it. Wines with high feeling should always be served with food to balance out/absorb the feeling of acidity and/or tannin. Wines with low feeling are pleasant to consume by themselves because they don't have that tartness or dryness that demands food. That's why when I'm doing the laundry or mowing the lawn, I'll choose a low-feeling wine because there's no food around. But with a meal, I prefer a wine with high feeling.

So Feeling is 3a.Now it's time for 3b: Flavor. The tongue isn't a big player in tasting wine. The salt, sweet, sour and bitter receptors make some difference, but the flavor of wine really happens in your nasal cavity. If you have a cold, you can't taste wine — but that's no reason not to drink it. Anyway, the trick is to get the wine to your nasal cavity. If you could drink wine through your nose, that would work. But since that is hard to do, the best way is to put wine in your mouth and while it's still there, you suck air into your mouth. The air crossing over the wine "opens up" the wine and sends the aroma up your retro nasal passage to your nasal cavity. That's where you taste wine. It sounds goofy, I know, but it works.

CAUTION: If your chin is up when you suck air in, you'll choke and probably spew. Spewage is not good. To avoid that, put the wine in your mouth, put your chin down against your chest and suck the air in. Because your chin is down, the wine won't get into your throat.

Let's do another "before and after" exercise with flavor. Put some wine in your mouth and just swallow again, as if you were drinking it.

Now for the next step, you may want to sit up straight, assume the position and put some wine in your mouth, put your chin down and suck like crazy. Go.

You'll see that you get a lot more flavor out of the wine. Maybe even a head rush.

So the third step, Taste, has two parts: feeling and flavor. When the third step is done in the real world, the same mouthful of wine is used for both feeling and flavor. You would put a bit of wine in your mouth and mouthwash, then suck air in. You got it.

AFTERTASTE

Aftertaste is how long the flavor lasts in your mouth after you swallow the wine. The cool way to refer to aftertaste is the "finish." Most wine writers will say the finish of the wine is long, or assign a time to it, like 30 seconds. Generally speaking, the longer the finish, the better the wine. But a great wine, when it's young, may have a short finish because it hasn't evolved yet. That's why the finish is not a big deal in critiquing a wine. I mean, not a lot of points are allotted to the finish when scoring wine. However, when a great wine is at its peak, the finish can go on forever (okay, like 45 seconds instead of the average finish of 15 seconds).

All four steps done in succession probably take 10-15 seconds to get through. But when do you do it? I mean, it's got some odd actions, like swishing the wine in your mouth and sucking air in.

Yes, it does, so it's really only done at a real wine tasting, not when you're having dinner with friends.

However, the tasting process can be done in a very subtle manner to avoid detection. It took months of practice in my closet before I was able to perfect it so I could pull it off in public without making a scene.

No matter when you decide to do it, you'll get so much more out of the wine. Typically the process is done for the first sip of the wine. After that, it's drinking time. Maybe when you get a second glass from the same bottle, you might want to try the four steps again to see how the wine has changed ... and then you're back to drinking.

In a tasting environment, that's when you can really go at it because everyone else is doing the same. All the wine is being tasted, 1-2 ounces of each wine. Take more time in smelling the wine. Smell, reflect, repeat ... over and over again, if the wine merits it.

Ideally, I think it's best to taste every wine you try, and then drink. You'll learn more about wine by tasting it than by reading every book on the market. To understand wine is to know how to taste and describe it ... which leads us to the next chapter.

6

Describing Wine
is for Geeks

THE EASIEST WAY TO SEE if someone is a Club member is to observe how they describe wine. The more adjectives they use, the higher office they hold in the Club. They also try to make the descriptions obscure and sophisticated as well as including geek terms like "nuances," hints," "notes," and "accents." So textbook. So ridiculous. I've included a few descriptions by wine writers.

Descriptions by Cindy and/or Scott Greenberg of *The Examiner* in Washington, D.C.:

"Creamy lemon scents mingle with floral notes and hints of brioche on the pretty nose. Approachable flavors of ripe apples and pineapple on well-textured frame with almond accents on the soft finish."

"A seductive nose of chocolate, cassis liqueur and black cherry. Full meaty flavors, blackberry, black raspberry jam and smoky meats cover the palate. The cigar box finish almost demands a sirloin steak."

"Honeysuckle, apricots and honeyed orange rind seduce the nose and keep peach and pear nectar notes plenty of company on the unctuous, sinfully silky finish. A perfect ending with a pear tart."

Compliments of Robert Parker:

"Big, sweet nose of tapenade, ground pepper, kirsch, blackberry and licorice. A full bodied palate with a hint of truffle emerging."

This one by Michael Franz, who used to write for *The Washington Post*:

"Subtle in aroma and flavor but highly nuanced as well, this very well made wine is ripe enough to show no hard edges but yet remains fresh and zesty. Notes of green apples and limes are very appealing, with accents of hay and wet stones."

Yeah, and get obscure with *Wine Spectator*'s description:

"It offers apricot and cherry flavors and the *goût de terroir* of flint, wet soil and matchstick notes."

"Amazingly ripe, complex and elegant, with tiers of black cherry, currant, raspberry and spice aromas and flavors. Shows tremendous balance between elegance and concentration, suppleness and structure, intensity and finesse. Picks up toasted oak notes and fine tannins on the finish."

All those were written by Club members. But some folks realized those kinds of descriptions were obviously too geeky. They tried to make the wine descriptions hip, to appeal to the younger generation. Look what they came up with:

"Imagine Bob Vila soaking in a tub of gardenias - woody, floral, and well-built."

"More grass and acid than a Led Zeppelin reunion concert."

Sure, they didn't have all the geeky adjectives, but they replaced them with just as useless information.

I don't have any idea what that wine smells or tastes like from any of the above descriptions. When a writer lists multiple aroma and taste sensations for a wine, how are we to know what that means? If we put all of the flavors they listed into a blender, would we then get the taste of the wine? I doubt it. And knowing how each person has a different sense of smell and taste, it's even more useless. It seems like wine writers get paid by the number of adjectives they use. The Traditional Approach of describing wine with lots of adjectives,

wine jargon and obscurity is so ineffective that it's a
wonder it's still being used.

The Progressive Approach offers a much different
strategy. It makes describing wines easier and suggest-
ing terms that can be understood by everyone else. The
key to describing wine is using profiles. There are two
parts to a profile, the facgs and the description.

FACGS

The facts are what you KNOW about the wine, and
there are four facts: the cost, the year it was made,
where it was made and the grape variety(s).

Now I'm saying the "facts," spelled f-a-c-t-s. But I
spell that word F-A-C-Gs, to help me remember what
the four facts that you want to remember.

F is for from – where the wine is from.

A is for age – the year the wine was made.

C is for cost – how much the wine costs.

Gs are for grapes that made the wine.

So let's pick a Riesling from Alsace, France, the
same one I used in my PBS special.

F: it was from Alsace, France.

A: the vintage was 2004

C: $12

Gs: it's made from the Riesling grape.

Knowing the FACGs is easy, because the label gives you the information. But describing a wine is tougher, especially after hearing the Traditional Approach with all of the adjectives.

The Progressive Approach is all about C.B.S. Although I do prefer Letterman to Leno, this is an acronym for Complexity, Body and Style.

DESCRIPTION

COMPLEXITY: A good wine is one that you like. We can agree on that. But what makes a wine great? It's complexity. You've had wines that you've liked. We all have. Those are good wines. But some wines stop you in your tracks. Something about that wine makes you excited. Typically, that "something" is complexity. A wine that makes you stop and think because so much is happening in your mouth, that's complexity. An aroma that just doesn't go into your nose all at once but has a long trail of aroma ... that's complexity.

Complexity is what makes a wine great. When describing wine, you want to determine the complexity of the wine. Is it a simple wine that goes down easy? Or is it a wine that makes you stop and think? Is the flavor one dimensional in your mouth or do flavors and sensations burst open in your mouth? After you swallow, does the flavor dissipate quickly or does it linger?

Wines that catch your attention are ones that are

complex, but it's purely subjective. As you taste more and more wine, you'll get a better grasp on what is complex and what is simple. Regardless, you'll want to think about the wine you're having by describing it by its complexity as a sliding scale — not "complex," "sort of complex," or "wow, it's really complex."

BODY: TAs you attend seminars, you're bound to hear the body of wine compared to milk. (CJA) Every Club member I've heard talk about the body of wine has used it. Here's what they say:

The body of wine is like the different types of milk. Skim milk is very light in body and you can sense that in your mouth. Whole milk is much thicker and has more substance, like a medium-bodied wine. And heavy cream has even more richness and thickness, like a full-bodied wine.

So what?! When I'm looking at a wine on the shelf, how is the milk analogy going to help me know if the wine is light, medium or full-bodied? It's just another one of those bits of education from the Traditional Approach that has no practical application.

The Progressive Approach alternative is this: The Body of the wine is determined by one or more of three characteristics: alcohol, oak, and tannin, with the alcohol being the most important.

Alcohol – The more alcohol a wine has, the more body it has. When you see a wine at 14+% alcohol, you can make a good bet that it will be full-bodied. 12.5%-14% = medium-bodied. Less than 12.5% is light-bodied.

Oak — If a wine is put into oak barrels to age for a while, the oak barrels gives it more oomph, more body. Oak is used in almost all red wines and some white wines, like Chardonnay and Sauvignon Blanc. For example, a Chardonnay that is unoaked (hasn't been put in oak barrels) will be a light-bodied wine. Add some oak to it, and it becomes medium-bodied; and if new oak barrels are used, it could even be a full-bodied wine — but refer to the alcohol, as that is the most important for body.

Tannin — Tannin comes from the skins of the grapes, and grapes that have thicker skins usually will have more body, like Cabernet Sauvignon, Zinfandel, etc. The sensation of tannin is that dry feeling in your mouth after you swallow the wine. Winemakers will allow the skins to sit with the juice longer if they want a full bodied wine and/or a wine that can age longer. Wines that are meant to be consumed right away typically won't have a lot of tannin. The more expensive a wine gets, typically the more tannin it has. That's just for red wines. Since the skins aren't used to make white wine, one doesn't find tannin in white wine.

It's easy now for you to have a pretty good idea of the body of a wine before buying it. The alcohol level is on every wine label, so that's the easiest way to find out how much body the wine has. The back label often states whether the wine has tannin and/or has been put in oak barrels, which helps you define the body even better.

STYLE: There are two main styles of wine: Old World and New World. Old World wine is any wine made in Europe. New World wine is any wine made outside of Europe. That's it. Put the book down. You're done. Get a glass of wine and relax.

Oh, we'd better not quit this soon. Let's cover just a little bit more.

Old World wine generally has higher acidity and less fruitiness than a New World wine made from the same grapes. So an Old World Chardonnay will generally have higher acidity and won't be as fruity as a New World Chardonnay. New World wine is just the opposite. New World wine generally will be lower in acidity and really fruity. Same for reds.

Since you're an inquisitive person, you're asking why that is. When a grape is under ripe it is high in acidity, like all under ripe fruit. An under ripe apple is very tart. Tartness is the manifestation of acidity. As that apple ripens, the acidity decreases. An under ripe piece of fruit also has very little sugar. As fruit matures, the sugars increase; it gets much fruitier.

One mistake people make in describing wine is calling a wine sweet. "Sweet" in wine means it has residual sugar in it. But in most table wine, the stuff we drink every day, has been fermented to be completely dry. That is, the yeast has eaten up all of the sugar in the mature grape leaving no sweetness. So it's called dry. But in a really fruity wine, the fruitiness often seems sweet. Just describe that sensation as "fruity" instead of "sweet" when at a wine tasting.

If a grape is grown in a region that has a short growing season and/or never gets very warm, the grapes don't ripen as much. That's Europe. So grapes grown in Europe usually get picked with higher acidity and less sugar. Thus, the wine made from those grapes won't be as fruity and will be higher in acid.

In the New World (the United States, Australia, New Zealand, South America and South Africa), those areas are quite warm and have a longer growing season. Thus the grapes there are high in sugar and lower in acidity, resulting in wines that are really fruity without much acidity.

The weather clearly makes a difference, but the winemaker does too. In Europe, food is king. Wine is there to complement the food. A wine that is too fruity or high in alcohol can overpower the food. So although winemakers could change the style of their wines, the winemakers that are more interested in having the wine complement the food will keep the wine higher in acidity meaning lower alcohol and less fruitiness.

Although acidity and lower fruitiness are the two main components of Old World wine, they have an earthy component too. The reds from Europe often have an aroma of the earth or dirt while the whites often have a minerally aroma. The earthy component is more obvious in certain wines from Europe but is always a good thing to look for.

Quick review:

Old World wine: Any wine made in Europe. It will be higher in acidity, not as fruity and will have a more obvious earthy component.

New World wine: Any wine made outside of Europe. It will be lower in acidity and more fruit-forward, with less of an earthy component.

Those are the two main styles, but a couple of others are worth mentioning. Because of technology and a better understanding on how to make wine, winemakers can manipulate wines dramatically. So although the categories of New World and Old World still are valid as far as the wine's origin is concerned, they don't accurately reflect the actual style of the wine. A New World winemaker has the ability to make a wine that has some Old World characteristics as well as New World characteristics. An Old World winemaker can do the same. Since this type of wine doesn't truly reflect the definition of Old World or New World, I had to come up with a new classification: *international style*.

International style wine is a wine that is made with both New World and Old World characteristics — a blend, if you will, that does not lose all of its identity. A well-made International style wine should still feature the characteristics of its origin. If it is made in Europe, it should be more Old World than New World, and one should be able to recognize that. It will just have a little more fruit and maybe lower acidity than a wine made in 100% Old World style. International style wines are becoming increasingly popular, and here's why.

The manipulation of wine is happening in all regions. It is more of a factor in Europe than it is in the New World. More Old World wines are being made to be more like New World wine than *vice versa*. Some people blame this phenomenon on the "Parkerization" of wine, after Robert Parker. Parker seems to prefer New World style wines and because of his influence, a wine made in the traditional Old World style will receive a lower rating. So Old World winemakers are doing everything possible to make their wines with a darker color, fruitier aromas and flavors — the style of New World wine.

Nowadays, wineries just can't afford to leave things to chance as they did in the old days. Winemakers can't control the weather, but that's about it. And even if the weather isn't that great, they can manipulate the wine to make up for much of what Mother Nature didn't provide in a certain year.

In fact, the winemakers' ability to manipulate the wine is so great, they can make a wine that has absolutely no identifying features of where it's from. It's origin-less.

Those wines fall into a fourth and final category: *manipulated wine*. Most wines under $15 per bottle fall into this category. They are very drinkable, but have no defining characteristics of origin. If you did a blind tasting of wines all made from the same grape variety priced under $15 a bottle, it would be very difficult to pick up where the wines were made.

That's not necessarily bad. Ten years ago, it was a real crapshoot to choose a wine that was drinkable. That was the case for two reasons. First, very few winemakers had adopted the technology to manipulate wine. In years when the weather was perfect, technology wasn't needed. But when there was bad weather, the winemakers were dinked because they didn't have the means to correct it.

Second, back to Parker. Robert Parker didn't really change the wine drinker's palate. He just enforced it. He, like most wine drinkers, preferred fruitier wines. Since he is so influential, winemakers could either make fruitier wines and get better ratings from Parker or hold on to their own, maybe traditional, way of making wine and not sell much. Most winemakers, in order to survive, made the switch to technology to ensure their wines were fruity year in and year out.

So now it's just the opposite of the crapshoot ten years ago. Now it's hard to walk into a wine shop and find a wine that is just terrible. Sure, I may not like it much, but it still would be drinkable. It's hard to find a bad wine (excluding wines that were ruined by shipping or storage). Decent drinking (manipulated) wine is everywhere, and that's good.

The downside is that the wines all start tasting

alike. Technology makes good wine in spite of the *ter-roir*. Technology often masks the *terroir*. For a wine geek, the tradition, the uniqueness of wines from certain areas is fading away. Sure, a few winemakers are hanging in there still trying to make wines that reflect their origin, but it's tough because making wine that way is often counter to making a profit. There is so much competition today because so many wineries are making wine; a winery has to do everything it can to squeeze out a profit. And usually that requires standardizing the winemaking process (kind of like the assembly line did for making cars). It's more efficient and produces more profit, but there is no customization. The wines all come off the assembly line tasting the same. So although I can find a lot of decent wine, it's hard to find unique wine.

Now you have learned the four categories of wine styles:

Old World: higher acidity, not as fruity, earthy

New World: lower acidity, real fruity, not as earthy

International Style: a mix of both Old World and New World characteristics

Manipulated wine: No sign of New World or Old World characteristics — just decent wine.

Whew, that was a lot, but it's so important in understanding wine. Let's apply it.

When you taste a wine, all you need to say about it is the Body and Style. For that Riesling from Alsace, I'd say it was a light- to medium-bodied (no oak, 12.5% alcohol) wine and was Old World in style because it had high acidity and wasn't very fruity. Done. No adjectives. No obscure references. You can describe a wine like that to any wine expert and they'll know just what you mean.

Now we can put the FACGs and the CBS together, and that's a profile. The 2004 Riesling from Alsace was $12, not very complex; pretty straightforward, light- to medium-bodied, and Old World in style. That's all there is to it.

If you can remember a Riesling from Alsace that is around $12 (give or take a couple of bucks), is pretty simple, light to medium in body and is Old World in style, it's a pretty safe bet that if the FACGs are the same between two or more wines, the wines will be pretty similar. In other words, if you can't find the particular Riesling on the shelf or wine list but see another one that is from the same vintage, about the same price and is from Alsace, the odds are it will be pretty close to the wine you know. That helps you so much when you don't recognize wines that you have to choose from.

But remember, if any one of the FACGs changes, the wine won't be the same. If that Riesling was six years old, it will taste different. Or if it costs $25 instead of $12, it will be different. If it was a Riesling from Germany, it might be sweet. If the wine is the same price, same region, same age but is made from a Gewürztraminer grape, it will be completely differ- ent. Once any of the FACGs change, the profile will change. What separates wine experts from you is that they know a zillion profiles, so they can know what almost every wine tastes like before having it because they've developed a profile for that wine.

You can probably deduce that there are a lot of wine profiles to learn, and that's true. But instead of it being overwhelming, get excited about it; the more you taste wine and associate what you get from the wine with the facts about the wine, the more you will understand wine.

My charge to you is that every time you have a wine, make a profile. The FACGs are easy to determine, and then describe it using CBS. If you do this for every wine you have, you'll learn about wine so quickly you won't believe it. Soon you will be able to walk into a wine shop, look at the wines and have a pretty good idea what the wines will be like because you've developed profiles for wines. You'll look at a Chianti Classico that is three years old and $15 a bottle and have a pretty good idea what that wine will be like, assuming you have developed a profile for that wine already. And if you've developed a profile for Chiantis in the $25 range, you'll know what the difference is between the two. And so on.

It makes buying wine at a store and ordering wine off of a restaurant wine list much easier the more profiles you know about wine. Even if you don't recognize the names of the wines, if you have a similar profile, you will have a good idea what the wine will be like. Bonus!

Second, if you are looking for guidance in selecting a wine from a salesperson in a store or a waiter, if you tell them the type of wine you want using the terms from a profile, they'll know just what you are talking about. No need to remember adjectives or tasting notes.

And last, when you are at a tasting, there is no more pressure of what to say when someone asks you how you like a particular wine. Just respond by describing it by CBS, and you'll be just fine. Let the Club members in the room spout off the adjectives.

ADVANCED WINE PROFILING

To help a wine profile stick in your mind, it is best to associate the wine with someone or something. Often that is an experience you had or want to have. For instance, when I have certain Chardonnays that have a medium amount of oakiness to them, it makes me think about sitting on a patio overlooking a vineyard at sunset. Or when drinking an older Vouvray, I remember having lunch at a castle in the Loire Valley overlooking a pond with swans floating about. Tying a wine to some experience or person will help you remember the wine and its qualities. That's why keeping a journal of the wines you drink and the context in which you had them is so much fun, to look back and remember all of the wine drinking experiences.

HOW TO MESS WITH A CLUB MEMBER

Nothing is more fun than messing with a member of the Club. The easiest way is to share the Progressive Approach to wine. They'll react like a vampire who is exposed to daylight. Really. It will be so foreign to them; they'll freak — and then walk away. They may argue for a bit, but then they'll bail because they don't know why they believe what they believe. They've been spoon-fed the information, believing it's true, but they've never thought about it on their own.

When they run, don't chase them. It's not worth it. But if they don't run, and you have a chance to actually drink wine with them, let the games begin.

It's easy for a Club member, anyone, really, to agree with the expert's rating when they know the wine they are drinking. If someone knows the wine is rated highly and/or costs a lot, then they believe it's a great wine. Think about it. When you are given an expensive wine, do you ever say it tastes bad? No. It's a self-fulfilling prophecy. If you know the wine is expensive and/or rated highly, then you make yourself believe it is a great wine. But in a blind tasting, I could serve that same wine to you or even Club members, and they would probably have a completely different opinion about it and maybe not even like it.

It is very unlikely — next to impossible, in my opinion — for a wine drinker, no matter how experienced, to taste wines blindly and come up with the same rating as

Parker or the *Wine Spectator.* I'll bet you dollars to donuts that a member of the Club will never rate the wine as highly or guess the retail price to be as high as the actual price. When people taste wines blindly and there is no information about price or ratings to influence their opinion about the wine, they will recognize their tastes are not at all like those of experts.

Try this experiment on a Club member or someone who thinks they know a lot about wine. Get an empty bottle of expensive, highly-rated wine. Instead of wasting your money buying one, next time you're in a restaurant, ask them to save a bottle that was ordered by another table. Try to get a bottle that costs more than $100 on the restaurant wine list, or just the most expensive wine you can get. Take a decent wine under $10, pour it into the empty bottle of expensive wine, and serve it. The Club member should recognize the wine by the label because they are into expensive wine. If not, tell them how much it costs, and if it got a high rating, mention that, too. Then ask them to explain to you what qualities about the wine merit such a high rating or high price. The member will go on and on about the complexity, the concentration, the region where it was made and who knows what else, letting that self-fulfilling prophecy brain loose.

Since I don't eat donuts, I still should have some left over from the bet in the last paragraph to bet that the member won't say that the wine isn't worth the price or doesn't merit the high rating. Since they have been trained to believe that expensive and highly-rated wines are good, whether they like it or not, they'll make themselves believe they like it.

I was at a tasting and put Almaden Mountain Burgundy from a box in a fancy bottle of wine and served it to wine experts, one who was just about to become a Master of Wine. The almost-Master thought it was a $35 bottle of Italian wine; a Valpolicella, he thought. When I told him it was a box wine that cost the equivalent of $1.50 a bottle, he was crushed. But that's how it goes. Very few people can accurately guess the FACGs about a wine without knowing anything about it. And even fewer have the guts to give a true analysis about a wine they believe is expensive and/or highly-rated.

CONCLUSION OF TRADITIONAL VS. PROGRESSIVE

I hope you have a better sense on the two approaches to wine. Let's reviews.

Traditional Approach:
1. It's all about knowing a lot of information even though most of it is useless.
2. It's a top down system where the authorities rule.
3. A belief that a different shaped glass is needed for different types of wine.

4. The use a lot of adjectives to describe wine
5. Good wine are ones that are rated highly by *Wine Spectator* or Robert Parker — or worse yet, justify the quality of a wine because of its rating.
6. Disparage wines and people that drink those wines as being unsophisticated.

Progressive Approach:
1. Who cares what anyone else thinks about wine. It's the drinker's opinion that's the most important.
2. Good wine is defined by the person drinking it.
3. A glass designed for a certain type of wine is not needed to get the most out of a wine
4. Profiling wine is the most practical and useful way to describe wine
5. Instead of rules, provide guidelines and options that will help individuals enjoy wine better.
6. Not taking wine so seriously

Now let's move on to some factual stuff that one must learn to understand wine.

7

Wine Basics

HOW WINE IS MADE

WHY DOES EVERYONE make such a big deal about wine? It's just grape juice with alcohol. In fact, anyone can make wine. You pick grapes, put 'em in a bucket, and smush 'em. The yeast, which is already on the grapes, interacts with the sugar in the juice and fermentation begins. The yeast converts the sugar into alcohol, and there you have it: happy hour!

Okay, there's a bit more to it. But it's my belief that to know much more than that is a waste of brain cells, and believe me, I need all I can spare. So I'm not going to pollute your brain with too much information that is, in my opinion, superfluous.

First, you probably need to know how wine is made, which involves a little more than what I mentioned in the opening paragraph, but not much more.

The winemaker picks the grapes and puts the grapes in a de-stemming machine that gets rid of the stems, which would make the wine bitter.

Now the process takes a fork in the road, depending on if a white or red wine is being made. If it's a white wine, the grapes are put into a press and the juice is separated from the skins and seeds. The yeast is added and fermentation begins. A winemaker could use the natural yeast that is on the grape, but using cultured yeast makes the process much more predictable. The difference between wine made years ago and modern winemaking is all about predictability and having control over every step, so nothing is left to chance.

Like little Pac-Men (does that date me?), the yeast "eats" the sugar in the grape juice and converts it to alcohol and carbon dioxide. The carbon dioxide is released into the air so that all you're left with is the alcoholic fruit juice, sometimes called wine. If the yeast eats all of the sugar, then the wine is called "dry" — not sweet at all. We'll talk about sweet wines and sparkling wines later.

The wine is usually put into stainless steel tanks or oak barrels to rest and age a little just to integrate the flavors. This process may last from as little as a few months to as long as a few years.

Before the wine is bottled to go out into the market, the wine is fined and filtered to get all of the dead yeast cells out of it so you don't get a wine with stuff floating around in it. Egg whites, bentonite (a clay-like substance) and gelatin are just a few of the agents used to fine the wine. When a fining agent is put into a barrel of wine, the solid particles attach themselves to the agent and that settles on the bottom. The winemaker siphons off the clear wine to bottle.

Fining may not get all of the solid matter out of a wine. If that bothers the winemaker, he'll filter the wine as well. Filtering a wine guarantees that no solid material will be floating in the wine. However, filtering also strips some of the flavor from the wine, so more and more winemakers aren't filtering their wines to keep as much flavor as possible in them. You may have some stuff floating around in an unfiltered wine, but it won't hurt you.

In red wines, after the stems are removed, the winemaker adds the yeast and ferments the wine with the skins still mixed in, for two reasons. First, skins give the wine its red color. The juice of a red grape is clear. Not red. The way the clear juice turns red is from the pigments in the skin. The skins left in with the clear juice eventually turn the clear juice red. For blush wines, like white Zinfandel, the Zinfandel grape, which is red, is smushed and the red skins are left in the clear juice just long enough to turn the clear juice a blush color. Then the juice is drained away.

The second reason the skins are left in with the clear juice is to impart tannin into the wine. Tannin is the bitter component that gives a wine structure and allows it to age. The skins aren't used to make white wine, because there is no need for the color from the white skins and winemakers don't want the bitterness from the tannin.

In the old days, before electricity, there was no way to control how much tannin got into the red wine. The skins were left in with the juice to give the clear juice color, and at the same time tannin was getting into the juice. If it was hot in the fall, more tannin got into the wine because the warmer it is, the more tannin gets leeched from the skins. Now, with electricity, winemakers can cool the wine down, which inhibits tannin from getting into a red wine. The color still gets in, but not the tannin. This is great for making reds that are ready to be drunk right away.

A winemaker who wants more tannin or color in the wine can let the skins stay with the juice for a longer time, which is a process called maceration. The fad right now is to make highly extracted wines like the big California Cabernet Sauvignons, Zinfandels and Australian Shiraz. These wines are often high in everything: dark color and lots of tannin. Usually they are high in alcohol also. That style of wine doesn't do much for me, but it often gets very high ratings.

The red wine is usually aged for a few months to a year before it is bottled, long enough to let the flavors blend together. That's really all you need to know. You'll hear lots of terms thrown out by Club members at wine tastings. Probably the most popular question to a winemaker or sales rep is if the wine has seen oak; if so, what kind of oak, French or American, and if the oak was new oak. *(CJA – Club members often use the word "seen" when referring to if the wine has been put in oak barrels.)* Oh and then how long was the wine aged in barrel *(CJA – Club members wouldn't ask how long it was aged in the barrel or aged in barrels; they ask how long it was "aged in barrel")*? They'll ask if the wines have gone through ML *(CJA – ML is the Club term for malolactic fermentation, which is when the malic acid in wine is converted to lactic acid, making it less acidic, and often gives the buttery component to wine)* and throw around other terms like *sur-lie* aging, maceration, extraction, etc. It's all geek talk that doesn't get you anywhere. Either the wine is good or it's not, and it doesn't depend on any of the above topics.

SULFITES

Let's get the facts out there about sulfites. Sulfites are used in wine to preserve it. ALL wines have sulfites. A few are made with no sulfites added, but even those have sulfites, because sulfites are in grapes.

Anyone who thinks they are allergic to sulfites probably isn't. So many foods have a lot more sulfites in them than wine; you wouldn't be able to eat almost anything, including canned pineapple, fresh tomatoes and potatoes, tomato juice, and some frozen juices. If you can eat those, then you are not allergic to sulfites.

European wines also have sulfites. I hear the comments all the time about people who travel to Europe and drink a lot of wine but never get a headache, and they say it's because the wines over there don't have sulfites. Wrong. All wines have sulfites. However, I too seem to be able to drink more wine, and cheaper wine, in Europe without getting a hangover. My explanation for that is because the wine is fresher. You heard it here first. I can't document that, but I do know that when a product travels and is exposed to temperature variations, it isn't at its best. I've had wines in Europe that I loved. Came back to America and bought the same wine, and it wasn't nearly as good. I think the shipping can affect a wine enough to make it taste different than it would in Europe.

I think the context makes a difference too. When you are on vacation and loving the surroundings, everything is better. Whatever makes wine taste better in Europe, I know it's not the lack of sulfites in the wine.

Typically, there are more sulfites in less expensive wine and more in white than in red. But again, the amount is so insignificant that it is not a factor for anyone other than the folks who are truly allergic to sulfites (and you know who you are).

If sulfites don't give you a headache, then what does? Some people only get headaches from red wine. Some only from certain brand names. Yet no one knows what causes negative reactions from wine. Several scientific studies have addressed this, but none has come back with anything conclusive.

One day my dentist, an avid wine drinker, announced to me as he had his hands in my mouth, that he had to quit drinking. What!? I couldn't believe it. But he said that he gets an allergic reaction to wine — all wine. Out of the blue! He met with several doctors to discover the cause, but they couldn't find one. After a year, the allergic reactions stopped. Out of the blue. And now he's drinking wine again.

There seems to be a lot more going on in wine than we know, which leaves us with unexplained reactions and consequences. I'm sorry I don't have a better answer for you. But I do have one bit of advice to wrap up this section: how to avoid hangovers.

Hangovers are caused by dehydration, so the easiest way to avoid a hangover is to drink water. I believe that if you alternate a glass of water between glasses of wine — one ounce of water for every ounce of wine you drink — you'll greatly reduce your odds of getting a hangover.

8

The Grape Varieties

IT WILL HELP YOU A LOT if you can memorize the names of the grapes (at least the most common ones). Then when you see a name of the wine, you will at least know if the wine is named after a grape variety or not.

Thousands of grapes are used to make wine, but knowing the ones I list below will suffice. Once you are familiar with the names of the grapes, it is up to you to try to remember the characteristics of each grape. It might seem like a lot, but once you start, you'll see it's not that tough.

WHITE GRAPE VARIETIES

Albarino – Grown in Spain and Portugal (Alvarinho) under the same name, it makes a dry white that is pretty high in acid and perfect with shellfish.

Aligote – The other grape of Burgundy, which has been mostly replaced by Chardonnay. Grown in Bulgaria and Romania also.

Chardonnay – The major white grape variety, grown just about everywhere. Most famous in Burgundy.

Chenin Blanc – A French grape found in the Loire Valley, which makes the wines Vouvray and Saumur. Also grown in the USA and Australia. Known as Steen in South Africa.

Cortese – A simple, prolific grape variety from the Piedmont region in Italy. It is best known for Gavi, the name of the wine.

Gewürztraminer – Most famous in Alsace, France but also Germany and the USA. It is usually lower in acid.

Malvasia – The name that covers a dozen strains of grapes. It is widespread in Italy.

Marsanne – Found mostly in the northern Rhône valley in France.

Muscat – A very old grape variety, it is grown around the world. It often makes a sweet wine.

Pinot Gris – A number of wines are produced from this grape. Called Pinot Grigio in Italy and Grauburgunder in Austria.

Prosecco – The grape that makes the sparkling wine in Italy under the same name.

Riesling – Most famous in Germany and Alsace, but

also grown in Australia and the US.

Sauvignon Blanc – Grown almost everywhere. In Bordeaux, it is often blended with Semillon. It is the grape that makes the wines Pouilly Fumé and Sancerre in the Loire Valley. New Zealand has been especially successful with it making very fruity wines that are also fairly high in acidity.

Semillon – Often blended with Sauvignon Blanc or another grape, it is grown all over.

Trebbiano – The Italian name for Ugni Blanc in France. It's bland.

Verdejo A noble Spanish grape making white wines from the Rueda.

Verdicchio – The grape in Italy that makes an easy-drinking white.

Vernaccia – An old grape variety grown in Italy that makes average wine.

Viognier – An old variety best known for making a wine called Condrieu from the Rhône. It also has become popular in California and Australia.

RED GRAPE VARIETIES

Barbera – Grown in the Piedmont region of Italy, it makes a pretty high-acid wine.

Gamay – The grape that makes Beaujolais

Dolcetto — The grape and name of the wine from the
Piedmont region in Italy. Simple and easy-drinking.

Nebbiolo — Also grown in the Piedmont region, it is
the grape that makes Barolo and Barbaresco. Big, powerful grape.

Pinotage — A cross between the Cinsault and Pinot
Noir grapes. Grown in South Africa.

Cinsault — A grape grown in the south of France, it is
often blended with Mourvedre.

Petite Sirah — Not related to Syrah, this grape is
grown in California and usually makes quite a powerful wine.

Montepulicano — Grape and name of the wine in the
Abruzzi region in Italy. Good value food wine.

Malbec — Grown in France in Bordeaux and south of
there, but is most famous in making Argentine wines.

Cabernet Sauvignon — Grown almost everywhere. The
main grape in Bordeaux, France, where it is blended
with Merlot, Cabernet Franc, Malbec and Petit
Verdot. In warmer wine-growing regions (California,
Australia, South America), the grape produces more
flavorful, "bigger" wines.

Merlot — Known for its soft and fruity characteristics.

Mourvedre — A grape that is usually blended in the
south of France.

Pinot Noir — A lighter grape variety, but very important. It's very difficult to grow successfully, so it's usually quite expensive. Mostly grown in California, Oregon, the Burgundy region in France and New Zealand.

Syrah/Shiraz — This grape is known for its peppery, spicy flavors, which makes it a nice match for any food that is spicy or grilled. It's the main grape in the northern Rhône Valley, and blended with Grenache in the southern Rhône Valley in France. It's also popular in Australia and now in California.

Grenache/Garnacha — As Grenache, it is the main grape of the southern Rhône Valley and it is also grown in Australia. As Garnacha, it is a major Spanish grape variety in Rioja and the like.

Sangiovese — The main grape of Tuscany, Italy where Chianti is made. Usually has pretty high acidity.

Tempranillo — Spain's most highly regarded grape. It is the main grape in Rioja.

Zinfandel — Mostly grown in California. It usually makes a very fruity wine, often quite high in alcohol It is used to make white Zinfandel by using only the juice of the grape, with the skins mixed in with the juice for just a couple of hours.

9

The World's
Wine Regions

THE TRICK TO GETTING A HANDLE on the wine regions requires a little memorization. I'm sorry. I hate to memorize stuff too, but if you want to be able to know how wines from region A compared to region B, you have to know what the characteristics of each region are. Once you read through this, you'll find that the amount of information isn't too overwhelming.

But here are a few things to know:

1. Wines from Europe typically seem drier. Now, "drier" is used two ways in the wine world. Dry can be used to describe a wine that isn't sweet. Dry is also used to describe the texture of wine.

The two textures in wine are acidity and tannin, what I called "feeling" in the four-step process. Both

acidity and tannin dry out your mouth. We know that
Old World wines have higher acidity than New World
wine, so they are often called drier. Tannin is not a
characteristic associated with origin. Red wines made
anywhere in the world can have a lot of tannin or very
little. Tannin is controlled in the winemaking process,
so it's up to the winemaker how much tannin goes
into the wine.

2. Every country has laws about how a wine can
be labeled. In the New World growing areas, it's pretty
easy to understand the label because the name of the
grape is on it more times than not. It's just the opposite
in Europe, where the label gives the region where the
wine is made instead of the grape used. Thus European
wine is a little more difficult to get a handle on, because
you need to memorize the grapes that are grown in
each region to know what the wine will be like.

3. Each European country has classifications, kind
of a hierarchy for wine. In Italy, it's DOC, DOCG, IGT
and Vino da Tavola. In France, it's AOC, Grand Cru,
Premier Cru, Vin de Pays, etc. I'm not going to go into
all of that; it is more information than one needs to
know, and it won't help you find a wine that you like.
Every other wine book discusses those classifications.
If you finish this book and find that your brain still
doesn't have quite enough wine information in it, read
the other books.

ARGENTINA

Argentina is a country to watch. There is a flood of foreign money coming into the wine business, which brings knowledgeable winemaking practices and technology. Argentina has so much going for it, because it has the perfect climate for growing grapes. Every year is a good year. All they needed to build great wineries was a little know-how and the money, and they got them. Because the economy is depressed there, prices for land and labor are low. That's a great formula for good value wine. The cheaper it is to make wine, the cheaper it is to buy the wine, so Argentinean wine can be a great value. Even though Argentina is in the New World, many of their wines have an international style to them — one of the few New World countries where I find that — and I like it.

White wines: In general, the white wines are nothing special. Good values. You'll see Chardonnay most often. Torrontes is a white grape that makes a simple dry white wine that is usually quite affordable, which is the primary reason to buy it.

Red wines: This is where the action happens. There are a couple of lesser-known grapes that are producing some very good wines.

Bonarda is one that you won't see that often on wine shop shelves, and that's too bad. Every time a trade tasting happens where Argentine winemakers bring samples for prospective importers of their wine, the trade always gets excited about any Bonardas that are presented, yet we still see so few on the shelves.

The other grape that you can find is Malbec. Argentina is the only country that really is doing something with Malbec, and it's worth seeking out. Cabernet Sauvignon, Merlot and Syrah are also grown with Cabernet performing the best.

Summation: If you want a good value wine and have no other information to make a decision, remember AA. No, not Alcoholics Anonymous: Argentina and Australia. Almost any wine you buy from those two countries will be a decent drinking wine.

AUSTRALIA

Geez, what country is hotter when it comes to wine than Australia? None. They're on fire! They might have been a relative newcomer in winemaking, but they sure caught on fast. When it comes to easy-drinking, fruit-forward, good value wines, no other country is even in the running compared to Australia.

What you are getting are manipulated wines. They have no sense of origin. They're usually pumped out by huge winemaking operations. A handful of monster-sized companies make the majority of wine in Australia, and they have perfected their system. Once you get past the inexpensive wines, let's say less than $12, the prices jump up dramatically to the next level. You're talking $30 and up very quickly. Sure, those wines might offer more flavor, but with all the good values under $10, it's hard to justify spending 3-4 times the money for what you get. When you do get to the high-end wines, you won't be getting wines with finesse. Oh no. That's not the style of Australia. You'll be getting in-your-face wines, usually with high alcohol, full-bodied and powerful flavors.

White wines: Chardonnay clearly leads the way. Semillon is sometimes blended with Chardonnay, which is an odd combination but seems to work. You'll also find some tasty dry Rieslings, Semillon on its own, and Viognier.

Red wines: Once again, red wine is where the action is. Shiraz and Cabernet Sauvignon are the two grapes that dominate. Whether on their own or blended, they make some kick butt wine. Merlot makes an appearance on its own, mostly in less-expensive wines. The Grenache grape is pretty popular. It's usually blended with other red grapes (typically Shiraz) in less expensive wines but also makes some very full-bodied, big, powerful reds in the higher price brackets.

Summation. THE country for good value Chardonnay and fruit-forward reds.

AUSTRIA

An up-and-coming wine region. Oh, they've been making wines for a long time, but they had one hell of a setback in 1985.

That year wasn't the best vintage. In addition, there was a growing trend by folks to drink sweeter wine. So some enterprising winemaker had the bright idea of adding glycol, the key ingredient in antifreeze. I guess antifreeze is sweet, although I know better than to try it. Dogs love it because of its sweetness, but they don't know better than to drink it. (Unfortunately, my dog Squiggy found some in a neighbor's yard, drank it and died. It's quite toxic.) Needless to say, when the public found out about the antifreeze being added to the wine, they stopped buying Austrian wine.

Kudos to the Austrian government for taking action. They enacted a set of wine production laws that are very strict, and the winemakers have also worked hard to change the world's perception of Austrian wine.

White wines: The grapes that are used in Austria are not well known here, but are quite tasty. Grüner Veltliner, a white grape, can be very aromatic, peppery and spicy. Riesling and Welschriesling, although not related, produce very nice wines also. Oak is rarely used in making Austrian whites, so you're getting a crisp, clean style.

Red wines: Because Austria is so cool (in climate), it's not the best spot for reds. But the Zweigelt red grape produces wines that are medium-bodied and meant to drink young.

Summation: The Grüner Veltliner is worth seeking out for something different.

CHILE

Chile is where it all started. No, not winemaking, but good value wines. Chile has been making wine for centuries, but it wasn't until the late '80s that they hit their stride. Because of low land and labor costs and a perfect climate for growing grapes, they were able to make boatloads of inexpensive wine. Chilean wines were the first batch of inexpensive, New World style wines that came to the United States *en masse*. The wines offered more flavor and structure than California wines, but at a fraction of the price.

But that was the rise before the fall for Chile. The demand for their wines increased dramatically, and they desperately tried to keep up with it. Wine 101: The more grapes you grow on an acre of land, the lower the quality of the wine. Chile had to make more and more wine to meet the demand and without the time to plant more vineyards (a vineyard takes 4-6 years before it starts producing grapes that will work for wine), they just harvested more grapes from each vineyard. Well, the quality went down in the mid '90s. But they have recovered nicely as more vineyards are in use and foreign money has brought training and technology.

Chile has made a change in direction. It looks like they have given up trying to recapture the leading position in value wines. They'll let Australia and Argentina have that. Instead, they are making a push to offer better wines. Many of Chilean wines you see on the shelf

are over $10, and more and more are in the $20 range
and up. They are trying to show the world that they
can make serious wine. In general, I don't think they've
gotten there yet, but things look promising.

White wine: Usually on the low end, with Chardonnay
leading the way, followed by some Sauvignon Blanc
here and there. Doesn't do much for me.

Red wine: Cabernet Sauvignon is the leader in red
wines, with Merlot taking second. There is no question Chile makes some good/great wines, but the trick
is to figure out which ones are really worth the price.
One other red grape is getting some hype, and that's
Carmenère. No Carmenère I've had has thrilled me for
the price, but if you have a chance to try it, maybe
you'll like it, as some wine writers have.

Summation: Chile's identity from a value-wine
leader to a producer of more serious wines is still being
worked out. Good values in all price ranges can be had
for the savvy consumer.

---

*Remember, cooler regions favor whites. Any reds
that come from cooler regions will be easy-to-
drink wines, usually without much tannin and
with a fair amount of acidity.*

GERMANY

Every time I go to a tasting of German wines, I walk out thinking I need to have these wines more often. The wines offer amazing complexity for the price. But German wines have several things working against them:

1. The labels are a mess, impossible to pronounce and even more difficult to understand. (Actually, once you learn how the labels work, it's not that bad.)

2. The wine is usually sweet and not oaky, and most folks want dry and oaky. If people want sweet and no oak, they can buy white Zinfandel at a fraction of the cost.

3. Do you ever see German wines in the store? No. Store owners, for the few German wines they feel obligated to carry, usually stick them in the back somewhere.

4. And last, they're too expensive. I know I said they give you amazing complexity for the price, but you'll have to pay at least $15 (and usually over $20) per bottle to experience that.

If you can get past all of that and have the money, German wines are a joy to drink. They have several advantages over other white wines:

1. They usually have fairly high acidity, which is a key component when matching wine and food. Other whites that have acidity often taste too sour

or tart. The acidity in German wines is countered by sweetness. In fact, a lot of sweet German wines will actually taste dry, un-sweet, because the sweetness is balanced by the acidity.

2. They are lower in alcohol, typically between 7-10% compared to other white wines that are 12% and up. That may not look like a big difference, but it is when it comes to having a few glasses of wine.

3. German whites are probably the most versatile wines with food. They do come dry, and even the ones with some sweetness to them may seem dry because of the acidity, which balances out sweetness.

With so much going for German wines, it's worth taking a few moments to learn how to read a German wine label and some of the terms used.

Ripeness level: German wines use terms to let you know how ripe the grapes were when they were picked. Riper (sweeter) grapes usually produce more interesting wines. The longer the grapes stay on the vine, the riper they get and the less juice they have. The less juice the grape has the less wine that can be made and the more expensive it becomes because there is less wine to pay for that vine.

Ripeness levels start at *Kabinett* and go up from there. You can generalize that the riper the grapes, the sweeter the wine. Without any other designation on the label, *Kabinett* would be slightly sweet; *Spätlese* sweeter; *Auslese* can be close to a dessert wine; and

Beerenauslese and *Trockenbeerenauslese* are really sweet, and damn expensive.

Two designations will tell you the wines will be not as sweet as usual: *halbtrocken* (half dry) and *trocken* (dry). A trocken wine (kind of the trend now) is a dry wine and a halbtrocken has just a bit of sweetness.

One word about sweetness. A couple of paragraphs ago, I said if someone wanted a sweet wine, instead of paying the money for German wine they could just buy white Zinfandel. I know German wine lovers are grabbing voodoo dolls, writing my name in blood on the doll's forehead and sticking pins — no, spikes — into it. It's true that both white Zinfandel and most German wines are sweet, but the similarity stops there. Club members don't like white Zinfandel not because it's sweet, but because it has no acidity. It's cloyingly sweet. Some folks like that, and more power to them.

But what most wine lovers want in a wine, whether they know it or not, is a balanced wine. A white Zinfandel tastes out of balance because nothing is counteracting the sweetness. In German wines, acidity balances out sweetness. In fact, the sweetness in German wine is hardly noticed when balanced by acidity. So although German wines do have higher residual sugar than dry wines from other countries that you might be used to, the wines at the Kabinett and Spätlese levels may not taste that sweet because they are balanced out by acidity. At Auslese and above, you're talking sweet — no two ways about it — but never cloying sweet.

Kabinett (ka bih nett) - these are the simplest German wines. Usually slightly sweet.

Spätlese (shpayt lay sah) - more complex and flavorful than Kabinett.

Auslese (ows lay sah) – hand-selected grapes from the vines, these can be sweet to really sweet like dessert wines.

Beerenauslese (bear in ows lay sah) - late harvested grapes. Very sweet. At this level and up, the wine is usually sold in half bottles.

Trockenbeerenauslese (troh kin bear in ows lay sah) - a fun word to say, once you learn to pronounce it. This is the sweetest of the bunch, even sweeter than Sauternes. The grapes have shriveled up like raisins, they've been on the vine so long.

Eiswein (ice vine) - the wine is made from frozen grapes.

White grapes: Riesling is the king of grapes here, and all you need to worry about. (Okay, Sylvaner isn't bad, but never on the level of Riesling.)

Red grapes: Spätburgunder (Pinot Noir) — but what are you doing buying red from Germany, if you can even find it? This is white grape country.

Summation: German wines are something you should give a try. Refer to the chapter on how to buy wine for clues on which German wines to get.

FRANCE

The 900-pound gorilla of wine. Actually, this gorilla has lost weight and is probably down to 600 pounds. France is no longer the major player in wine for the average wine drinker. As more and more affordable wines have come in from Australia, South America and even the two-buck Chuck type wines from California, France has been losing market share like crazy

The political world crossed into the wine world when France didn't back George W's move into Iraq. Americans got revenge by boycotting French wines, and the French took another hit that they still haven't recovered from. And then just to add some salt to their wounds, the dollar lost value against the Euro, making European wines even more expensive.

But even though France might be losing ground in sales in America, I'm trying to keep them in business because I love its wine. On the high end, most of the greatest wines I've had have been from France. Sure, they've all been over $100 a bottle, but they were worth every cent. Orgasmic. If I had only a few months to live and had the money, I would be drinking only expensive Bordeaux and Burgundy. If I had a few months to live but didn't have the money, I would steal them, because I think I could avoid capture for three months. Of course, if my doctor was wrong about my illness being terminal, I'd be dinked.

On the low end, there are some great values from the south of France. They may not be able to compete dollar for dollar with Australian or South American wines, but the French wines have a desirable flavor profile that you can't get from New World wines.

And even in the mid-price level, it's hard to beat the whites from the Loire or Alsace or the reds from the Rhône. So although France has lost a little market share, it still has wines that can wow you at all price levels.

BORDEAUX: I say, don't bother with the wines from Bordeaux unless you are willing to shell out some bucks. The reds start getting good at $20, $30 and up. But there is a lot more lousy wine than good wine, so the odds of getting a good wine are not in your favor. I wouldn't count on getting a show-stopper wine for less than $100. And if you want to move up to an orgasmic wine, double that, and the wine should be at least four years old.

There are some spectacular expensive whites from Bordeaux, but you rarely see them. Usually you'll find inexpensive ones, under $12, that are pretty simple, fairly acidic, similar to a Pinot Grigio.

White wine: White Bordeaux is a blend of Semillon and Sauvignon Blanc grapes.

Red wine: The reds are a blend of at least two of the following grapes: Cabernet Sauvignon, Merlot, Cabernet Franc, Petite Verdot and Malbec.

Summation: Inexpensive whites can be good value. The expensive reds are some of the best in the world. You'll buy more misses than hits, but when you hit, ooh baby.

If you want to take the risk on the reds, be sure to go to a very good wine shop that specializes in Bordeaux to get good advice. Refer to the chapter on "Buying Expensive Wine."

BURGUNDY: If I had to choose one type of wine that is the Holy Grail for wine geeks, I would say red Burgundy. Folks who can afford any wine in the world usually collect both red Bordeaux and red Burgundy; but red Burgundy has the edge over Bordeaux, because great Burgundy is more ethereal than Bordeaux. There are great wines made all over the world, but red Burgundy has complexity, finesse and depth that go unmatched by any other wine.

Now the bad news. The wines are stupidly expensive, and the odds of finding one that's worth the money is next to impossible. It's called a rich man's wine region because a person will have to buy dozens of bottles of Burgundy at $60 a pop and up before finding one that is worth it. But once you have a great Burgundy, you're addicted. Then you have to experience that kind of wine again. The cycle starts over again ... buying dozens of bottles at $60 and up before you find a winner. Oh, it's a vicious circle.

Burgundy is also the most complicated of France's wine regions to get a handle on, but only if you're into buying the expensive stuff. Otherwise, it's pretty simple. White Burgundy is made from Chardonnay. Red Burgundy is made from Pinot Noir. Done. Not so hard.

Like most European wines, the labels state the sub-region where the wine is made, not the grape variety, so as long as you can see the wine, you'll know what grape variety it is. From that point on, Burgundy is just about how much money you want to spend. The more you spend, the better the wine.

The difficult aspect about Burgundy is that there are so many sub-regions. And knowing those isn't good enough. You have to learn the producers also. But in many cases, you don't know the producer because a guy called a *negociant* makes the wine. It's a mess. For me to go through all of the different sub-regions, producers and *negociants* of Burgundy would be useless. Too hard to pronounce, and next to impossible to remember. Just remember this: Burgundy provides probably the greatest payoff in wine, but also at the greatest cost.

White wines: Chardonnay is the grape, but the wines from Burgundy are "drier" than California Chardonnays. As the price goes up, oh! the wines get so good. For those of you who are in the "ABC" club (Anything But Chardonnay), you probably have never tried great white Burgundy, because it will knock your socks off — more so than any other white in the world, from any grape. (Okay, a great white Bordeaux might compete, but you never see those on the market.)

Red wines: For some reason the French made the region of Beaujolais (bo szoh lay') a sub-region of Burgundy, even though they are nothing alike except for the initial consonant. Beaujolais is made from the

Gamay (gah may') grape. Most folks know Beaujolais from the Beaujolais Nouveau celebration each fall. The grapes are picked in September and the wine is done and out the door by early November, in time for the worldwide release each year on the third Thursday of November. Because the wine is made so quickly, it's basically grape juice with alcohol. I've rarely tried a Nouveau that was worth paying for. The spin by the winemakers is that it is meant to be a drinking wine, not a sipping wine, so it's not meant to be "serious." Maybe so. But I can name a zillion other wines that cost the same or less that I would much rather drink. No matter, because the hype happens every year and millions of bottles of Beaujolais Nouveau are sold for parties celebrating the release.

The Beaujolais to try is not the Nouveau. It can be a simple fruity wine that has a decent level of acidity, which means it goes well with food to a more medium body, food-friendly wine and often a great value.

Moving north from Beaujolais, we move into the areas where the more prestigious red wines of Burgundy are made. As mentioned above, Burgundy makes great wine, but it's very expensive and you'll buy a lot of dogs before you find one. Red Burgundies under $20 are not worth it, in my opinion. If you're ready to make the quest to try some great Burgundies, go to the best wine shop in the city, find the sales clerk who knows about Burgundy and let him advise you. But know this: if he starts saying that you should buy this or that bottle because Robert Parker rated it highly, go somewhere else because he's got no brain of his own. That applies to all wine. Sales folks who try to sell you wine based on the ratings are lazy and don't care about you.

Summation: The whites are more affordable and can provide you a nice alternative to California Chardonnay. The reds are for the rich. Plain and simple.

LOIRE VALLEY: The Loire Valley is one of the prettiest wine regions to tour, with all of its castles. Because the region is in the north of France, the wines, both white and reds, will be medium-bodied with a fair amount of acidity — great food wines.

White wines: You'll see two grapes from the Loire. Chenin Blanc is used to make Vouvray, a sub-region of the Loire. Vouvray can be made dry, semi-dry or sweet like a dessert wine, and often the label doesn't give you any info to know which version you're buying.

The grape that is more commonly found on shelves is Sauvignon Blanc, which is used to make Sancerre (sahn sair) and Pouilly Fumé (pooh ee foo may'). Again, Sancerre and Pouilly Fumé are the sub-regions, but they're each made from 100% Sauvignon Blanc. Don't confuse Pouilly Fumé with Pouilly Fuissé, which is a sub-region of Burgundy and is made from Chardonnay. Sancerre and Pouilly Fumé are quite different from Sauvignon Blancs made in other parts of the world. They generally have more finesse and a flinty, stony character.

These two Loire wines paired with goat cheese are one of the top ten wine and food matches. Beyond goat cheese, I believe that the Loire Sauvignon Blancs are one of the top three most versatile white wines to match with food (the other two being German Riesling and Champagne).

Red wines: You'll find a Chinon on the shelves occasionally. That's the sub-region. Chinon is made from the Cabernet Franc grape. It's kind of wimpy, and usually not worth the money.

Summation: Skip the reds and buy Sancerre or Pouilly Fumé.

ALSACE: Another region in the north (the northeast in this case), so the wines will be mostly white and high in acidity. This is the only wine region that has traditionally put the name of the grape on the label, not naming the wine after a sub-region. They are the only French wines in tall bottles, taken after the Germans as Alsace used to be a part of Germany.

White wines: Several grapes are grown here, but each makes its own wine and it is usually made dry. The main grapes are Riesling (rees ling), Pinot Blanc, Gewürztraminer (geh vurtz' trah mee ner) and Pinot Gris (pee no gree). Riesling, Gewürztraminer and Pinot Blanc are also made into a high-level wine called a Grand Cru. The label still has the grape variety on it, but it will be followed by a vineyard name. There are 50 or so vineyards that are Grand Cru, too many to remember but

the label will always read Grand Cru. These are worth
trying because the difference in taste is significant. The
regular wine will usually sell in the teens. The Grand
Crus will be in the $20s and up, but that's pretty rea-
sonable for a top-level wine. Geez, the Grand Crus from
other regions are usually over $100 per bottle.

Red wines: Pinot Noir is grown here but it is rarely
seen in the U.S.

Summation: The regular whites go well with food
because of their acidity. In fact, they are often too acidic
to have on their own. They need food and will taste
better with it. Also, give a Grand Cru a try and see how
much more action there is in those wines.

CHAMPAGNE: As much as I love red wine, I think if I
had that illness where the doctor says I can only drink
one type of wine for the rest of my life, I would choose
Champagne. It's fun to drink anytime, anywhere, with
anything and anyone.

Champagne fits under the category of sparkling
wine, but only sparkling wine made in the Champagne
region in France can be called Champagne (according
to the French). Some non-French wineries don't honor
their wish and call their sparkling wine Champagne,
which I'm all for. But so not to piss off the French, in
this book I'll use the term Champagne the way the
French want me to use it.

Champagne has a lot of misinformation associated with
it. The biggest misconception is that Dom Perignon, the

French monk, invented Champagne. That isn't the case. (News flash.) It was the English who invented Champagne. (Ouch. What a shot to the French. But it's true.)

Back in the 17th century, the English were importing French wine. It seems some of the English thought the wine was a little bland. In the early 1660s, they came up with the idea of adding sugar and molasses to the bland wine to make it "brisk" and "sparkling." It's conceivable that the French had the same idea, but they had two strikes against them. They didn't have the glass making technology to make a bottle strong enough to withstand the pressure of sparkling wine. Second, they didn't use corks. The French were still using wooden bungs wrapped in hemp. The English, on the other hand, used corks and invented the glassmaking technology that uses coal instead of wood-burning fires to make glass stronger.

Dom Perignon arrived at the Hautvillers Abbey in 1668. Not only was sparkling wine made in England before he arrived at the abbey, it isn't even clear that Dom Perignon ever made Champagne. A paper written by his successor at the abbey attributed to him the first use of several winemaking practices, but never mentioned he made a sparkling wine. However, Dom Perignon did contribute several key practices in the making of Champagne. He was the first person to:

1. make a white wine from red grapes;

2. develop the concept of cool harvesting of the grapes;

3. make several passes through the vineyard to harvest only the grapes ripe at the time;

4. create the idea of assembling grapes from several
   vineyards to make a consistent wine; and

5. reintroduce the use of the cork as a stopper for wine.

I guess it would be tough for the French to say an
Englishman invented Champagne. They had to choose
a Frenchman, and Dom Perignon did more than any-
body at the time, so he got the honors. Fine by me.

By 1695 sparkling wine was being regularly produced, but it was still a hit-or-miss proposition because
the winemakers still didn't have a clear understanding
of what was going on. It really wasn't until the early
1800s that the process of making sparkling wine was
understood clearly and could be controlled (nearly 100
years after the death of Dom Perignon).

The way Champagne is made is called *méthode
champenoise*. The key aspect of *méthode champenoise* is
that the second fermentation happens in the same bottle
that will be sold on the market. In a nutshell, here is
how Champagne is made:

1. A regular wine is made from three grapes: Chardonnay,
   Pinot Noir and Pinot Meunier, another red grape. The
   skins are not left in with the juice when the grapes
   are pressed, so the juice stays clear. The color of wine
   comes from the skins.

2. The wine is put into the Champagne bottle, the

same bottle that you will be sold. To the wine, sugar and yeast are added. A second fermentation happens when the yeast starts consuming the sugar. But this time, the CO2 gas has nowhere to go but into the wine, so you get carbonated wine.

3. The dead yeast cells are removed from the bottle. A little more wine is added to top off the bottle, and it's done. The wine added at the end may be sweetened, so there are different terms to let you know if the Champagne is sweeter or drier.

SWEETNESS LEVELS FROM DRIEST TO SWEETEST

Extra Brut or Brut Nature
Brut - this is the most popular way Champagne is made
Extra Dry - this always gets me, that extra dry would be sweeter than Brut
Sec
Demi-Sec
Doux

TYPES OF CHAMPAGNES: Most Champagnes are made from a blend of vintages. Wine made in previous years is saved to be used in blending future wines. These Champagnes are called non-vintage. Easy enough.

Vintage Champagnes are made when the grapes used to make the wine all come from the same year. Vintage Champagnes are made only when the grapes are great. Well, that's what they say. I think it has more to do with supply and demand. You never see two vintages in a row. The wineries want a year or two between vintages, so that they can sell out of the current vintage before bringing another one along.

The regular way to make Champagne is from three grapes, Chardonnay, Pinot Noir and Pinot Meunier. These grapes are used whether it's non-vintage or vintage Champagne, unless you see some other terms on the label that state that the wine is made from just one or two of the grapes.

Blanc de Blanc - Literally, "white from white." A Champagne made only from Chardonnay. I think this is the best, most expressive style of Champagne.

Blanc de Noir - Literally, "white from black." A Champagne made from only red grapes. In Champagne, the finished wine shouldn't be pink. The goal is to make it as clear as possible. Usually kind of wimpy.

Rosé - White and red wine are blended together. The rosé version of non-vintage Champagne usually isn't that great. But the rosé versions of the luxury cuvées are orgasmic.

Luxury Cuvées - These are the most expensive Champagnes sold. The most famous are Dom Perignon by Moet & Chandon, Cristal by Roederer, Grand Année by Bollinger, Cuvée Louise by Pommery, La Grande Dame by Veuve Clicquot and Comtes de Champagne by Taittinger. Two Champagnes that don't get much press but are spectacular are Salon and Krug.

The luxury cuvées typically sell for $100-$150. The rosé version often sells for $250 and up. These are orgasmic wines.

Summation: Drink as much Champagne as possible. You'll be happier, have a better sex life and make more money in your job.

RHÔNE VALLEY: The Rhône Valley is divided into two sections, the north and the south.

White wines: In the north, the grape used is Viognier (vee o nyay'), which makes a pricey wine called Condrieu, rarely seen on store shelves and usually not worth it anyway. In the south, the whites are made from a blend of Grenache Blanc, Marsanne and Roussane and a few others, but they are nothing special.

Red wines: Rhône is for reds. In the north, the Syrah grape is used to make: Côte Rôtie (coat roh tee), Hermitage (er mih taj), Saint-Joseph (sahn jo sef') and Crozes-Hermitage (crohz er mih taj), the names you'll find on the labels which are sub-regions. You can find Saint-Joseph and Crozes-Hermitage in the $20-$30 range but they're often wimpy and not worth it. The Côte Rôtie and Hermitage cost upwards of $50 and can be stunning — but and then again, maybe not.

The south is where you should focus your attention. The reds are made from a blend of grapes: Grenache, Syrah and Mourvedre.

The wines are labeled by the sub-regions where they are made. If the label just says Côtes-du-Rhône, that means the grapes can come from anywhere and will probably make an easy-drinking wine. A step up from that are some specific areas that will be labeled as Châteauneuf-du-Pape (sha tuh nuf do pop), Lirac, Gigondas (szee gon dass) and Vacqueyras (vak ah rass).

Summation: The reds of the south are usually a great value. A Côtes-du-Rhône is often quite good and costs from $7-$12. Decent Vacqueyras and Lirac are somewhere in the teens, while Gigondas will be in the $20s. However, you'll get so much more action out of a Châteauneuf-du-Pape. They can be found in the $20s, but most will be $30 and up. They rarely will be full-bodied like a big California Cabernet or Zinfandel, but they still have enough oomph to satisfy someone who wants a more substantial red wine. A pretty safe and reliable buy.

LANGUEDOC: This region used to be the region for jug wine until a few folks recognized that good wine could be produced here. This region, in my opinion, offers some of the best red wine values in the world. If you want fruity wine values, Australia can't be beat. But if you want an earthier style of red, a good wine from the Languedoc can easily be bought for under $10. The labels will state the sub-region, and those include Faugères (fo szair'), Saint-Chinian (sahn shin ee ahn), Minervois (min air vwah) and Corbieres (core b'yair') and Fitou (fee too). All are made from a blend of two or more of the following: Grenache, Carignan (care ree n'yan), Syrah, Mourvedre (moor vay' dreh) and Cinsault (sin so).

Summation: Great value reds that are worth buying by the case.

I've just listed the regions in France that you will run across 98% of the time. But feel free to explore others if your local wine shop carries them.

ITALY

Italy has a ton of different wines and many less well-known ones that are worth trying. As is the case for most European countries, the wines are labeled by the region where they are made, not by the grape varieties, so a little memorization is needed on your part to understand the wines.

The majority of the wines you'll see from Italy come from two regions, Tuscany and Piedmont. While most of Italy's great wine comes from these areas, they are quite expensive. For the real wine values, you have to seek out wines from the lesser-known regions.

PIEDMONT: Just behind Tuscany in fame, Piedmont produces some note-worthy whites and reds.

White wines: Moscato d'Asti is a sparkling, sweet white wine made from the Moscato grape. It's actually not a sparkling wine because it only has about half of the carbonation, so they call it a *frizzante* wine. It is also low in alcohol, around 5-7% so you can guzzle it and not get looped. I love this wine, especially for summertime. Give this one a try.

The term for sparkling wine in Italian is *spumante*. And a sparkling wine from Asti, a city in Piedmont, is called, strangely enough, Asti Spumante. Recently, they called it just Asti, because some folks think Asti Spumante is just a cheap wine. This too is made from the Moscato grape and is sweet, but this is fully sparkling and higher in alcohol. It is not a "cheap" wine, though. I like it and I think you will too.

Gavi is a still white wine made from the Cortese grape. There are a few good ones out there, but most are kind of wimpy.

Red wines: Barbera is the name of the sub-region and the grape variety. The label will say Barbera d'Alba or Barbera d'Asti. The "d'" means "from," so in this case it's a Barbera from the city of Alba or Asti. Barbera that sells for $15 and under is probably a medium-bodied wine with pretty high acidity, which means it will be a lot more enjoyable if you drink it with food instead of on its own. Once the price gets over $15 or $20, Barbera is usually a lot more full-bodied. It still will have pretty high acidity, but just have it with heartier food.

Dolcetto is the grape and also the name of the wine region. It's often pretty simple, even wimpy, so good for guzzling.

The big boys made here are Barolo and Barbaresco. They are both made from the Nebbiolo grape and cost a mint. Barbaresco is usually not quite as full-bodied as Barolo, which makes it easier to enjoy when it's young. Barolo can be consumed young, but it gets so much better with age and can age almost indefinitely. Barolo has a very rustic, earthy, manly kind of flavor. Fortunately, there have been a string of good vintages from 1996 on, with 1996 and 1997 being the best. Since Barolo just starts coming into its prime 8-10 years after its vintage, the '96 and '97 vintages would be great years to buy now and enjoy. Barolo isn't inexpensive, but once you have one that has been aged and is from a good producer, it will change your life.

Summation: Barberas are great for easy-drinking wine with food. Barolo is a wine you MUST try.

TUSCANY: The most famous of the Italian wine regions, Tuscany is such a beautiful place, and it's a great place to speak Italian.

White wines: Why bother? Oops. There are some decent Chardonnays, but they usually are pretty expensive. And then there's the Vernaccia di San Gimignano (ver na chah dee san jee mee nyah no - whew!), which can be a good value at under $10 a bottle.

Red Wines: Sangiovese (sahn gee oh vay zee) is the main grape of Tuscany. It makes up about 90% of Chianti. You'll find several versions of Chianti on a store's shelf. If the wine just says Chianti on the label, that means it's from anywhere in the Chianti region and will be a light-bodied, high acid wine to guzzle with pizza. The next step up is Chianti Classico, which means the grapes are grown in a designated area that the government says has the best vineyards. Chianti Classico Riserva is wine that is aged at the winery for several years and will command a higher selling price.

Brunello di Montalcino (bru nell oh dee mon tul chee no) is 100% Sangiovese and is expensive. It was the first Italian wine I ever tried and fell in love with. Brunello can't be released from the winery until four years after the vintage, or five years for Riserva. Whenever a wine is kept at the winery for a while, you know it's going to be expensive. The problem with Brunello, like French red Burgundy, is that it is expensive and the quality is erratic. You'll buy so many Brunellos that aren't worth the money before you get one that knocks your socks off.

The better way to go is the Rosso di Montalcino, Brunello's baby brother. Made from the same grape and from the same area, the only difference is that it doesn't need to be aged as long and is ready to drink much younger. A Rosso will never match a Brunello, but you're spending a fraction of the price.

The last red wine to know is my favorite to say: Vino Nobile di Montepulciano (vee no no' bee lay dee mont teh pul chee' ah no) is also made from Sangiovese, but I have found it isn't worth the price compared to Chianti.

Super Tuscans: In the 1970s some winemakers

revolted against the regulations the Italian government put on winemaking, like which grape varieties were allowed to make wine from Tuscany. These winemakers wanted to experiment with French varieties like Cabernet Sauvignon, Merlot, Syrah, etc., varieties that weren't allowed in Tuscany. Since wines made from these grapes didn't fit under any of the sub-region designations, the winemakers bottled them as lowly table wines. But they were anything but. These were magnificent wines, even better than the traditional Tuscan wines. Thus the name Super Tuscans.

The Black Rooster Chiantis - You may notice that on certain bottles of Chianti, you'll see a black rooster on the foil covering the neck of the bottle. The rooster means that the winery is a member of the Black Rooster Consortium. The Consortium was formed in 1924, a time when there was a lot of counterfeit Chianti Classico being sold. To protect the integrity of Chianti Classico, the Consortium invited wineries to join and then put a black rooster on the neck of the bottle as a guarantee to consumers that the wine in the bottle was really Chianti Classico. Nowadays it doesn't mean much, as the counterfeit issue is not as prevalent. The rooster is more of a marketing program and has nothing to do with the quality of the wine in the bottle.

OTHER NOTABLE ITALIAN WINES

WHITE WINES: *Soave* is from the Veneto region made from the Garganega grape. Not much happening in Soave.

Verdicchio (ver dick' ee oh), from the region of The Marches, is the name of the sub-region and the grape. It can be a pleasant wine at a pretty low price.

Orvieto (or vee eh' toh) is made in the Umbria region from the Trebbiano grape. Another usually pretty bland wine.

Pinot Grigio is Italy's most popular white wine, grown in several regions. It usually has fairly high acidity, so it is best to have with food.

Chardonnay is made in several regions and although it is often put in oak, it usually has higher acidity and is a little leaner and fresher than Chardonnays from other parts of the world.

RED WINES: *Valpolicella* (val pole ih chell ah) is a sub-region of the Vento region where wine is made from the Corvina grape. It can be a simple, guzzling red under $10, or made in the Ripassa method, which means they take the regular Valpolicella and put it in barrels where the skins of the grapes that made Amarone are still present. The Amarone grapes add tannin, color and body to the simple wine, making it a full-bodied wine that is worth trying.

Amarone (am ah rone' ee) is a type of wine made in the same region and from the same grapes as Valpolicella, but the winemaker dries out the grapes on straw mats for a few months until the grapes shrivel up. The juice is more concentrated and makes a full-bodied wine with lots of flavor. It's kind of a wine geek's wine that can have a cult following. You should try it sometime.

Montepulciano d'Abruzzo (mohn tul pool chee ah no dah bru tso) is made from the Montepulciano grape in the region of Abruzzi. It's often an easy-drinking wine that is a safe bet to buy. It's rare you'll get a loser.

Salice Salentino (sah lee chay   sal en tee no) is gaining popularity in the U.S. because it's got a rustic, dark berry flavor. It's made from the Negro-amaro grape in the region of Apulia, the boot of Italy.

Primitivo (pree mih tee vo) is another wine made in Apulia, and is the name of the sub-region as well as the grape variety. The Primitivo grape is related to the Zinfandel grape. It can be a good value red, although I haven't had too many that have been inspired.

The real value in Italian red wines often doesn't fit into a category or sub-region. Look for wines from Sicily and Sardinia that are good value reds from grapes you never have heard of. Then there are a zillion wines on the shelf that are blends of regional grapes with Cabernet Sauvignon, and are made in many different regions. They are often under $12 and offer the best values in Italy.

Summation: Look for the blended wines that aren't labeled by sub-regions for the best value in almost any price range. Most are being made in the south of Italy.

Worthy reds that are labeled by the sub-regions that are worth trying are Montepulciano d'Abruzzo, Amarone and Barolo. The whites are all pretty simple and best for guzzling.

SPAIN

Spain is another region that is on the rise in making quality, good value wine. The regions and grapes might be unfamiliar, but don't let that get in your way of trying out the wines. You'll be a convert once you do.

White wines: The whites of Spain are usually pretty wimpy, except for Albariño, which is both the grape variety and what the wine will be called on the label. It's from the Rias Baixas in the northwestern corner of the country.

Red wines: Spain is producing some great value wines. You may find those from the best known regions of Rioja and Ribera del Duero, but you're better off trying wines from the lesser known regions like Toro, Campo de Borja, Navarra, Yecla, and Jumilla.

The two most popular grapes are Tempranillo (tem prah nee yo) and Garnacha (gar notch ah), which is the same as the Grenache grape. Most of the red wines you buy will be from one or a blend of these two grapes. Another red grape that you might run across is Monastrell, which I've seen as the lead grape on several best buy wines.

Like most European countries, the Spanish label their wines by the regions or sub-regions they're from and not by grape variety. You'll also see the terms *Crianza*, *Reserva* and *Gran Reserva* on the label. This tells you the wine has been aged before it's released. That's the handy thing about Spanish wine. The wineries age the wine for you, so you don't have to. Great concept. Crianza has been aged for one year, Reserva for three years and Gran Reserva for five years.

Most Spanish reds are medium-bodied wines. The exception is the reds from Priorat, which can be full-bodied. Also, once the wine costs $30 or higher per bottle, you can count on getting a pretty full-bodied wine.

Summation: Just start buying them. Since they are mostly made from the same two grapes, it's not an issue so much to focus on the regions. Try the inexpensive ones first and work your way up.

PORTUGAL

Famous for Port, which is covered in a different chapter, Portugal is making some great value wines. You may not have seen many Portuguese wines in the past, because most of the wine made in Portugal is consumed by the locals. As the winery business has grown, more wine is being made and now it's making its way to the U.S.

White wines: In the northwest of Portugal it's all about Vinho Verde, which translates to "green wine."

It's called this because the grapes often don't ripen very much. Vinho Verde comes in red and white, and it's meant to drink young. The white is better than the red. Don't worry about the grape varieties that are used.

Red wines: Most Portuguese wines are blended from indigenous grape varieties like Tinta Barroca, Tinto Cao, Touriga Nacional and Touriga Frances. The three key regions are Dao, Douro and Alentejo, which will be stated on the label.

Wines from Dao are generally pretty smooth and a good deal. It's hard to find a bad Dao. Douro reds are usually more full-bodied and rustic. The reds from Alentejo are often quite fruity because it's so hot in the region, and the grapes ripen completely.

Summation: For chugging, try the Vinho Verdes. The red wines from other regions are often tremendous buys, and I highly recommend that you seek them out.

SWITZERLAND

They make decent whites, but they are hard to come by and are quite expensive.

EASTERN EUROPE

Hungary, Croatia, Romania, Slovenia, Slovakia and Bulgaria — If you live near a big city, you may see some wines from these countries. In the past all the wines from these countries were low-priced, jug type wines. Now we are seeing more serious wines, mostly reds, and at affordable prices.

Summation: Still a novelty and a little iffy, but we are seeing more and more wines coming from Eastern Europe, and I think they're worth considering if you can find them.

NEW ZEALAND

New Zealand made a big splash in the U.S. market years ago with its Sauvignon Blancs. Typically, a Sauvignon Blanc is either really fruity with low acidity (what you would usually see from New World countries) or a leaner style (not that fruity with higher acidity), the kind from Europe. But lo and behold, New Zealand produces Sauvignon Blancs with lots of fruit AND high acidity. Unbelievable.

I'm not a big fan of the style, but many fans are, and you owe it to yourself to try a few Sauvignon Blancs from New Zealand.

Chardonnay is also made there, but I haven't found that to be as good a value as the Sauvignon Blancs.

Some writers hail the Pinot Noirs coming from New Zealand as the next competitor for Burgundy. If I were a winemaker in Burgundy, I wouldn't be nervous. The Pinot Noir made in New Zealand is fairly expensive, like Burgundy, but it is very clearly made in the New

World style (pretty fruity). I've only had a few that got my attention, but when I found out how much they cost, they just didn't seem to be a good value.

Summation: Sauvignon Blanc is where the action is.

SOUTH AFRICA

I visited South Africa recently and fell in love with the country. I was there when the Rand was 12:1 to the dollar. I was buying good wines for $.50 a bottle. Two of us had a wonderful meal at a nice restaurant and ordered the most expensive wine on their list, and the total for the whole meal was $20. No wonder I fell in love with the country. Now the exchange rate might be 6:1, but it's still a heck of a place to visit.

The South Africans are not stupid. Instead of charging the normal markup for their wine, which would make the wines a great value in the U.S. market, the wineries and/or importers add a huge markup on the wines to fit into the cost of other wines of like quality. The same wine that costs $2 in South Africa will cost $16 or something here. It's crazy. Someone's making a ton of money.

White wines: They do pretty well across the board, whether it's Chardonnay, Sauvignon Blanc or Chenin Blanc (called Steen). Very few of the wines fall into the outstanding category. They mostly are easy-drinking wines, but are often overpriced compared to what you can find from other countries.

Red wines: There are some beauties made from Pinot Noir, Pinotage (a cross of Pinot Noir and Cinsault), Cabernet Sauvignon, Shiraz and Merlot. There are a lot of wines under $12 and they are like manufactured wine (good for guzzling). The noteworthy reds are over $20 a bottle and often much higher. They don't seem to justify the price to me, but they sure taste good.

Summation: Good, easy-drinking wine across the board in the $12-and-under category. Better yet, visit South Africa and get great wines for a fraction of what you pay here.

GREECE

Greece has certainly been making wine for a long time, and they do a pretty good job of it. But who buys Greek wines in the U.S.? I don't think I have ever bought a Greek wine in a store. At a Greek restaurant I drink Greek wine and at various wine tastings, I always try all the Greek wines that are being presented. But to go out and buy one is a different story.

Retsina was all we knew when it came to Greek wine for the longest time. Retsina is a wine to which small pieces of pine resin have been added. To me, Retsina tastes like I'm drinking liquid wood. Ugh.

Although Retsina is still being made, the story now is in the wonderful wines being made without the pine resin. The Greeks are making wines from familiar grapes such as Cabernet Sauvignon, Cabernet Franc, Chardonnay, etc. and they're good; but to me, the ones worth trying are wines made from the indigenous grapes, even if they are next to impossible to pronounce.

White wines: The main white grape is Assyrtiko and makes a fresh, easy-drinking style of wine with good balance.

Red wines: The two most popular indigenous varieties are Xynomavro and Agiorgitiko. You'll find red wines made just from one or the other or blended with international varieties like Syrah, Cabernet Sauvignon and Grenache. They can be easy-drinking or more full-bodied, with a rustic edge.

Summation: The Greek wines have two big things going for them. One: they are some of the best wines with food, and two: on the whole, they are true to their heritage. They haven't been corrupted by the International style of making wine.

CANADA

News flash: It's cold in Canada. And cold is not good for growing grapes, unless you want frozen grapes, which is just what Canadian winemakers want: frozen grapes to make ice wine. Canada is the largest producer of ice wine in the world. Because of the volume, the very sweet ice wine is often much less expensive than ice wine produced in Germany, where it is more of a rarity.

There are some pretty good regular wines being made in Canada, but you never see them on store shelves. The government just doesn't seem to care about marketing Canadian wines to the U.S.

MEXICO

No, I'm not kidding. The Mexican wines are really quite good, and good values besides. The wine region is right around Ensenada in Baja. Although still rarely stocked by a store near you, Mexican wine is worth trying.

CALIFORNIA, WASHINGTON AND OREGON

So I got to this section, and I thought about what I should say about wines made in the United States. The labels are easy to read; no problem there. Would it be worth listing the regions in each wine producing state? No. Would it even make sense to name the regions of California, Washington, etc. and what they're good for? I don't think so. Despite what the winemakers might say from each of the states, it is very difficult to guess a wine from a particular wine-growing region in those states, let alone the state itself. I challenge someone to be able to tell a Chardonnay from Santa Barbara vs. a Napa Chardonnay — or a Cabernet from Sonoma vs. Washington State. The geeks are fuming right now as they read this, but the heck with them.

Two generalizations I can make is that I think Washington State has a smoother, more appealing style of wine than the other two states. Oregon Pinots get a lot of hype, but so many are too expensive.

ALL OTHER STATES

Every state has wineries now. Scary, in some cases, but there are some decent wines being made. I'm most familiar with Virginia wines, and they're doing a great job. The problem with the wines made in most states is that they are expensive compared to a wine of the same caliber that you can get from the west coast (maybe), but certainly from other countries. But it's fun to go to a winery and hang out drinking their wine.

Okay, that's all I have to say about American wines.

10

All About
Sparkling Wine

SPARKLING WINE IS GOOD ANY TIME, anywhere. If you drink sparkling wine as just a special event beverage, you're missing out on so much. You should flip your thinking around, because sparkling wine can make even an average event special. I prefer different wines depending on the mood I'm in, but sparkling wine always seems to work, no matter what my mood.

Lily Bollinger was once asked, "When do you drink champagne?" She replied, "I only drink champagne when I'm happy, and when I'm sad. Sometimes I drink it when I'm alone. When I have company, I consider it obligatory. I trifle with it if I am not hungry and drink it when I am. Otherwise I never touch it - unless I'm thirsty."

Napoleon said, "In victory, you deserve Champagne; in defeat, you need it."

And look what Mr. Copycat Winston Churchill said: "In success you deserve it, and in defeat you need it."

And last, I say, "Sometimes I have too much Champagne, but I never have enough."

Anyway, the point is that many insightful people have recognized that sparkling wine is an appropriate beverage any time.

Now, I'm saying "sparkling wine," because one is supposed to call a sparkling wine Champagne only if it comes from the Champagne region in France. I know the rules, but I think of the term Champagne like "Kleenex" or "Frisbee." I know if it isn't really Kleenex® or Frisbee®, it should be called "tissue" and "flying disc," respectively. But, hey, the brand names should be happy they are being referred to at all. I usually refer to all sparkling wine as Champagne, but for the sake of education, I'll stick with the proper usage in this chapter.

So Champagne is a sparkling wine that comes from the Champagne region in France. Any bubbly outside of that region should be called sparkling wine. You can read all about Champagne in the chapter on Wine Regions. I'll cover sparkling wine in general in this chapter.

It's all about the bubbles. There are several ways bubbles get into sparkling wine, but in almost every case, it's done through a second fermentation. Regular wine is made first. Then yeast is added along with some sugar to start a second fermentation. Fermentation has two byproducts, alcohol and carbon dioxide. The second fermentation only adds about 1.5% more alcohol, but the carbon dioxide is not released as it is in the first fermentation, and that's how the bubbles get into the wine. The differences in sparkling wines come from where that second fermentation happens.

1. *Méthode champenoise* (method shahm pehn wahz) — the way Champagne is made. The first fermentation is in some container, stainless steel tanks, oak barrels, a bathtub, wherever. Then the wine is put into the actual bottle that you buy, and that's where the second fermentation happens.

2. Transfer method — The second fermentation happens in a bottle, but not in the same bottle that it is sold in. Once the second fermentation happens in the bottle, the wine is transferred into a tank, under pressure, filtered, and then bottled under pressure into the bottle you buy. Filtering in a huge tank instead of individual bottles saves money.

3. Charmat method — The second fermentation happens in big tanks, and then the wine is put into bottles under pressure. An even less expensive way of making sparkling wine.

4. Carbonation — CO2 is injected into the wine, as is done for sodas.

Does it make a difference to me how a sparkling wine is made? No. The technology has come along so far that each way can make very good wine. If a sparkling wine isn't good, it's because someone is cutting corners by choosing lousy grapes or the system they used to make the wine. The way it works out practically, though, is that the better sparkling wines are almost always made in *méthode champenoise*.

TYPES:

Champagne – Made from Pinot Noir (red), Pinot Meunier (red) and Chardonnay (white) grapes.

Crémant – A sparkling wine made in France from other regions; it has half the fizziness as Champagne.

Cava – The Spanish sparkling wine made from the Macabeo, Xarel-lo (sha REL oh) and Parellada grapes (all white grapes) and is usually made in *méthode champenoise*. The Spanish sparklers are usually under $10 a bottle, and are great for guzzling.

Asti Spumante or *Moscato d'Asti* – Both are sweet and made in the Piedmont region in northern Italy from the Moscato grape. The Charmat method is most commonly used. The Spumante has the same fizz as Champagne, while the Moscato has just half the fizz and is much lower in alcohol, usually around 6%. I can drink a bottle of Moscato d'Asti like it's water. It is the drink of choice when I'm mowing my lawn on my riding mower.

Prosecco – Also made in Italy, Prosecco is the name of the grape and the wine. The Charmat method is often used. Prosecco is growing in popularity and may actually catch up with Champagne in number of bottles sold. I haven't been too impressed by Prosecco, but because it sells for $10-$20 and has had a huge marketing campaign, people are buying it. Good for them. I think one can do better, though, with Spanish sparklers.

Sekt – German sparkling wine usually made in the Charmat method. Who knows what kinds of grapes are used. It could be Riesling or whatever they feel like.

Sparkling wine in general – There are sparkling wines made in many countries that don't have a specific term other than "sparkling wine." The grapes used run the gamut from the traditional Pinot Noir and Chardonnay to anything else under the sun. There's even red sparkling wine, like Brachetto from Italy or the Australian version made from Shiraz. The sky's the limit ,and most are pretty good. Definitely worth a try.

OPENING A BOTTLE OF SPARKLING WINE: First you have to decide the purpose of having sparkling wine.

1. If you are celebrating a victory, you want to shake the bottle vigorously first and then pop the cork, and continue to shake it while you spray everyone around you.

2. If it is a more reserved celebration, don't shake the bottle but let the cork fly out of the bottle with a big "pop." Pour and guzzle.

3. If you're buying decent sparkling wine and you want to really enjoy it, the removal of the cork should

make as little noise as possible when opened. You're paying for the bubbles when you buy sparkling wine, so you want to keep them. The more of a pop when a bottle is opened, the more gas gets out of the bottle and the more bubbles you lose.

The following is the way to open a bottle of sparkling wine:

a. Remove the foil. Typically there is a tab that you can pull that takes it right off.

b. The next step is to undo the cage. Grab the metal circle and turn it until the cage is loose. It will always require six turns to get it undone. Once the cage is loose, this is where trouble can happen. The cork can "blow" on its own and really do some damage. The pressure inside of a Champagne bottle is 90 pounds, or equal to three times an automobile tire. *(CJA – this is the analogy always given by Club members: the auto tire. Some Club member started using that years ago, and now everyone repeats it. One is supposed to imagine an auto blowing up, which would seem huge. But a bicycle tire on a road bike — those really skinny tires, less than an inch wide — is filled to over 90 pounds. Now the analogy isn't so amazing.)*

Just a couple of days before I wrote this chapter, Robert Kearns died. He was the guy who invented the intermittent windshield wiper. He got the idea for it on his wedding night in 1953, when a champagne cork struck him in the left eye, which eventually became blind. The blinking of his eye led him to wonder if he could make windshield wipers that worked the same way — that would move at intervals instead of in a constant back-and-forth motion. A little crazy, but you can see that the flying cork can be dangerous.

So as you loosen the cage, you never want to take your hand off the top of the cork. Thus, you don't want to remove the cage. You'll pull the cork out with the loosened cage still around it.

c. To pull the cork out, you grab the bottle with one hand and the cork with the other. Tilt the bottle at a 45-degree angle and slowly turn the bottle, not the cork. As the cork starts coming out it will gain in pressure. Don't let it just pop out. Slow it down and just before it's ready to come out, tilt the cork a little so the gas sneaks out on one side of the cork. It should make a quiet "pssst" sound.

There is a saying that the sound of a properly opened bottle of Champagne is the sound of a satisfied woman. The saying is not referring to a sexually satisfied woman, although that makes for a better story. Rather, it's satisfied as in content. The sound should be like a sigh or a deep breath of content.

Now that the bottle is open, the traditional way to pour sparkling wine is to put your thumb in the dimple on the bottom of the bottle (called the punt) and to rest the bottle on your hand. The neck of the bottle should never hit the top of the glass. Pour a little bit in and when the foam goes down, top it off.

So that's the traditional way to open a bottle of Champagne. But there are much showier alternatives. Some people use a saber to whack off the top of the bottle. It's pretty neat as the top of the bottle is launched across the room and Champagne foams out the top of the bottle. But my favorite way to open a bottle is to use a Champagne flute. I have a video of it on my website at www.winetasting.org that shows just how to do it. What you're doing is using the base of a Champagne flute or wine glass to knock the top of the bottle off. It is the coolest thing you can do with wine. It takes very little effort and anyone can do it. The best part about it is that the wine doesn't foam out of the bottle so nothing goes to waste. You will get so giddy with excitement once you try this trick. Visit the website to learn how.

GLASSWARE: The Champagne flute started out as a coupe, the flat and shallow glasses that are often plastic. It is said that that shape was originally modeled after the breast of Marie Antoinette, who loved Champagne. Others say the coupe shape was to pay tribute to the breasts of Madame de Pompadour. I don't care who the woman of honor was, I'm just glad there are breasts in the story. Champagne has always been the beverage loved by women. Historically, men usually choose Port or Claret, which is another term for Bordeaux. The coupe isn't a good choice because the wide, shallow shape dissipates the bubbles too quickly.

The best shape is a flute. I'm not sure whose breasts were the inspiration for the flute, but they probably weren't proud of it. The taller flute allows you to see the bubbles rise and the narrower opening retains the "mouse." Some flutes are etched in the bottom of the bowl, so the bubble streams form there and go up in a pattern. Way cool.

No matter what the glass, the key is to make sure they're clean. Any soap residue will ruin the bubbles. After washing, rinse the flutes twice with really hot water and let them dry or dry them with a lint-free cloth.

DRINKING SPARKLING WINE: Sparkling wine is so enjoyable when you're drinking it, but it can cause a major hangover the next day. Two things to do to avoid a bubbly hangover: drink plenty of water, which really applies to all wine, and drink slowly. If you drink sparkling wine too quickly, like guzzling, the bubbles get into your bloodstream and wreak havoc. It's better to take small sips and let the wine dissipate in your mouth before swallowing. Follow those two rules and you'll be feeling bubbly the next day.

Sparkling wine is a great starter to a meal or an evening. Even if you drink it slower, the bubbles make the alcohol get to your brain quicker. So if you want to loosen up a crowd, your guests or yourself, sparkling wine does it for you physically — and also emotionally, because just the idea of drinking sparkling wine makes one more lively. And it beats doing a shot of tequila.

WHICH SPARKLING WINE SHOULD YOU BUY?

Here's how I choose what to drink:

When I want to guzzle or if I have guests over who really don't appreciate the finer stuff, or if I am mixing it for Mimosas, I choose Spanish, Prosecco, South American or Australian at under $10 a bottle. Anything American under $10 scares me.

When I'm mowing the lawn or want to blow the socks off someone: Moscato d'Asti. It's sweet, fizzy and low in alcohol, but damn good. While Prosecco is the most overrated sparkler in my book, Moscato d'Asti is the most underrated. When folks try it, they're hooked. About $15 to $20 a bottle. Asti Spumante is similar and could work too, but it doesn't have quite the finesse of Moscato d'Asti.

When I want a good quality sparkling wine for everyday consumption, which I try to do, I go with one of two: Segura Viudas Aria Brut from Spain (around $9) or Korbel Brut (around $11) from California. (A shout out to Michelle McClendon, a winemaker who makes Korbel. She's one of my favorite people in the wine business.) Both of these sparklers are clean and fresh and won't break the bank. Aria is by far my favorite and the best value of any wine that fizzes.

For a little bit more sophistication, I choose American sparkling. I like Roederer Estate, Mumm Cuvée Napa, and Domaine Carneros (all in the high teens to high $20s).

The next level up is non-vintage (NV) French Champagne. I think that Rosé is the most romantic, but the Blanc de Blanc is the most sophisticated. You're looking at $50s and $60s.

There are many more Champagnes available in stores than just the big names. The big names buy grapes from grape growers and then make the wine. There are two letters in small print on every label of Champagne. The major Champagne producers have NM on the label, which means they buy the grapes. The grape growers that make their own Champagne put RM on the label. These can be the real buys.

Then we hit the luxury cuvées like Dom Perignon, Cristal, etc., which usually cost around $100 and some change. The Champagnes are certainly better, but I have rarely found that it's worth spending the money unless you want to make a real impression on someone. To me, these wines offer more impact for show than for taste.

The last level is for the real high-end Champagnes, such as special bottlings and luxury rosés. It's the luxury rosés that will knock your socks off. Hell, they will knock every bit of clothing off. For me, if I were to choose one wine to celebrate something, I would choose a luxury rosé Champagne every time. I love red wine, but it's always iffy to know what will be in the bottle. A Champagne is much more reliable. The luxury rosés will set you back from $120-$300.

11

Sweet Wines

THERE ARE THREE TYPES of sweet wines: fortified wines, dessert wines and regular table wines that are sweet, like white Zinfandel.

The latter doesn't need too much discussion. There are sophisticated sweet table wines, like some German Rieslings, and the guzzling type to satisfy a sweet tooth, like white Zinfandel.

This chapter is about fortified and dessert wines, as they are made in a special way.

FORTIFIED WINE

A fortified wine is a table wine to which a spirit (brandy, typically) has been added, so these puppies can make you silly very quickly. The alcohol is 18-22%. That's why they are typically consumed in small quantities.

There are a few different fortified wines you should be familiar with. The big one is Port. Port with a capital "P" is made in Portugal. Other port-style wines are made in California, Australia and South Africa, and can be quite tasty.

Let's get through real Port first. Port is made from a blend of grapes, none that you have heard of nor should you care about, but here they are: Touriga Nacional, Tinta Barroca, Touriga Francesca, Tinta Roriz and Tinta Cao. (See, I told you so.)

The grapes begin to ferment, just like it's done to make a regular wine. But before fermentation is done, a neutral spirit kind of like a brandy is added. The high alcohol kills the yeast, so fermentation stops. Since the fermentation didn't finish, there is still sugar in the juice (all the sugar typically gets eaten up by the yeast). So now you have a wine that is sweet and high in alcohol as a result of the brandy being added.

What happens next is what makes the different styles of Port. There are two different types of Port. I don't like the terms used by other writers, so I'm going with "big barrel" and "small barrel" Ports.

Big barrel Ports are ones made when the wine is put in huge wood barrels (bigger than my bedroom). Small barrel Ports are put in usual-sized wine barrels. Within each of these categories, there are sub-categories. I'm feeling encyclopedic here, but hang with me because I think this will be worth it.

BIG BARREL STYLES:

Ruby Port — Ruby style is the least expensive. The wine is put into the big barrels for two to three years and bottled. The wines are very fruity and are really good for guzzling—but watch out for those calories. They are usually priced in the teens.

Vintage Port — The Big Kahuna of Port. I can't say enough good things about Vintage Port. Although it's good when it's first released from the winery, it can last forever. I've had Vintage Port that has been over 50 years old that was as fresh as can be. That's why folks buy a Port the year a child is born and open it on the child's 21st birthday. No problem keeping a wine that long. The odds of a regular wine lasting that long are very low. (Dessert wine can age like a Port, so that could be bought also — like a Sauternes.) Vintage Port is put in the big barrels for two years and then released. Since Vintage Port doesn't really hit its peak for at least a decade, it's up to you to age it. Again, it's still okay to drink it young, but you'll never use the word "orgasmic" to describe a Vintage Port under 10 years old. A Vintage Port is made from grapes grown only in that vintage year. Wineries usually choose 2-3 worthy vintages per decade.

Late Bottled Vintage (LBV) Port — You can probably recognize the problem with Vintage Port: it takes forever to mature. Who has time to wait? So the clever wineries came up with Late Bottled Vintage, or LBV as it is referred to. This is a wine the winery ages for you.

How nice of them! Thank you, winery. LBVs are still from one vintage, and they'll state the vintage on the label. They differ from Vintage Port in that the winery ages LBVs for 4-7 years in big barrels to expedite the aging of the wine with the idea of creating a wine that tastes kind of like a Vintage Port that has been aged. It doesn't work. I mean, an LBV will never taste as good as a Vintage Port that has been aged, but I believe the LBVs are a great deal. They do taste good and they're quite affordable. I give them the best buy rating of Big Barrel Ports.

Single Quinta Vintage Port — This is the new thing in Port, making a Vintage Port with the grapes from one vineyard. Traditionally, Vintage Port is made from the grapes from a bunch of vineyards. The fact that Single Quinta Port is made from grapes from just one superior vineyard is supposed to give the wine cachet.

WARNING: Vintage Port, Single Quinta Vintage Port and some LBVs Ports are unfiltered. That means that there will be a lot of sediment in the bottle once the wine gets five or more years old. You'll have to decant it. The easy way to decant a wine is to pour it through a coffee filter. Then you can take the sediment and make a Port wine jelly out of it. Tasty.

SMALL BARREL PORTS:
Tawny Port — Tawny Port is a wonderful wine. All Tawny Port is a blend of several vintages. Basic Tawny is aged in small barrels for a few years; and with more

wood contact and some oxidation, Tawnies develop a brownish color and nutty taste. It's hard for me not to finish a bottle of it (blimp alert!). This is one style of Port that the Portuguese may not be better at making than other parts of the world. There is some great tawny port being made in Australia, and you should give it a try. The inexpensive basic Tawny Port is drunk chilled by the French in the summer time. What are they thinking? Can you imagine pumping down an 18-22% alcohol wine in the summer with the sun beating down on you? Pass-out-ville. But I will say that Tawny Port, Portuguese or Australian, chilled or not, summer or winter, is good anytime. You can't lose with it.

There are also the more serious and more expensively-aged Tawnies. On the label they will designate 10, 20, 30 or 40+ year old Tawny Port. Here's a chance for you to win some money in a bet. Most wine geeks or even experts believe that the age stated on the label, 10, 20, etc. is the average age of the different wines used in the blend. That's not true. Because these wines are all tasted by a panel of independent experts in Portugal before they're released, the wines get the designation of 10, 20, 30 or 40+ based on if the wine tastes like the respective aged wines should taste. In other words, the wine is labeled based on the taste profile, not the average years of the wines in the blend. It's impossible to make a 20-year-old Tawny Port from a blend of wine where no wine in the blend is older than 20 years. It just won't pass the taste test. These tasters are good!

Colheita Port — Okay, so I lied. I said that all Tawny Port is a blend of vintages. Colheita (coal hay tah) Port is an exception. These are Ports from one vintage aged in small barrels for a long time. They're good, but I think I'd take an aged tawny over a Colheita.

White Port — Don't bother.

OTHER FORTIFIED WINES:

Madeira — This is a wine made on an island off the coast of Portugal. It can age as long as Vintage Port and can be quite good. It's mostly used for cooking, but the high quality Madeira is worth a try if you can find it.

Marsala — From Sicily, it is used in zabaglione and tiramisu. Best used for cooking. Hard to find any Marsala worth drinking.

Sherry — Sherry doesn't do it for me, but a lot of wine geeks think it's the greatest. Most Sherries are dry and high in alcohol. The types are Fino (dry); Amontillado, a fino on steroids (dry, more potent and nutty); Oloroso, even more fortified than a fino; and Cream sherry, the sweetest of the bunch, resembling a Port.

Vin Doux Naturel — Vin Doux Naturels (VDN) are fortified wines from France that are made like Port is made. The wine is fermented and then a neutral spirit is added to bump up the alcohol. VDNs can be white, made from the Muscat grape, or red, made from the Grenache grape. The best known are White Vin Doux Naturel, Muscat de Beaume-de-Venise, Muscat de

Frontignan and Muscat de Rivesaltes. The best known Red Vin Doux Naturels are Banyuls (the best wine with dark chocolate in the world), Maury, Rasteau and Rivesaltes.

DESSERT WINE

Dessert wines are sweet like most fortified wines, but dessert wines don't have alcohol added to them. They are made from sweet grapes. Some grapes are affected by a fungus called noble rot, or *botrytis cinerea*. The fungus appears in the autumn on the grape and dehydrates the grape, concentrating the sugar in the grape. If the weather turns cold and damp, the noble rot turns to black rot and destroys the grapes. It's a high-risk venture, and that's why *botrytis* wines are usually quite expensive.

I don't think it's necessary to list all of the different styles of dessert wine. Most wine shops will have a section of dessert wines. Most dessert wines are not made in large quantities, so you never know what you'll find in a store. For that reason, it's hard for me to recommend a style or type. Consult with the sales clerks at the shop to let them know how sweet a wine you want, and they'll take care of you.

12

How Wine Shops Work

WINE SHOPS ARE IN BUSINESS to make money. Okay, duh, you knew that. But as basic as that concept is, it isn't easy. The market is down in general, and it has become very competitive. So how does a store survive?

There are only a few ways a shop can survive. Let's review:

1. It can mark the wine up a ton. When shops are in affluent areas, that's a common strategy.

2. It imports directly. Depending on the jurisdiction and if it is even allowed, it tries to cut out the middleman, the distributor, or even the importer. Fewer hands that touch the wine means a higher profit.

3. It has to focus on wines that no other shops sell. The shop knows it can't make any money off Kendall-Jackson Chardonnay. Everyone carries it, so they have

to cut the price to remain competitive. The shop carries wines that no one else does, and its sales staff sells the bejesus out of them. When a shop carries a wine that no one else carries, there is no way for you to compare the price. Perfect. It has a monopoly.

4. It buys closeouts for pennies on the dollar. Throughout the year, there are vintage changes for wines. The new vintage comes in and the wholesaler/distributor has to unload the previous vintage if they still have some left. They cut the price way down and a store buys all of it, so it is the only one that has the deal in town. The store sells it for the usual price or maybe at a discount, but still making a higher profit.

Here's a blurb by a store that bought a closeout: "A faithful supplier is going out of business. We have the last of about 225 cases of delicious, current vintage and reasonably aged, well-stored XXXXX wines which retail for $9.99 to $21.99. About 180 cases of Cabernet, Merlot, Chardonnay and Sauvignon Blanc selling for HALF PRICE @ $4.98. All the others, their Reserva wines, which should be $16.99-$21.99, will be $7.98 till they are gone."

Any wine marked down more than 20% is probably a closeout. Watch out for inflated retail prices also, so they can offer an even "bigger" discount. When anything seems too good to be true, it often is.

Options 1, 2 and 3 are not bad things. The wine may or may not be worth it. It's all up to you.

Try to attend the store's free tastings to see what the wine is like before buying a bunch of it. This is another reason you need to know the wine salespeople intimately. Sleeping with them would be better, but just getting to know them is good enough. They will give you the straight scoop on what the deals are in the store and which ones to stay away from.

A dishonest action by the store that I've seen quite often is putting up shelf tags with incorrect ratings or recommendations for the wines. *Wine Spectator* may have given the 1999 vintage of XXX wine 90 points, but the wine on the shelf is the 2000 vintage. The wine shop will often leave the vintage off of the tag and just say *Wine Spectator* rated XXX wine 90 points. This is quite common. If the promotional tag does not state the vintage, ask the sales clerk for proof that the wine on the shelf was actually the year that was rated the point score stated. The store usually has a list of the ratings from *Wine Spectator* and Robert Parker. If you find a store has done that, find a new store. If they lied about that, they probably will lie about other stuff too.

Discounts. Ask for them. The store rarely publicizes discounts, because it wants to get the full price for the wine. But there is almost always wiggle room. If you are a regular shopper there and get to know a sales clerk, it's more likely they'll give you a discount. But ask even if you're not a frequent shopper. Ask how many bottles you need to buy to get a discount, and then you can decide if it's worth it.

It certainly is more convenient to buy your wine at the grocery store, since you're already there. Grocery

stores usually stock the mass-produced wine. If that's
good for you, then go for it. But if you want to really
have fun drinking wine, your best bet is to make the
extra trip and stop by a wine shop where they have wine
salespeople who know something about wine. Not only
will you have a much better chance of getting a wine
you like, you'll learn about wine at the same time.

GETTING GOOD WINE EVERY TIME

Let's face it; the most important part of enjoying wine
is being able to buy wine you like. There's nothing
worse than buying a lousy wine and having to pour it
down the drain. Expecting to get a good wine based on
its numerical rating, the attractiveness of its label or its
price is not a very good strategy. Using any of those as
a guide to buying wine is as good as closing your eyes
and picking out a wine. The only real strategy to buying good wine every time is to shop at a store where
there are staff to assist you.

If you ask them for recommendations on what a
good wine is, then you haven't accomplished anything.
You might as well buy wine by the ratings. The key is
not to find a wine that someone else likes; it's to find
a wine that YOU like. That can be accomplished only
if the sales clerk knows what you like. But it can work
even better if the salesclerk likes you. So I recommend
you say the following four sentences to the sales clerk:

1   "Hi, my name is Mark." Well, you might want
    to use your own name, but feel free to introduce

yourself as me if you like. Regardless, you'll build a rapport and connection if they know your name.

2. "I want to find a wine that *I* like," with emphasis on the second "I."

3. For the third sentence, you'll want to use a swear word because you really want to drive this point home. "Damn" should suffice. "I don't give a damn about the ratings." Do the fingers thing for quotes when you say "ratings." They'll like that.

Why say this sentence...and say it in such an emphatic way? The sales clerks are so used to referencing the numerical ratings as a sign of quality, but you and I know that ratings are a useless standard to go by for quality. So you have to drive into the sales clerk that you don't want the numerical ratings as a criterion to finding a wine you like. Now I'm not saying you shouldn't buy any highly rated wines, but the wine should be chosen based on being a good wine for you, not because someone else rated it well.

4. And lastly, say, "Will you help me?" This completes the circle, inviting the sales clerk to join with you as a team to help find good wines for you.

After you say those four sentences, if the salesperson doesn't hug you or fall down in a crying heap kissing your feet, I'll be surprised. Those are the best four sentences they could ever hear. Except maybe if you said that you just inherited a million dollars and you want to spend it all in their store.

True story: I told one of my agents to do this, and she didn't believe me. She had been shopping at the same store for 10 years and knew the owner. The owner wasn't a real talkative guy, but he took care of her when she needed help with buying wine. She walked in and said the four sentences. His eyes lit up and he talked to her for hours. The four sentences endeared her to him. He was so excited to find someone who really "got" wine. Believe me, it works.

Since you are asking for wines that YOU like, the sales clerk will be forced to ask you what kind of wines you like. You'll name wines by name that you've had and liked or maybe go with types of wine, white or red, whatever information you can give to help the clerk understand your palate. Then they'll suggest a wine or two for you to buy. You'll take their advice, go home and try them, and then come back and report to the sales clerk what you thought about the wines. The more wines you buy on that sales clerk's recommendations and the more you tell them what you think about each wine, the better the clerk will know your preferences. And then they'll be able to suggest good wines each time you shop there. It's Mission Accomplished when you walk into the store and the sales clerk runs over to you and says that they just got a wine in that you'll like. That's the ultimate, when a clerk knows your palate and is thinking about your well-being.

But it gets better. Once you become bosom buddies with a sales clerk, more benefits will come your way. You'll start getting discounts on wine. They'll give you the opportunity to buy allocated wine, wine that the average customer doesn't even know exists. Every wine shop has access to special wines, but they may get only a few bottles, so they want to offer those to their best customers (the ones who buy the most) and their friends. Even if you don't buy a lot, you'll be a friend of the shop. You'll also be offered to taste samples brought in by the wine suppliers and you'll be exposed to such a variety of wines without spending a dime.

I'm not against buying wine at Costco or other stores where there is no staff to help you. If you know the wine you want and that store sells it, then go for it. But if you want to find the best value wines that you like, the only way to go is to say the four sentences to a sales clerk and stick with them.

13

What Wines I Like
and How I Buy Wine

F IRST OFF, LET ME REMIND YOU that the foundation of
the Progressive Approach is "Who Cares?" So who
cares what I like and how I buy wine? You're right. I
didn't have this chapter in the original version of the
book, but a few of my test readers asked me to put it in.
Maybe you might get something out of it.

There are very few wines that I don't like, but I
would never say I didn't like a category of wines, *i.e.* a
grape variety, a country's wines or a style of wine. So
many people, when asked what kind of wine they like,
or dislike, they name a category: they prefer Californian
wine or they like Pinot Noir, etc. That doesn't make any
sense to me, because there is such a variety in any category. Even Miles, from the movie *Sideways*, who made

the disparaging comment about not drinking Merlot, knew that there are wonderful Merlots being made that would thrill even the most ardent Club member. There are tremendous oaky Chardonnays and spectacular sweet wines. There are also some terrible wines from Bordeaux and Burgundy, awful-tasting Napa Cabernets and insipid Brunellos — all categories the Club member favors. Good and bad wines are not defined by the grape variety, country of origin or color. A wine is either good or bad on its own. So when someone asks you what kinds of wine you like, you might want to rethink your answer only because it sounds naïve to say a category.

The main criterion of a wine I like is that it is balanced — for me. That rules out white Zinfandel, not because it's sweet, but because it's out of balance. It's sweet without acidity, which makes it cloyingly sweet. I like Chardonnay and like it with a little bit of oak, but not out of balance. I like box wine and jug wine if they're in balance (and sometimes they are). Of course, what I call balanced may not be what someone else thinks is balanced, and that's fine.

The next step up is one that has personality. Typically, I prefer an understated, sensual personality in the wine, which I find more often in Old World wines. The big, powerful, in-your-face wines don't do it for me. But when I taste a wine like that and rate it, I don't rate it poorly, because a lot of people like that kind of wine. If the wine is balanced, it gets a good rating and I'd recommend it to folks who like that style. I just don't find any sensuality from the big wines. They don't call me back for more. They don't tease me and seduce me to have another glass. I may choose to have another glass of a big, powerful wine, but only because it's pounding me into submission ... and on occasion, that's okay.

My mood and the context of the situation is a major factor on what wine I choose to drink, as you will see in the "Wine and Activities" chapter. Just as you put certain music on depending on your mood and the context, I choose wine the same way. And when you get all of the variables in sync, *i.e.* the music, lighting, food, wine, temperature, glassware and the company, it's a glorious experience. The context makes a huge difference on how you enjoy wine. One of my New Year's resolutions was not to drink better wine *per se*, but to enjoy wine in more appealing contexts; that makes even the average wine taste better.

As much as I like to match the wine to the context, I do have one type of wine that I like anytime, anywhere: sparkling wine. I LOVE sparkling wine, and I'm always in the mood for it. It might be my house sparkling, Aria, or one with more character, up through the more complex Champagnes. It's something about those bubbles. And if it's a good rosé, I'm in heaven.

The advice I gave you in the previous chapter on how to buy wine is for someone who doesn't have many profiles developed. When I go to a wine shop, there are a ton of wines I haven't had. I'm in the same boat as you. The difference between you and me is that I have a lot of profiles developed, so I have a pretty good idea what most of the wines taste like. But I still rely on the assistance of a salesperson.

First, though, I have to "vet" them to see if they're a Club member. If so, I'll usually decline their help because one, I probably won't agree with their choices and two, it makes me ill to hear their Club jargon.

If I can't find acceptable help, I'm on my own. I rely on the profiles that I have developed, but I also use other bits of info.

The label, for instance. I'm serious. So many people (mostly women, it seems) seem to base their buying decision on the label. I'm guessing they choose a particular wine because the label is pleasing to their eye. Of course, that doesn't have anything to do with whether the wine is good or not, but more power to them. But the label can give you information about the style of the wine. The labels that are more colorful, non-traditional and maybe whimsical, mean that the wine is probably a fruit-forward wine. A traditional label means that the wine is trying to be true to its place of origin in its style. Neither tells you about the quality of the wine — just the style.

When it comes to wines with the fun, non-traditional labels, I prefer the wines be from Europe. The fruit-forward style in Europe is not as fruity as the fruit-forward wines from the New World. The fruit-forward wines from Europe end up being more International Style, which I like. I'm not a big fan of the "fruit bombs" that one often finds in the New World. Spain, in particular, seems to have a nice selection of good value wines in the International Style.

Besides the style of wine, I look at who produces or imports the wine. As you drink more wine, you'll learn the style of the producers and importers. Wines produced by Turley, for example, are favorites of Club members. They are big, powerful and "thick," and it seems you are eating the wine more so than drinking them. Not my style at all....but Parker loves them. When I see a Turley wine, no matter which one, I can bet that it's going to be in that style.

Importers are the same way. The wines they import are usually a pretty consistent style. Once you know an importer's style, it makes choosing wine a lot easier. Some of my favorite importers are Michael Skurnik, Terry Thiese Selections (a division of Michael Skurnik Wines), Winebow/Leonardo LoCascio Selections, Louis/ Dressner Selections, Eric Solomon Selections, Robert Kacher and Fran Kysela.

One importer, Jorge Ordonez, is a Club favorite and one that I have liked for years, until recently. The wines he brings in almost all get silly high ratings from Parker and *Spectator*, but they are monster wines. Huge. Over the top to me. There's no sensuality to them like there used to be. I feel the same about the Grateful Palate. Again, their wines get high ratings but so many just don't do it for me. Both Jorge and the Grateful Palate have some good wines in their portfolio, but I wouldn't buy one of their wines just because they are the importer — as I would with the importers I listed above.

I wrote the majority of this book while living in the Washington, D.C. area. As I traveled more to other cities, I found a zillion regional importers that I had never heard of, so the sky is the limit. Give them a try. If you like a wine, try other wines from the same producer or importer.

And finally, I buy cheap. Not all the time, but my mission in life is to find the cheapest wine possible that I like. So I'll buy inexpensive wines, really inexpensive wines. Oh, I show some discernment, but the loss of buying a few "dogs" is offset by finding the one that is a really good value. I like to buy a range of wines just to continually be exposed to new wines. Other times, I'll try to find values in a certain category, like Pinot Noirs under $20.

There is a lot of good, inexpensive wine out there. And it feels so much better to find a good value than to spend $30, $40 or more and get a wine that is disappointing. As the wine price goes up arithmetically, my expectation of what the wine should deliver goes up exponentially because I know there are so many good wines under $20. An expensive wine has to be so much better to justify the price, and it rarely does. I'm constantly looking for values, and I'll let you know when I find them. Visit my website to learn about them as I do.

14

Does the Vintage
Make a Difference?

THE VINTAGE OF A WINE is simply the year the grapes
were picked. If the weather is lousy, *i.e.* rain at
the wrong time, extreme temperatures, etc., then the
grapes don't ripen properly. There's a saying that you
can't make good wine from lousy grapes. The exception
to the saying is that there are so many things a winemaker can do to manipulate the wine, that one can still
make a decent wine from lousy grapes.

Generally speaking, wines that are less expensive
are manipulated more than more expensive wines. So
if you're buying a wine under $20, let's say, don't worry
about the vintage. But as the price increases, the more
you should be aware of the vintage and the consequences for wines over $20.

1. Wines from great vintages will cost more. All the wine buyers in the know flock to the better vintages, so the demand pushes up the prices. Better grapes make better wine.

2. One thing you should know is when the grapes are really good, the wine typically is meant to age. So if you are buying a wine for immediate consumption, you might want to either buy a wine from an Average or Good vintage or buy an older wine that has been aged. On the vintage chart below, people naturally look for the Excellent or Superior vintages to influence their buying strategy. But the better value and more accessible wine are usually found in a vintage that's Good. At least, that would be my strategy for wines that I know are meant to age.

For wines in the $20-$40 range, I'd still choose a wine from a better vintage that may be relatively too young to drink than a wine a year or two older from a lesser vintage. But for the $40+ wines that I know really need to age, and are just too closed (*CJA – closed refers to a wine that isn't showing much flavor because it's either too young or just going through a phase in its evolution. A closed $50 bottle of wine tastes like a $15-$20 of wine*), then I'd look for the Good vintages, because I wouldn't be getting my money's worth in flavor if I drank the closed wine immediately.

3. The vintage chart is a generalization. There are many microclimates within a region that could be better or worse than the rating I gave for the region as a

whole. Great wines can still be made in Good vintages if a particular vineyard got the right weather. Conversely, just because the vintage is Excellent or Superior, doesn't mean you can just close your eyes and buy any wine from that vintage and expect it to be good. An incompetent winemaker can screw up a wine even with good grapes from a Superior vintage.

As you can probably tell, with microclimates, winemakers and wines being closed, there are enough variables that lessen the impact of vintage in your buying decisions. However, I've included the vintage chart below for you to take it or leave it.

Wine Region	2008	2007	2006	2005	2004	2003	2002	2001	2000	1999	1998	1997	1996	1995	1994	1993	1992	1991	1990	1989
Argentina	G	E	E	E	E	E	E	G	G	E	P	E	G	A	E	E	G	A	A	
Australia		G	E	E	E	E	E	E	G	G	S	G	E	G	E	G	G	E	E	G
Chile		G	E	E	G	E	A	E	G	E	P	G	E	E	E	E	A	P	E	
France, Alsace				G	G	A	G	E	E	G	E	G	G	G	E	G	P	P	S	E
France, Bordeaux		G	G	S	G	E	G	G	S	G	E	A	G	E	G	A	P	P	S	E
France, Red Burgundy		G	G	S	G	E	E	G	A	E	A	G	E	G	P	G	P	G	S	E
France, White Burgundy		G	E	E	E	G	E	G	G	G	G	G	E	E	G	P	E	P	E	E
France, Champagne					S	G	E	A	G	G	G	G	E	E		G		G	S	E
France, Loire			A	G	E	G	G	E	G	G	A	E	E	E	G	G	A	P	E	E
France, Northern Rhône		G	E	E	G	E	P	G	G	S	E	E	G	E	G	P	P	E	E	S
France, Southern Rhône		S	E	S	E	S	P	E	S	E	S	P	P	E	G	A	P	P	S	S
Germany			E	S	E	E	E	S	P	E	G	G	E	G	E	G	E	G	E	E
Italy, Tuscany			E	E	E	G	P	S	G	S	E	S	G	E	A	A	P	A	S	P
Italy, Piedmont			E	E	E	G	P	S	S	E	E	S	S	G	P	G	P	P	S	S
New Zealand			G	G	A	P	G	P	A	A	E	E	E	P	S	A	G	S	A	E
Portugal, Port					E			E			E			E		E	E			
South Africa		G	G	E	G	E	A	G	E	G	E	A	P	P						
Spain		G	E	E	E	G	P	E	G	A	A	A	E	E	E	G	G	P	E	G
California																				
Napa Cabernet		E	G	E	E	E	E	S	P	E	A	S	E	S	S					
Sonoma Cabernet		G	A	A	A	A	A	G	P	G	A	G	G	G	G					
Napa Zinfandel		G	G	G	A	G	G	G	P	G	A	G	G	E	E					
Sonoma Zinfandel			G	E	G	G	G	G	G	A	A	G	A	E	G					
Napa Chardonnay		E	G	G	E	G	E	G	G	G	A	S	S							
Somoma Chardonnay		E	E	S	S	G	S	E	G	E	G	S	S							
Santa Barbara Chardonnay			P	G	G	G	E	G	A	E	A	S	S							
Carneros Pinot		G	G	G	G	G	G	G	G	G	G	A	A							
Monterey Pinot			G	E	E	E	E	G	G	G	G	A								
Sonoma Pinot			G	G	E	E	E	G	G	G	G	G	G							
Oregon		E	E	G	G	G	E	G	G	E	E	A	E	E	S	E	E	E	E	
Washington		E	E	E	E	E	E	E	E	G	E	G	G	A	E	A	G	G	G	

15

Top Wines
in the World

DO YOU EVER WONDER WHAT the Club members long for? You may not play in this league, but knowing what the big time wines are will allow you to "play along" if you're around Club members. And it would also be great if you could try some of the wines, to see if all the fuss made over the wines is worth it.

The big collectable wines are California Cabernets, red Bordeaux and Burgundy. Next in the pecking order would be Italian red wines from Tuscany (Brunello and Super Tuscans), Piedmont (Barolo and Barbaresco), vintage Port, Northern Rhône, Australian reds and Spanish reds. Whites don't get too much play at auctions. When included, they'll probably be white Burgundy and Sauternes. Listed below are the producers that sell for top dollar.

FRANCE

Red Bordeaux: Mouton Rothschild, Lafitte Rothschild, Haut Brion, Latour, Margaux, Montrose, Lynch-Bages, Cos d'estournel, Palmer, Petrus, Ausone, L'Angélus, Cheval Blanc, Le Pin, La Conseillante, Clinet, Lafleur Red Burgundy: Leroy, Romanee-Conti, Comte de Vogue, Dugat, Meo-Camuzet

Northern Rhône Valley, Hermitage, Côte-Rôtie: Guigal, Jaboulet, Chapoutier, Chave

Southern Rhône Valley, Châteauneuf-du-Pape: Beaucastel, Les Bosquet des Papes, Rayas, Marcoux, Clos de Papas

Champagne: Salon, Krug, Bollinger R.D. and Grande Année, Moët & Chandon Dom Pérignon, Mumm René Lalou, Laurent-Perrier Grand Siècle, Louis Roederer Cristal, Taittinger Comtes de Champagne, Veuve Clicquot La Grande Dame

Sauternes: d'Yquem, Raymond-Lafon, Climens

ITALY

Barolo and Barbaresco: Ceretto, Clerico, Conterno, Gaja, Giacosa, Voerzio
Brunello di Montalcino: Altesino, Azienda, Constanti, Castello Banfi, Campogiovanni

Super Tuscans (now called IGT): Solaia, Tignanello, Sassicaia, Ornellaia, Masseto

PORTUGAL

Vintage Port: Dow, Taylor, Fonseca, Quinta do Noval

USA

Screaming Eagle, Shafer Hillside Select, Dunn Howell
Mountain, Joseph Phelps Insignia, Grace Family,
Caymus Special Selection, Harlan Estate, Mondavi
Private Reserve, Ridge Montebello, Neal Family,
Peter Michael, Colgin, Lewis, Pride, Arrowood, David
Arthur, Bryant Family, Dalla Valle, Diamond Creek

AUSTRALIA

Penfolds Grange, and that's really the only real cult
wine. Elderton, Henschke, Torbreck, Clarendon Hills,
D'arenberg are other big names.

SPAIN

Vega Sicilia, Pingus, Pasquera

Here are some recent auction sale prices of these
super wines:

Château d'Yquem Sauternes 2001 12 bottles $8,400

Comte Georges de Vogüé Musigny Cuvée Vieilles
Vignes 1990 9 bottles$4,200

Dominus Estate Napa Valley Napanook Vineyard 1991
12 bottles $1,800

E. Guigal Côte-Rôtie La Mouline 1989 12 bottles $6,600

Giacomo Conterno Barolo Monfortino Riserva 1997 12 bottles $3,480

Tenuta San Guido Sassicaia 1988 12 bottles $4,800

Château Léoville Las Cases St.-Julien 198612 bottles$2,868

Comte Georges de Vogüé Chambolle-Musigny 200112 bottles$1,434

Harlan Estate Napa Valley 199212 bottles$4,780

Krug Brut Champagne 198512 bottles$3,107

Louis Latour Corton-Charlemagne 200512 bottles$1,554

Louis Roederer Brut Champagne Cristal 19836 magnums$3,107

Paul Jaboulet Aîné Hermitage La Chapelle 199012 bottles$3,585

Tenuta San Guido Bolgheri-Sassicaia Sassicaia 200012 bottles$2,151

Bryant Family Cabernet Sauvignon Napa Valley 2004 12 bottles $2,057

Château Latour Pauillac 1982 12 bottles $14,520

Château de Beaucastel Châteauneuf-du-Pape Grande Cuvée 1989 6 bottles $3,630

Comte Georges de Vogüé Bonnes Mares 1971 2 bottles$4,840

Moët & Chandon Brut Rosé Dom Pérignon 1975 12 bottles $3,933

Penfolds Shiraz South Australia Grange 1990 12 bottles $4,538

Château Petrus 2000 1 Imperial $41,825

Château Ausone St.-Emilion 199812 bottles $5,019

Château Cheval-Blanc St.-Emilion 2000 12 bottles $11,950

Château Lafite Rothschild Pauillac 1982 12 bottles $22,705

Château Léoville Las Cases St. Julien 1986 12 bottles $3,346

Château Margaux Margaux 1990 12 bottles$10,158

Château Pichon-Longueville-Lalande Pauillac 2000 6 bottles $1,195

Domaine Leroy Nuits-St.-Georges Aux Vignerondes 1993 12 bottles $3,346

Domaine de la Romanée-Conti La Tâche 1996 12 bottles $15,535

Joseph Phelps Cabernet Sauvignon Eisele Vineyard 1989 12 bottles $1,135

Screaming Eagle Cabernet Sauvignon Napa Valley 1997 3 bottles $8,365

16

Buying Expensive
Wine is Stupid

BELIEVE ME, I LOVE DRINKING expensive wine ...
especially if someone else is paying for it. I'm talking about wines over $50 a bottle in a store. Expensive
wines can be so wonderful. And then there are those
wines that are beyond wonderful. They're orgasmic.
The pinnacle of winedom. Orgasmic wine. I say orgasmic because a wine that good makes one feel the same
way as having a sexual orgasm. The body is super-
stimulated. Your brain seems to shut down, and that
unbelievable feeling engulfs your body from head to
toe. Yep. That's the same feeling that you get when you
have an orgasmic wine. Obviously, once you have one
orgasmic wine, you want another and another.

The problem is cost. The least expensive orgasmic bottle of wine I have ever had was maybe around $60 per bottle, but that was a freak situation. More times than not, the bottle will easily be over $100, and often over $200. However, if I knew that if I spent $200 I would get an orgasmic wine, great. Unfortunately, there are no sure things in wine.

There are so many variables that have to be right to make a wine orgasmic, the odds are against you. Even a wine that someone else thinks is orgasmic may not be orgasmic to you. So you have to buy bottle after bottle of expensive wine with the hope that one will be orgasmic. I hope you have a chance to have orgasmic wine.

But what if we set the bar a little lower: having a great bottle of wine, a step below orgasmic, for that special occasion? People generally believe that the more money they spend on wine, the better it will be. But that's rarely the case.

Here's why:

1. More expensive wines taste different than wines one drinks on a daily basis.

True story: A man walked into a wine shop and announced to the clerk that he and his wife were celebrating their 40th anniversary that night. She was making an exquisite dinner, and he was going to provide the wine. The man said they usually drank red Bordeaux in the $20 range, but he wanted a more expensive Bordeaux at its peak and he had money to spend.

The sales clerk went to the shelf and chose a ten

year old Bordeaux that he said would be wonderful. The man didn't blink at the $250 price, because this was a special occasion.

The next day, the customer came back with a nearly full bottle of wine in his hand, and was steaming mad. He complained to the sales clerk, "That wine you sold me was terrible! It ruined our evening." The clerk felt horrible and asked if he could try the wine. He did and it was marvelous, a truly great manifestation of Bordeaux.

The problem was that the man had never had old wine, and didn't appreciate the taste. Old wine is not as fruity. Its strength is that the flavors are integrated and the wine has such finesse — something a younger wine can't match. It's like making a great sauce. It takes time to reduce and meld the flavors together. Wine is the same. You can get some great-tasting young wines, but it usually takes five years or more for the flavors to really begin to integrate.

Most people drink wine five years old or younger, usually at under $25 a bottle. It's a big difference to go for a ten-year-old bottle that costs $250. The odds are they won't like the wine. But even if they do like it, it is even rarer, nearly impossible, that they'll think it is worth the cost.

2. So let's say you stay away from the older wine, but spend $50 or $100 on a young California Cabernet, for example. You still aren't out of the woods.

True story: I was in a store years ago and a wine salesperson highly recommended a wine for me to try, which cost about $60 a bottle. It was a little out of my price range, but I got it anyway. I opened it for dinner and it was good, but not that good.

I thought it just might need to breathe a little, so I decanted it to let as much air as possible hit it to open it up. I waited 15 minutes. No difference. I waited 15 more minutes, and still no difference. By this time I was needing a fix of wine badly, so I had the first glass. The remainder of the bottle was finished in about 45 minutes. By the last drop, the wine still hadn't gotten any better.

The next time I went back to the store I mentioned that the wine was good, but certainly not worth $60. The clerk asked me how long I let it breathe, and I said almost an hour and a half by the time we finished it. He laughed and said that that particular wine needed to breathe for eight hours. Eight hours! What's that about? Who would have ever guessed?

The moral of the story is that young expensive wine usually is meant to age. If you have it before it has reached its peak, the wine will be "closed," meaning it won't offer much more than a $20 bottle of wine. It always dumbfounds me to see wine dinners featuring expensive wines that have just been released. They are way too young to get the full value from them. They'll still be tasty, but is it really worth spending a bunch of money for just a tasty wine?

On the flip side, I was given a bottle of 1945 Mouton Rothschild. I opened it but didn't decant it, because wines that are soooo old will go bad with a lot of air contact I poured out a one-ounce sip and drank it. It was really quite good, considering its age. I poured another sip, and it had already gone bad — in less than a minute. The air contact was just too much for a wine that was so fragile. I should have guzzled the whole bottle as soon as I opened it. Drat.

3. Another thing to consider when buying expensive wine is the vintage, the year it was made. The year a wine was made is a huge deal in expensive wine. Even the best wineries don't make great wine from a year when the weather was terrible for growing grapes. But they still make wine — they have to pay the bills.

So let's say you are at a restaurant and you see a Mouton Rothschild wine on the list, and see that it only costs $100. Mouton is a great producer from Bordeaux and its wines usually cost hundreds of dollars, so $100 in a restaurant seems like a bargain. If it is too good to be true, it usually is. The wine is probably from an "off" vintage; if it is, the wine will not be worth the price you paid. But who can remember all the good vintages? Most people can't, unless they are way into wine. So don't waste your money on expensive wine unless you know it is from a good vintage.

4. Let's say you find a wine from a good vintage, it's at its peak and you like that style of wine. Sounds good, but I'm sorry to say you still don't have all of the bases covered. An older wine is only as good as its storage conditions. The recommended storage conditions are

55°F, give or take, with dark and decent humidity so the cork doesn't dry out. Very few wines are stored that way. Even if the wine you find is being stored in a temperature-controlled environment, where was it stored before it got to that location? If it sat in a hot warehouse for weeks or months, the wine could be terrible.

I've had repeated bad experiences with one national steakhouse chain (whose name I won't mention, but will say it rhymes with Norton's). I've visited several locations on different occasions, and every time I ordered a bottle of red wine, it came out warm. I mean actually warm to the touch, as if they'd been cooking it along with the steaks. I would never spend money on an expensive wine from that restaurant because they don't have the right storage conditions.

5. Even if the wine is orgasmic, it can still be a mistake to order expensive wine.

True story: I had been dating this gal for a while, and it was time to take the relationship up a notch. I thought a weekend at a bed and breakfast and dinner at the Inn at Little Washington would be nice. For those of you who don't know, the Inn at Little Washington, in Washington, Virginia, is considered by many as one of the great restaurants in America. It's about 50 miles west of Washington, D.C., in the middle of nowhere. (This is a restaurant you only go to once ever or even once in several years, so it all hinges on the experience you have at that one special time. Some folks think it's totally overrated. Others rave about it. I'm in the middle.) At the time, it was the place to go for a special occasion.

I got the wine list and it was massive, as one might expect. I didn't think it was necessary to spend a ton of money on wine, so I was counting on getting a medium-priced wine.

We each had ordered a glass of Champagne and had some nibbles. No hurry, of course. I wanted to milk this situation as long as possible. We were in the groove. Soaking up the sensuous atmosphere. Enjoying the moment. Everything was perfect!

I looked back at the list and there it was. It jumped out at me as if it was talking just to me. On the list was a Domaine de la Romanée Conti La Tache 1990. Domaine de la Romanée Conti (DRC) is one of the great producers in Burgundy. The wine is next to impossible to find, and it is very expensive. La Tache is a famous vineyard and 1990 was a superb year for Burgundy. This had all the signs of being an orgasmic wine.

Up until that time I had never had the privilege of having a DRC wine, so I was very excited. But the best part was that it was only $500 per bottle. Yes, only $500. Sure, that's expensive and I had never spent that kind of money for a bottle of wine, but it was DRC La Tache 1990. C'mon! I really couldn't afford it, but I had to have it and worry about monthly payments on the credit card later. Believe it or not, $500 is a great price for that wine. You can't find DRC wines in wine shops; if you were to find a 1990 La Tache, it would sell for $3,000 a bottle.

I ordered the wine, and when my date saw the price she almost fainted. I told her I had to have it since it was one of those great wines of all time, and because she was worth it. That did the trick.

Until the wine was brought out, my date and I were having a great time. Laughing. Enjoying the Champagne. The atmosphere. Then the wine came out. A $500 bottle of wine! We both were so eager to try a wine that expensive.

But here was where everything went south. Oh, the wine was truly outstanding. But it instantly became the focus of the meal. It took over. We were so intent on analyzing its development and nuances, that we stopped laughing and enjoying each other's company.

The wine was so important that when my date bumped her glass and a splash came out of her glass on the tablecloth, I put the tablecloth in my mouth trying to suck out that $20 worth of wine. It was crazy!

The dinner was a wonderful experience, but cost $1,100. Was the La Tache really worth $500? No. It sure was good, but not $500 good. But then again, my date and I had a great time later back at the B&B, and maybe the wine had something to do with that.

But here's another story when it definitely wasn't worth it. An old girlfriend who had moved away moved back into town and called to say hi. We talked and talked, getting all excited about seeing each other and maybe to start dating again. She invited me over for dinner and I was to bring some wine. I decided to go for all of the marbles, so I bought a bottle of Cristal Champagne. I had a relationship with a wine shop, so it only cost me $200. Yep, *only* $200 — but hey, you only go around once.

I arrived at her home and I announced that I had brought a bottle of bubbly to celebrate reconnecting. I showed her the bottle, but she didn't have the reaction I was hoping for. She asked if that particular bubbly was any good. Ouch. That hurts, when you splurge on an expensive bottle of wine and the other person doesn't appreciate it. I told her it was pretty good, trying not to hype it too much. However, I was excited to give her the opportunity to try an expensive Champagne.

She didn't have Champagne flutes at her new place, so we used some pretty big wine glasses. Because they were so big, I poured just a half a glass for each of us, which was probably about eight ounces. She put her glass on the kitchen counter, opened the refrigerator, and pulled out a Red Bull. Popped it open and poured it into her wine glass, mixing it with the Cristal while mentioning she liked Red Bull and bubbly.

My heart almost stopped beating. Maybe it actually did stop. I got weak in the knees and had to reach for the counter to keep me from falling down. Smiling, she raised her glass to toast our date, and it took every bit of energy to raise my glass and smile.

I quickly regrouped and thought about my reaction to her adding Red Bull to a $200 bottle of Champagne. Sure, I was shocked — but not angry or insulted. In fact, I just smiled, thinking about the reaction of a wine snob if they would have seen that. Hey, she didn't know. And even if she did know how much it cost, she liked it better that way, so good for her. I reminded myself that I'm the wine guy who says drink what you like and who cares what others think. It was my fault for bringing over an expensive bottle of wine without considering the company. So clearly, if you are drinking wine with folks who don't appreciate expensive wine, don't open the good stuff.

So, is an expensive wine worth it? Well, if you're trying to impress someone, I would say yes, as long as they know the price of the wine and are impressed by someone who spends a bunch of money on them. When an expensive wine or highly rated wine is poured for them and they know the details, they always love it. In a blind tasting, over 90% of the time, the folks won't like that same wine. But the power of suggestion is very powerful. I've seen it happen a zillion times.

In summary, if all of the following are not right, it's stupid to buy expensive wine:

1. It has to be the right context;

2. If the wine is older, you have to know you like older wine;

3. The wine has to be from the right year;

4. You have to know how long the wine should breathe (or whether it's an old wine that shouldn't breathe at all);

5. You have to be able to recognize a dumb wine to know if you should let it breathe;

6. You have to know if the wine is at its peak;

7. You have to know if it was stored properly;

8. The people who are drinking it will appreciate it.

Will you appreciate it even if everything is right? All the criteria could be met, but the odds are still low that the wine will be worth the price. The more wines you have, the more you'll recognize that there are dozens of wines that are under $15 that are very, very good. Next time you are considering buying that $100 of wine that is unlikely to be worth it, you may want to remember that you could get at least six bottles of wine that you would really like for the same outlay of $100.

17

Wine at Restaurants

WHO DOESN'T CRINGE WHEN they see the prices restaurants charge for wine? Wine is marked up a whopping 300%, six times the markup of a retail store. Seems like highway robbery, but is it?

Let's compare the markup of wine to that of other beverages served in restaurants. A soda you buy in a restaurant has a 2,000% markup. Bottled water is marked up 600%. There's at least a 500% markup on beer and up to 800% markup on mixed drinks. Hey, compared to the other beverages, wine is a deal!

So should we offer restaurants an apology for complaining about their high wine prices? Heck, no. They're still too high. But this article isn't about what a restaurant charges for wine. A business can charge whatever it wants for its products. That's capitalism.

You have two options. First, seek out restaurants that have more reasonable wine prices: reasonable either by the restaurant offering more low-end wines in the teens or twenties for a bottle, and/or not marking up the wines as much as usual. Second, bring your own wine to a restaurant. Check your jurisdiction to see if that's allowed. The restaurant usually charges a corkage fee, anywhere from $2 - $50 per bottle. Obviously, at $50 per bottle, the restaurant is really discouraging you from bringing a wine. The restaurant may have extra stipulations, such as that the wine you bring in can't already be on their wine list. Others will waive the corkage fee if you also buy one of their wines. It's important to check the restaurant's policy by calling ahead before your visit.

If the restaurant sells wine, there's an unspoken rule that bringing a wine to a restaurant is only proper if you have an exceptional bottle, like something from your wine cellar to celebrate a special occasion. I say that's baloney. What difference does it make if someone brings in a $7 bottle of Yellow Tail Merlot or a $200 bottle of Château Lafite-Rothschild? Either way, the restaurant is getting its $15 corkage fee. A $7 wine with a $15 corkage fee is only $22, much less than what you would pay buying the wine from the restaurant.

Okay, bringing an inexpensive wine looks cheap and would make a terrible impression on a date. But I don't think the wine needs to be anything special to bring it to a restaurant. If you feel okay with bringing inexpensive wine, then go for it and save some money.

Speaking of inexpensive wine, why don't more res taurants offer inexpensive wines on their lists? There are so many great wines you can buy at a store for less than $10. Those wines cost a restaurant between $3 and $6. The restaurant could put some of those wines on their list, take their full 300% markup, and the wines would still sell for less than $20! It would be a win-win deal.

In some states it is legal to take home an unfinished bottle of wine. Since wines by the bottle are often a better value than wine by the glass, you can order a bottle without worrying about having to finish it at the restaurant.

But let's say you aren't bringing a wine to a restaurant. How do you navigate your way around a wine list? It's tough because so many wines on a list are ones you haven't heard of. There are two reasons for that. First, a restaurant likes to put unknown wines on the list so that you can't compare their prices to retail prices. Second, some wineries only allow their wines to be sold in a restaurant, not in a store.

Either way, if restaurants would offer more information on the list, the process would be much easier. For instance, I would like to see a restaurant have a description for each wine describing the flavor, body, style, even what dish would be a good match. The more information, the more help you'll have to make a decision.

Unfortunately, that's a pipe dream. When there is no description of the wines and the waiter doesn't offer much help, your safest bet is to stick with wines you are familiar with — what you drink normally. Restaurant prices are typically twice retail prices, so if you typically drink a $15 bottle of wine, look for wines on the list in the $30s. That way, you're getting a wine you're used to. To spend more money is okay, but know that you might be getting a wine that you're not used to, and may not like.

As the price gets over $40 per bottle, the year the wine was made becomes more of an issue. The vintage is more important the more expensive a wine is. I recognize that it's unlikely you'll know which are the good and bad vintages for any given wine region, but if the restaurant does not include the year the wine was made on the wine list, I wouldn't order a bottle over $40. It means the restaurant doesn't care about wine, and I would not trust how and where they bought the wines, how they stored them, etc.

Let's say, though, that you have either a waiter or sommelier who knows the list well and can help you in selecting a wine. There are two issues of concern for you: getting a wine YOU like and having it match the food you're having.

Regarding interacting with the waiter or sommelier, make sure you tell them what you usually drink so they know the style of wine you like. Remember, the waiter isn't there to pick out a highly rated, a popular wine or their favorite wine. They are trying to pick out a wine that meets your needs. The more info you can give them, the better off you'll be. And give a price

limit on what you want to spend. It's much more important to get a wine you like than to match the wine to
the food. It's rare that a wine is a BAD match with a
dish...no matter what the wine and dish. More about
wine and food matching in another chapter, but if you
like the wine and you like the dish, 95% of the time,
the two will work together.

HOW A RESTAURANT WOULD PRESENT
A BOTTLE OF WINE

There is certain etiquette for the tableside presentation
and approval of wine. First I'll list the basics that any
decent restaurant should do, followed by the ultimate
actions by a more sophisticated restaurant.

THE BASICS

1. The waiter will show the bottle to you and ask if it
is the wine you ordered. It probably is, but you might
want to look at the vintage. Very often a restaurant
will receive a new vintage of a wine and not reprint
the wine list.

If the vintage isn't the same, the dilemma is what
to do. It all depends if you know which vintage is better, which you probably won't. You can try to slyly get
the information from the waiter or manager by saying,
"This isn't the vintage we ordered. What's the difference between the two vintages?" If the waiter gives you
some BS or is clearly stumped, ask if anyone else knows
more about the two vintages. You may get someone else

with more BS or a qualified answer. Either way, you can always refuse the wine and choose a different one at any point in the process.

2. Next, the waiter opens the wine and presents you with the cork. Now what? What does the cork tell you about the wine?

a. If it is completely dry, you know it hasn't been stored on its side. But is that bad? Maybe. If it is a young wine, less than five years old, a dry cork is no problem. A cork can do its job of keeping air away from wine for five years easily even if it is dry. We have the idea that a wine should be stored on its side from guidelines decades ago, when all red wine had to age because they couldn't produce wine with low tannin (the aging ingredient in wine). So if a wine has to age for more than five years, it is better to store on its side because a moist cork can expand and contract easier. But even if you get an older wine and the cork is dry, it's still not a reason to send the wine back.

b. What if the cork is soaked through with wine? Not good. If wine has gone all the way up the side of the cork, that means air has gotten in, and air is no friend of wine. But still, a soaked cork is not a reason to send a wine back because the wine may still be fine.

c. If the cork smells moldy or even has mold on it, is that bad? Not necessarily. If a wine is stored in a humid environment, mold can grow. Still not a reason to send a wine back.

d. What if the cork crumbles, completely falls apart? It's so bad you have to push the cork into the bottle just to get the wine out. Nope. Still not a reason to send the wine back.

In fact, there is no reason to send the wine back based on the cork. So why do they give you the cork, you might ask?

True story: A group of businessmen went to a restaurant in D.C. years ago and the company was going to pick up the tab. When they sat down and looked at the wine list, they ordered the most expensive wine on the list. Why not? The company was paying for it. (Oh, the good ol' days.)

The waitress came out with six glasses on a tray along with the wine, which was already opened. She put the glasses down, poured the wine; they tasted it and gave it an enthusiastic thumbs-up. Well, six guys finished the first bottle in a heartbeat and ordered another one. The waitress took the empty bottle away and came back with the second bottle, already opened, and poured the wine. They tasted it, and it was just as good as the first. Beautiful. Great wine. The food was great. Atmosphere was nice. Everything was perfect.

One of the guys was smoking. He finished his cigarette and couldn't find an ashtray to put it out. The second bottle of wine was already empty, so he dropped the butt in the bottle. The waitress came over and asked if they wanted a third bottle of wine. The men said yes. She took the empty second bottle away and came back with the third bottle, already opened, and poured the wine.

Sure enough, the cigarette butt was in the bottle.

What happened was that someone had ordered this wine previously and the restaurant saved the bottle. When these men ordered it, they filled it up with jug wine and brought it out. Who would know? Who would even suspect a restaurant would cheat someone like that? Of course, you'd think the men could tell the difference between a jug red and an expensive red, but that's not true. Most folks can't. And it goes back to the self-fulfilling prophecy: once you know the wine is expensive, you'll like it. Everyone likes expensive wine, even if it's really jug wine.

That's why the second step of proper wine service is for the waiter to show you the bottle and open it right in front of you, so you know the wine in the bottle is the wine that is supposed to be there.

I was at a restaurant in Annapolis right by the city dock. It was a lunch on Saturday on a beautiful day and the restaurant was packed. My friends and I got a table, and I thought that we should celebrate. Nothing in particular, but it just felt like a time to celebrate. So I ordered a pretty expensive wine.

Our waiter was in the weeds, no question. We waited and finally he came out with a bottle of wine with the cork already out of the bottle.

Of course, the first thing that popped into my mind was the previous story. But I hate to distrust anyone. Geez, nothing is worse than going through life thinking people are trying to screw you. But this was a pretty expensive wine, so I politely asked the waiter why the cork was out. He said a co-worker opened the bottle for him because he was so far behind. That was probably true, but I thought, "You know ... well, you just don't know." As graciously and apologetically as I could, I asked if he could bring another bottle out of the same wine and open it in front of us. Boy, even as I write this I feel like that was kind of a jerk move, even though I was as nice as could be. But I guess I felt that if I were going to spend the money on a wine, I should be sure it was the wine that I expected. The waiter was nice about it, and everyone was happy.

Once the bottle is opened, the waiter has to do a few things to prepare for the third step, which is pouring the wine. First, he'll put the bottle down on the table so he can undo the cork from the corkscrew. The corkscrew goes in his pocket and the cork on the table. Since nothing about the cork can tell you if the wine is rotten, just leave the cork there. And now the waiter is ready to pour the wine.

3. The waiter pours a taste into the glass of the person who ordered the wine for approval.

I've been to some restaurants, usually high-end ones, where the waiter will sample the wine first, before he pours it in your glass. He's checking to see if the wine is okay. I have mixed feelings about this practice. I would wonder if the waiter really could tell if the wine is bad. I know many people in the wine business, even wine teachers, who can't recognize a bad wine. And if the waiter says the wine is good and then you taste it and say it's bad, then what? When I mean bad, I mean flawed, corked, not that you just don't like it.

On the other hand, since many folks don't know what corked wine smells like, if the waiter does know what he's doing, he can save you from having to drink a lousy wine when you might not have the guts to send it back.

I was at the Capital Grille in Washington, D.C. and ordered a wine for about $125. They had some-one there who was the wine guy (sommelier) and he brought me the wine. He opened it, took a taste and said the wine was not right and that he would fetch me another bottle. Not right? Wow. Did that mean corked, I asked? And he said no, it just wasn't at its peak. I tasted the wine and he was right. But how 'bout that? First, the guy could recognize that, and second, he offered to get another bottle. The second bottle was perfect. Now, that's great wine service.

Now for some not so good wine service: I went to a restaurant in D.C. and brought my own wine. (This is something that is legal to do in D.C., but not in Virginia or Maryland. But let me get back to that in a second.) The two bottles I brought were quite expensive, one white and one red. I was ready for the white wine and the waiter brought it to the table, opened it and poured himself a sample to taste it. Now, how goofy is that? It was my wine. I brought it. There was nowhere to send the wine back, except to my house. He shouldn't have been pouring him-self a sample of a wine brought in by a guest.

It got worse. He then poured a sample of wine —
and all these were pretty healthy pours - — into my
guest's glass and my own. He swirled the wine around
in each glass and dumped the wine out. I was wondering if any wine was left in the bottle after all of this.
He was seasoning the glasses. Seasoning looks cool, but
it is a waste of wine. Either the glass is clean, or it's not.
Seasoning is a waste of wine.

When the red came out, knowing what might
happen again, I mentioned it would be fine if he just
poured the wine into our glasses without tasting it first
or seasoning the glasses.

SENDING A WINE BACK

Let's say you got a wine that you thought you would
like, but it doesn't taste good. I don't expect you to
know if the wine is flawed/rotten or if you just don't
like it. No matter; when you get a wine that doesn't
taste good to you, send it back. Call the waiter over
and be as gracious, nice and humble as possible, and
say, "I'm sorry, but this wine just doesn't do it for me.
I'm not sure if it is flawed or not, but I just don't like
it. We would like to get a different wine." Notice I'm
not being an ass about it, making a scene and demand-
ing they take it back. I'm trying to be as gracious as
possible and asking for the privilege of returning the
wine and getting another.

Of the dozens of times this situation has arisen, I
have never had the restaurant give me a hard time. But

if they do, stick with it and know this: If the wine isn't flawed, the restaurant can sell it at the bar by the glass. If it is flawed, then they send it back to the wholesaler and get their money back. Either way, they are not going to lose money on it. You are not dinking the restaurant in any way. So you should never have a good meal ruined by a lousy bottle of wine again.

18

Matching Food and Wine

A DINNER WITHOUT WINE is like a day without sun-shine, so the saying goes. But what about lunch? Some of my best dining memories have been while on vacation, enjoying lunch with friends over a bottle or four of wine. Something about having wine at lunch validates an afternoon of relaxation. To me, having wine signals that the responsible part of the day is over. And if you can pull that off by lunchtime, you've got the life.

It's hard for me to have food without wine. What did I just say? No, it's impossible for me to have a nice meal without wine. But the flip-flop is not true. I like to have great wine without food. When I get a great wine, I just want to have it on its own or maybe with a few benign nibbles like some mild cheese and fresh bread. I want to focus on the wine. In fact, I prefer to drink great wine alone, by myself, with no one else to interrupt the bonding between the wine and me. Something about great wine makes me contemplate so many things in life. My mind just races.

So great wine without food is fine for me. Great food without wine is criminal. If I'm shoving a sandwich down my throat because I'm in a hurry to eat, sure, wine's not needed. But if I want to relax and enjoy a meal, wine is a key component, no matter what the food is. Whether it's simple food like pizza or a gourmet meal, wine is a necessary complement if the meal is to be relaxing.

If we can agree that food needs wine, the next issue is which wine to pair with which food. There are books written about just this topic and they all have so much information, rules and guidelines, it's impossible to remember it all. Can't wine and food matching be made simpler? Yes. I'm devoting just one chapter to it, but by the time you finish this chapter, you'll know how to match wine and food for any occasion.

There are several different approaches to matching wine and food, from very simplistic to ones that require more knowledge of both wine and food. I think the simple ones work pretty darn well for most occasions. But if you are really into wine and food, I have systems for you too. The first two are what I use more times than not when I'm by myself. If I'm choosing wines for others, especially professionally, I'll make more of a point of matching the wine and food. The first two aren't really "matching."

They're more about playing the odds of choosing wines that will satisfy you. Let's get to it.

DRINK A WINE YOU LIKE

Don't worry about how the wine will go with the food. There are very few disastrous wine and food matches. I've had Chardonnay with steak, Cabernet with fish, red Zinfandel with salads, etc. trying to find disastrous matches, and it just doesn't happen. Okay, maybe the matches weren't the best, but they certainly weren't bad enough to make me get another wine.

I can't emphasize enough that if you just drink the wine you like and order the food you like, you'll be in good shape 90% of the time. When I'm alone and am choosing a wine to go with food, this is the system I use most frequently.

Ordering a wine you like takes the fear out of trying to figure out what kind of wine to get when everyone at the table is eating a variety of dishes. Now you don't have to worry about what people are having. All you have to figure out is what people are in the mood to drink, and get a wine that makes everyone happy.

Your other option in this case is to let everyone order wine by the glass. However, sometimes the wine-by-the-glass selections aren't very good. You tend to get better wine by the bottle, and it's probably a better value as well.

DEPENDING ON THE CUISINE

This is a fun one to me because it's simple, but actually takes some components into consideration. You choose a wine depending on the cuisine. At its simplest, New World wine is best with New World cuisine. Old World wine is best with Old World cuisine.

Old World cuisine is the food of the European countries. New World cuisine is any food from countries outside of Europe. That's broad, I know, but it works pretty well.

The two New World cuisines would be Asian and "American," which includes foods like BBQ and West Coast cooking. Let's look at those a minute.

In Asian cuisine, spiciness is often a factor. Another place we find spiciness is with BBQ. One way that spiciness is balanced is by sweetness in wine. But if you don't want to drink a sweet wine, drink a fruity wine — a New World wine. Fruitiness can make a wine taste sweet. So a wine that's really fruity can often balance out the spiciness in food. A fruity white or red can work with Asian food. Wines that work well with BBQ are Zinfandel and Shiraz, because both are really fruity and both are kind of spicy on their own, so it's a nice connection with the food.

West Coast cooking uses a lot of fruit-based salsas and sauces, which can give a slight sweetness to the dish. A fruity wine matches well with the fruitiness in the dish.

Old World cuisine doesn't have the pronounced flavors of many New World cuisines. With the sauces in

French cuisine, the acidity in Italian cuisine, the fish used in many European countries, etc., the wines that work best are ones that are higher in acidity — Old World wines. Also, food is really the king in Europe, more so than wine. So when good food is made, the wine should complement the food so the food still is the star. European wines are not that fruity or high in alcohol, so they won't overpower the flavors.

I had the privilege to have lunch with Jacques Pepin, one of the most renowned chefs of our time. As Jacques was French (duh), I chose a French restaurant. When we were seated, the waiter asked if we would like some wine. I deferred to Jacques to choose the wine because he was the guest of honor. He didn't ask what dish each of us was going to order. No, he looked for a wine that would be a good match with just about anything and chose a Gigondas, a medium-weight wine from the south of France. He knew that if you got a food-friendly wine, you'd be in good shape.

PLEASE REMEMBER THIS: It's important to remember that if you prefer New World style wines, you shouldn't feel you should get a European wine because you're having European food. There's nothing worse than matching a wine with food because it's "supposed" to be a great match, but without any consideration whether the person actually likes the wine. Ugh! The number of times I've heard a wine expert recommend a Gewurztraminer for Asian cuisine, without any consideration that most people don't like Gewurztraminer.

News Flash: It's not a good match if the people don't like the wine!

The next two are actually matching the wine to food. The key to making these work is that you have to know the qualities of the wine, like you've had it before AND the quality of the food, like you've tasted it already.

May I just share one story before I explain the last two? Thanks. Most wine dinners at restaurants work the following way: The winery sends a bottle of each of the wines to the chef. The chef tastes them and supposedly creates a dish to match the wine. For many years, I hosted these kinds of events. What I found was that the chef didn't really understand how to match wine and food. They're chefs. Not wine guys (gals).

Another problem was that the chefs had egos. They wanted their dish to shine, more so than the wine. But in a lot of cases, the dish wasn't worth shining. The wine for that course was better than the food. I avoid dinners like that if the reason I'm going is for an orgasmic wine and food experience vs. just something to do. I've never been too keen on a dinner featuring the wines from one winery, as it's rare that all the wines are exciting.

And last, I think it's kind of nutty to go to a dinner with recently released wines that are meant to age. I remember an Italian wine dinner featuring recently released Barolos and Brunellos, high dollar wines that need years of aging to really appreciate them. The guests tasted them and all you could hear was the wines needed more breathing. Duh! It seems like a complete waste of money to taste wines that aren't mature.

When I am hosting a dinner at a restaurant, I meet with the chef and ask him to select dishes he wants to showcase his talents. Once I read the description of each dish, I bring a bunch of different wines to the restaurant and try them with the dishes. Then I have a very good idea what kind of wine will match with each dish; whether the wine should be the focus of the course, because the dish isn't that great, or *vice versa*. Those are the dinners where you can experience orgasmic wine and food matches.

ASSSF

No, that's not a typo. ASSSF is an acronym that I pronounce "As If." Remember that acronym and you'll be able to match wine and food AS IF you know what you're talking about. I'll go through each letter.

A stands for Acid: Foods high in acid (like goat cheese, tomato-based dishes or sauces, fish with lemon squeezed on it, etc.) need to be paired with a wine that is also high in acidity, or the wine will taste flat and boring. The more acidic the dish is, the more acid that needs to be in the wine. Some other wine folks say that you can't have wine with a salad because the dressing is too high in acid for any wine. I don't buy it. Rarely are salad dressings that high in acid, and there are plenty of high acid wines like Pinot Grigio that would be a nice match.

S stands for Salty: Salty foods are balanced out by
acidity. Think caviar and Champagne. Oysters and
Sauvignon Blanc. Old World Sauvignon Blancs are good,
but so are Sauvignon Blancs from New Zealand because
of their high acidity.

S stands for Spicy: When it comes to spicy foods,
sweet wine is the best balance for the spiciness. But
a sweet wine without acidity tastes cloyingly sweet;
flabby, as the wine jargon would say. Classic wine
matches with spicy Asian cuisine are Gewürztraminer
and German Riesling, both with some sweetness but
also with acidity.

To be honest, I don't really think that Gewürztraminer
is as good as a match as other folks make it out to be.
It's usually not that sweet, doesn't have very high acidity and has a flavor that a lot of consumers don't like.
Stick with the German Riesling. A New World Riesling
might have the sweetness but not the acidity, so Old
World is the way to go.

Most sweeter wines are white, so what do you do
when the food calls for red, like BBQ? Drink beer.
Okay, but if you want to have wine, choose something
fruity. Consumers often describe a really fruity wine as
sweet even when there is no sugar in the wine, because
fruitiness in wine tastes "sweet." So New World wines
are probably the pick, as they tend to be more fruit-
forward. Shiraz and red Zinfandel are usually fruity,
and they have a spiciness to them that works well with
many spicy foods. Pick one that is low in tannin, which

usually means an inexpensive one.

S stands for Sweet: Matching sweet food with sweet wine is one of the hardest matches, because if one is much sweeter than the other, it ruins the less sweet item. Typically, I would suggest that the wine be sweeter than the food, as most dessert wines are very expensive and that's what you want featured. The less sweet food would support the dessert wine.

There are also non dessert foods that are "sweet," such as mango salsas, cranberry sauce, etc. Those dishes also benefit from having a sweet wine with them — typically an off dry wine (semi-sweet), as the dish isn't very sweet. Of course, you can substitute a really fruity wine if you don't want sweet.

F stands for Fat: There are two types of fat in food: animal fat in meat and dairy fat, usually found in cream sauces. Cream sauces and other rich dishes need a wine that can cleanse the palate to get the mouth ready for the next bite. Acidity does that. One might consider putting a creamy, buttery Chardonnay with cream sauces because of the obvious similarities. But your mouth will be overwhelmed by the richness of both the wine and the food if the Chardonnay doesn't have any acidity. If you do choose a Chardonnay, make sure it's an Old World one that has the acidity to "cut through" the cream sauce.

Animal fat in meat is best balanced out by tannin. The more fat the meat has, the higher the tannin should be in the wine. Chicken has very little fat, so a red like Pinot Noir is a good match, as Pinot Noir is low in tannin. The very fatty beefsteaks require wines high in tannin, typically Cabernet Sauvignon, Zinfandel, Shiraz, etc. They can be New World or Old World. The fish that are served as steaks, like tuna, swordfish and salmon, often pair nicely with a red, especially if they're grilled, as the char calls for a red. Because those fish don't have much fat, you'd choose a red low in tannin. Once again, a Pinot is often chosen.

As with all systems, there are always exceptions. Play around with all types of wines to see what works for you. A chef suggested pairing rosé Champagne with a nice steak on the grill. I didn't get it until I tried it. It's awesome! The acidity in the Champagne matches perfectly to steak.

THE ESSENCE

The Essence is the last step in making a wine and food match, but it is also the hardest because you need to know the flavors of both the wine and the food intimately to match them up. The menu may list the ingredients and a description of the dish, so you have something to go on there. But without ever having had a wine, it's tough to know its real flavor profile. If there is a description of the wine on the wine list or on a shelf tag in a store, that will give you some idea, but it's more reliable if you try the wine first to know what flavors jump out to you.

Then you match the flavors of that particular wine to the flavor of a particular dish. There's no generalizing, like "have a spicy Shiraz with a spicy dish." It has to be XYZ Shiraz with Joe's BBQ. It's just like dating. It is very specific, but this is when you often get the orgasmic wine and food matches.

WHEN ALL ELSE FAILS

No matter what wine and food matching method you choose, you're bound to still come up with a wine and food match that just doesn't work. Don't worry, though, because one ingredient fixes every bad wine and food match: butter. Butter goes with all wines, and all wines pair well with butter. So when you have that disastrous match, take a bite of the food, then have some bread with butter on it, then have the wine. The last taste in your mouth before having the wine is the butter, a perfect match.

Good luck with your efforts in matching wine and food. Use the above systems and play around to discover matches you love.

Following are my orgasmic wine and food matches:

White Burgundy and lobster or escargot

Red Bordeaux and lamb

Sauternes and *foie gras* or *crème brûlée*

Muscadet and oysters on the half shell

Stilton cheese, Port and walnuts ... on a bearskin rug in front of a roaring fire

Aged Barolo and truffles

Banyuls and dark chocolate

Sancerre and goat cheese

Red Burgundy and duck or venison

Champagne and caviar

Sparkling wine with potato chips or popcorn

Rosé Champagne and a grilled steak

19

Parties

BRINGING WINE TO A DINNER PARTY

L ET'S LEAVE THE RESTAURANT and move home and discuss dinner parties. Either the dinner party can be
at your house and it's your responsibility to select the
wines, or you may be invited to a dinner party and you
are supposed to bring the wine. I'll start with the latter.

When you are invited to a dinner party, there are
two ways the wines can be supplied. The guests can
bring a bottle to be opened at the dinner, or the host
supplies it all. If the host supplies it and you know the
host is a wine lover, bringing a bottle of wine as a gift
is a nice gesture. Whatever wine you choose, the host is
under no obligation to open the bottle that evening.

It's choosing the right wine that can be tricky.
Obviously, if you know what kind of wine the person

usually drinks, stick with that type of wine but go up a notch. For instance, if the person likes California Chardonnay at home and usually pays around $12 a bottle, then bring a California Chardonnay that's more expensive, maybe $20-$30.The higher price makes it more special. Sticking with a wine the host usually drinks ensures they can actually enjoy it. I've seen too many wines brought that the guest likes but the host doesn't. What is the host going to do with it then? They're dinked. Oh, and if you bring a white wine, don't bring it chilled, because that looks like you are expecting them to open it while you're there.

If you are supposed to bring a wine that will be consumed that night, you should bring the white chilled. The trick to bringing wine to a dinner party is to bring a wine that *you* like. That way, if the other guests bring junk, you'll at least have something to drink. If it is an unknown name, it's even better because then the guests won't choose the wine, as most are scared to try wines they haven't heard of. That way you can have more of the wine for yourself.

If you really want to score huge, choose an expensive wine at home. Buy a wine that no one will choose, cheap and well known; a screwtop would be even better, because that way no one can really tell the bottle has already been opened. Empty the lousy wine out of the bottle and transfer the good wine into that bottle. Perfect!

HOSTING A DINNER PARTY

Now let's talk about you hosting a dinner party. You have two options: have the guests help out with the wine by bringing a bottle (or two or three), or supply it all yourself. If you think it's "cheap" to have guests bring a bottle, I can understand that, but you're no fun. I think it's fun to get folks involved in the dinner. And you can do it several ways.

Give them the food, and have them bring a wine that matches. No suggestions by you. Not white or red. Just let them sink or swim on their own. Almost any of your guests will probably go to a wine shop and ask a sales clerk for help so they can manage. Of course, folks who have read this book can do it on their own.

But maybe you have some exceptionally-challenged wine people coming. You can always give them the assignment of bringing a wine as an aperitif. Oops, better not use that word. It may throw them. They can bring a wine to have with the appetizers. If they have to have a suggestion, go with Champagne.

Of course, you can give the folks some more requirements. (Hey, it's your party.) You can set a certain price range, but that's a little touchy. You can say a certain country, if the dish is from there. Or tell them you want a white or a red.

Since any wine will go with about any dish, maybe you could just tell them to bring their favorite wine. And when all the wine gets there, you can decide which course to serve it with. I love doing that. It really drives home the point of how so many different kinds of wine can go with different dishes. AND, the guests won't be panicking about whether they're bringing the right wine to match with the dish.

If you want to do the cooking and supply the wine, more power to you. Know your crowd. When in Rome …If you have folks coming who aren't really into wine, it might be safe to stick with normal wines (Chardonnay and Merlot or Cabernet). No one goes home disappointed that way. If you have a more sophisticated group, then you can go nuts.

But let me tell you: EVERY dinner I've been to where the hosts have provided wine that was meant to be more upscale, it's bombed. Really. The best part about getting together, hopefully, is the conversation and just being relaxed. Once folks know that you have gone all out (and this applies to food too), then everyone seems obligated to talk about the food and wine forever to give it its due. What fun is that? It isn't to me.

For your sophisticated group, get a bunch of wines but don't break the bank. Put them all out on the table, white and red, and let the folks graze on them as they please. The more wines you have, the more chance they'll find a winner and you'll be the star.

I remember doing a wine tasting for a big medical meeting. They had me come to give the talk during dinner, and I supplied the wines to go with each course. I usually provide 2-3 wines per course with at least one white and one red, no matter what the course, and usually an Old World and a New World in there. It's a great chance to see how different wines work or don't work with the food. Every time I've done this, the less expensive wines were the most popular.

Remember, either the food is the star or the wine is the star. More expensive wines want to be the star, whether you like it or not. It's the way they're made. With less expensive wines, they play a great supporting role to any food — and thus, seem to go better. They don't compete with the food. If you are showing off your cooking prowess, I don't recommend providing great wine. Get some reasonably priced wine. I'd say under $10 a bottle, but that may scare you. Okay, under $15. All right, under $20 ... but no more than $25. Boy, you drive a hard bargain. But buy smart.

One bottle will serve 5-6 people, and generally you want to end up with at least as many bottles as guests. At my dinners, I try to have two bottles per guest. Some people, I won't say who, just love to put away wine.

Glassware: The nicer the glasses, the more nervous people get and the more not-fun your party becomes. Hey, I love nice glassware. I designed my own hand-blown glasses. But for almost any dinner party, regular wine glasses are fine.

To make a point, serve the wines in highball glasses, especially for a casual dinner. In Europe that's done all the time. And think of the money you'll save on carpet cleaning, since those glasses are much harder to knock over. Whatever you choose, make sure they're clean. Smell them to check for any residual soap or storage area aromas.

If you still have questions, give me a call and we'll work it out.

Home wine tasting parties can be a gas. There is nothing better than to taste lots of wine and then break out Twister. Even if you don't do Twister, home wine tasting parties are usually much more fun than going out to one.

But before you send out the invitations, you have to decide on the format of the party. Listed below are five formats that will work well no matter who is invited.

Following are a few things to consider no matter what format you choose:

Provide Clean Glassware. No matter what shape glass you use, it has to be clean. That might seem obvious to everyone, but glasses that aren't rinsed properly or that are stored upside down will have an odor in the glass that will make any wine smell bad. Make sure the glasses are washed thoroughly and rinsed with hot water. Store them upright so they don't pick up the aroma of a shelf, etc. You should get into the habit of smelling an empty wine glass before wine is poured into it, whether at a restaurant, at home or at a wine tasting. You'll find that it isn't uncommon to have a faulty wine glass. If you don't have enough glasses or don't want the hassle of washing them all, they can be rented for as little as $.50 each.

Smell: Since the aroma is the most sensual aspect of wine, it's helpful not to be in a house that stinks. Oh sure, people might know to clean their house before guests arrive and maybe remove the litter box, etc. But some common aromas can be distracting for a wine tasting. At professional tastings, there are a few no-nos: brewing coffee, fresh flowers or even people wearing too much perfume. I've seen people thrown out of a tasting of expensive wine because they had too much cologne on. At home, you'll probably not be that anal (at least, I hope). But just be aware, if you opt for a more serious home tasting, to make sure your house is aroma free.

Light: Because one of the four steps in tasting wine is looking at the wine, having enough light might be an issue. If your bunch isn't that serious, then don't worry about the lighting. But if you're at a level where each wine is in its own glass or if you are doing a blind tasting, you want to make sure there is plenty of light in the tasting area. At this level, dimming the lights to set the mood is a wrong move.

FORMAT 1: WINE FEST

Focus: Trying many different wines

Best for: A really diverse guest list of oenophiles and wine newbies

How many people: Sky's the limit

This is the loosest of the five formats. The bottles are put on a counter, and people pour their own. The bottles are visible, so no guessing or voting is being done — although it could be. The key element here that sets this apart from any ol' party that serves wine is that no more than two bottles of the same wine should be bought, so that people try as many different kinds of wine throughout the event.

A good thing to do is to have the name of each wine, where it was bought (and maybe the price) on a piece of paper or marker board so that folks who like that wine can know where to go to get it.

Glassware: Highball glasses, wine glasses, mugs, plastic cups – who cares? You're just trying to get the wine from the bottle into your mouth. You'll want a pitcher of water and dump bucket handy for folks to rinse out their glass between tastings.

Food: Anything goes here too. Just make it fun. There are so many different wines, it would be silly to try to match food to all of them.

Obtaining the wine: Two options: one person can buy them to ensure a good mix of wine, or you can have people bring a bottle or two. The problem with the latter is that you will have some guests who just bring junk. I've seen people state in the invitations that your name will be written on the label of the bottle you bring, so it holds folks accountable for their selection. And if they still bring a wine that sucks, you'll know whom not to invite to the next party.

FORMAT 2: PICK ME! PICK ME!

Focus: Having people bring wine and guests vote on their favorite

Best for: Any level of group, pretty casual

How many people: Best if fewer than 25. A bottle of wine is 25 ounces, so everyone could try a wine if people only pour a one-ounce taste ... but people often pour too much. If you have close to 25 folks, where the pouring could be an issue, have a one-ounce shot glass by each pitcher so folks know how much to pour.

You certainly could have more than 25 people, and thus more than 25 wines. It's just that people wouldn't get to try all of the wines, but that's okay. The guests would vote for their favorites from the wines they had a chance to try.

The goal of this tasting is for a person to bring a bottle of wine that everyone will vote as the best wine of the evening. I suggest narrowing the scope of what the wines can be, such as all one grape variety, or even one grape variety from one country. You can set the cost parameters, but I think it's more fun to leave that open. If someone wants to spend a mint on wine to try to win the contest, why not? On the other hand, to do a tasting of wine under $5 per bottle, that's fun too. You'd be surprised at how many good wines are out there that are under $5 a bottle or equivalent, like jug wines and box wines.

The one thing you should avoid is having both white and red, because reds will always win. Pick a color and stick with that. You can always serve a variety of wines before and after the tasting.

When people arrive, they should write their name on the label of their wine with a magic marker. The wines are tasted blind, so either bags can be put over the bottles or the wine can be poured into carafes or pitchers. Most wine shops have the one-bottle bags you can get, but I prefer transferring the wines from the bottles into a carafe or pitcher. Bagging wines is disaster waiting to happen. The bags can slide off the bottle, revealing the wine. The bottle can break through the bag, and then you have a real mess.

Carafes or pitchers cost pennies at the store. I've seen the colored plastic pitchers at Wal-Mart for $.50 each. You could even have folks bring a carafe or pitcher with their wine. Dumping the wines into another container ensures no one will know what the wine is, and it makes it much easier to handle. The pitchers/carafes can be plastic, glass or metal. Clear or opaque.

If you transfer the wines into the pitchers, you'll have to number them. Don't use the adhesive nametags or labels; the glue is hard to get off. And Post-it® notes fall off too easily. Just use a piece of paper and Scotch® Tape it to the pitcher. One person will have to make a record of what wine is going into each pitcher, but that can be the job of the non-drinkers in the crowd.

If all the folks want to participate, you could have each person open his or her bottle and pour the contents into a numbered pitcher. Of course, they'll know which wine is theirs, but that's only one vote. The problem with the person knowing which pitcher their wine is in is that they could "lobby" others to vote for their wine to win. Being the anal game player that I am, I think it's better if folks don't know which is their wine.

I would suggest that all the bottles should be opened and put into an empty wine carton. One at a time, a person walks into the room with the wines and pitchers and pulls a wine out of the box, pours the wine into one pitcher and writes down on a piece of paper the name of the wine and which pitcher it went into, folds the paper up and puts it into a basket. They are not allowed to select their own wine when they go into the room. The person then puts the empty bottle back into the wine box and goes out of the room for the next person to come in and do the same thing. That way, each person still only knows one wine out of all of them, but not which one is theirs.

Whites should be chilled first. It's fine for the whites to be in the pitcher for a while without being on ice.

Everyone should vote for their top three favorite wines, with 1 being their favorite, 2 their next favorite and 3 the next favorite. The wine with the lowest score wins. The person who brought the favorite wine should get a prize. (A new car! Something good. I think it's fun for everyone to put money into a pot and the first place winner gets 50% of the pot, the second place winner gets 30% and the third place person gets the rest.)

Glassware: Regular bowl-shaped wine glasses. Since you are probably going to be tasting only one color of wine, there's no need to rinse out your glass between tastings.

Food: Anything goes here, too. Just make it fun. There are so many different wines, it would be silly to try to match food to all of them.

Obtaining the wine: Easy. Everyone brings a bottle.

FORMAT 3: BE THE WINE, DANNY

Focus: Guessing aspects of the wine

Best for: People who are into wine

How many people: Best if fewer than 25. A bottle of wine is 25 ounces, so everyone could try a wine if people only pour a one-ounce taste, but people often pour too much. If you have close to 25 folks where the pouring could be an issue, have a one-ounce shot glass by each pitcher so folks know how much to pour.

This format is tougher and is probably best for folks who have some wine experience, but then again, anyone is able to guess. Their legs won't be cut off if they don't get any right, so it's fine if they don't have any wine experience.

This is a blind tasting, where people have to guess pre-determined aspects of each wine. It could be the price, the grape variety and/or the country it came from. The advantage this format has over the last one is that you can have a mix of white and red wines, since a favorite is not being determined. The wine should be transferred out of the bottle into carafes or pitchers (see the above format for details).

This is best to do in a more organized manner. The wine is poured from the carafe into everyone's glass at the same time. Each person has a piece of paper with the number of the wine and spaces for each aspect of the wine that you want to make part of the game: cost, grape and/or origin. People taste the wine and make their guess. When everyone is done, you move on to the next wine. Do the whites first in any order, then move on to the reds.

If you want to give out prizes, score each card with one point for each correct answer. You could make a range for the cost to be correct, say within $2 up or down, or $5, however generous you want to be. The origin is typically the country it comes from   unless you are so good that you want to make it the region within the country.

Glassware: Regular bowl-shaped wine glasses. One glass per person is still fine for this format. Since you will be moving from white to white, white to red and then red to red, there's no need to rinse out a glass between samples. It's only when you go from red to white that you need to rinse out a wine glass before pouring the next wine.

Food: Skip the food during the tasting. Have some mild cheese and French bread available, and that's it.

Obtaining the wine: This could be done as a BYOB, or by having one person buy all the wine with everyone pitching in. The advantage of one person buying the wine is that the person can get a range of prices from box wine to \$50+, depending on how much money each person is willing to pitch in. The fun is to see if a person can tell an expensive wine from a very inexpensive wine.

FORMAT 4: MATCHMAKING EVENING

Focus: Matching food and wine

Best for: Any level of wine drinker

How many people: Any number is fine.

Food changes the taste of any wine. The chapter on wine and food explains how wine and food match up, but doing a mouth-on tasting is better. There are many ways to structure a wine and food tasting. Following are just a few options:

1. Sit down tasting. When the food is going to be non-sweet items, here is a standard list of wines to have that covers the main characteristics in wine that affect the taste:

A. Sparkling wine – Brut

B. A white wine high in acidity. For white, that could be a Riesling (not a Grand Cru) from Alsace, an Italian Pinot Grigio, a zippy New Zealand Sauvignon Blanc or an inexpensive white Bordeaux.

C. If the food begs for a red, inexpensive wine, Chiantis and Barberas from Italy are usually high in acidity. If you do choose a red, switch the red with the oaky Chardonnay in order.

D. Fruity reds with no tannin. Your best bet would be to buy inexpensive reds from Australia or maybe California — under \$10 per bottle.

E. A wine with tannin. Only reds have tannin, and you'll find more tannin in a wine as the price of the wine goes up. Grapes such as Zinfandel, Cabernet Sauvignon and Shiraz from Australia usually have a fair amount of tannin once you get over $15 or $20 a bottle.

F. Slightly sweet wine, like a German Riesling (Kabinett or Spätlese) or an American Johannisberg Riesling.

With those six types of wine, you'll have most of the bases covered.

Now you need to choose a food to match. Don't get crazy here. The idea is not to have too many different food items to match to the wine, because the combinations get out of control. Say if you had six cheeses and the six wines above, and wanted to try each wine with each cheese, you would have 36 matches to try. Hmmm, one ounce of wine with each cheese and you will have consumed the equivalent of a bottle and a half of wine. Yowie! So narrow your food items down as much as possible. I'd keep the food to four choices: four cheeses, four sauces, etc.

Some fun and easy categories are cheeses, pasta sauces (remember it's the sauce that makes the difference, not the pasta itself), different types of salmon, different meats prepared the same way, snack food like chips, popcorn, pizza, etc.

It's best to be seated with each person having a plate of food, with the food items labeled if it isn't obvious (like the type of cheeses). For the progression of the tasting, it is best to present one wine with each food and then move to the next wine. The order the wines are listed above would be a good order. Depending on how much wine you have and how eager each person is, it's best to take a taste of wine then a bite of food, then a taste of the same wine to see how the taste changes. If that just seems like too much wine, you can taste each wine once at the beginning and then taste it after each bite of food.

If you want to do a sit down tasting with dessert items or chocolate, the wine lineup should be different. Here's what I suggest:

1. Banyuls
2. Ruby style Port that costs in the teens, or LBV to move up a notch
3. Tawny Port
4. Muscat-based wine
5. Sauternes
6. Sweet sparkling wine

Glassware: You'll want to have a glass for each wine. It's nice to put the glasses on a piece of paper with circles on it, so one doesn't get the wines confused. They can be either red or white wine glasses. If you can't come up with enough glasses and don't want to rent them, plastic cups or water glasses are fine.

Obtaining the wine: This is best done by one person, to make sure you get the right types of wine.

2. Reception-style. If a sit down tasting is just too formal for your group, make it reception style and have stations with a food item; it could be anything. At each station are two wines. The wines could be a white and a red, or two of the same color. If they are the same color, you want to be sure they are different styles. If you have two Chardonnays, for instance, have one be an unoaked version and the other an oaky Chardonnay. Or you can differentiate the two wines by where they're from, like one Old World and one New World — just so folks can see how two different styles match with the food.

A variation on this theme is to make each food station food and wine from a different country — kind of an around-the-world tasting. Or for the ultimate tasting, have stations with the top wine and food matches of all time.

Glassware: One wine glass will do for this. Because guests may be going from red to white wine, it's good to have a pitcher of water and dump bucket at each station to rinse out their wine glasses.

Obtaining the wine: If you are serving wines that are different versions, then this is best done by one person to make sure you get the right types of wine. If you are doing the stations by country, then you could assign each guest a country to get the wine. While you're at it, why not have the guests bring the food from that country too?

3. Wine and Dinner. Incorporate wine into your dinner. With each course, have two or three different wines. Once again, it's more interesting if each wine is unlike the others in some way.

Glassware: You can get away with one wine glass, but it would be better to have as many wine glasses as wines for each course.

Obtaining the wine: Since the host knows the dishes, it's best they buy the wine. However, the host could have guests each bring a style of wine that the host would designate. Or, if you want to walk on the wild side, you can have each guest bring a wine and just throw it in the mix and pair up the wine to the courses at random. Now that's exciting.

If you are doing a dinner and folks who don't drink are attending, the non-alcoholic wines on the market aren't bad. The wines that I've had from Inglenook and Sutter Home (Frei) are very drinkable, and that way your guest won't feel left out.

FORMAT 5: DON'T TRY THIS ALONE
Focus: Learning about wine by hiring an expert
Best for: Any level of wine drinker, but for folks who really want to learn more about wine
How many people: Any number is fine.

If you have folks who want to learn more about wine, this is the way to go. You have ultimate flexibility as far as the theme. It could be a tasting of wines from a certain country, grape variety, wine and food matching, etc. More times than not, I think it is best to do an "overview of wine" theme, as people find that to be the most useful.

The trick is to get a wine speaker who fits your style. If you are doing a high-level tasting with folks who are very serious about wine, a serious, knowledgeable wine speaker is easy to find. However, if you want a speaker who is fun and is not a Club member, that will be tougher. Of course, every wine guy or gal says they are fun and not snobby, but in reality it isn't so. Visit local wine shops to see if any of the sales clerks seem fun. If not, ask the clerks if they know of any sales reps for their wholesalers or importers who are fun. The defining question to see if someone is fun is to ask them if they ever drink box wine. They probably don't, but if they say anything derogatory about it, like they're too good for that, you probably have a Club member in your midst.

When you get a salesperson to come to do the tasting, oftentimes he/she will come for free. If not free, then maybe he/she will want $50-$200. The retailer wants your business and the wholesaler will probably bring the wines he/she sells so they are benefiting from the exposure. The downside is that you may not be getting an objective speaker or one who is any good at speaking in the first place.

Another option is to search the Internet for independent wine speakers, like me, who aren't in the business of selling wine. Depending on what part of the country you are in and who you get, the speaking fee may range from $50-$10,000. More times than not, it will probably be between $100 and $500. Make sure you ask the box wine question with these folks too, because there is even a higher likelihood these types are members of the Club.

Besides the speaking fee, you'll need wine. Figure a $15 a bottle average price and maybe 4-10 wines. If you pour two ounces per person, you'll get about 10 people per bottle, so you can do the math from there about the wine cost per person.

The talk can be any length and from casual (folks sitting on couches and chairs) to a more formal tasting at tables. The content usually is 30-60 minutes. In addition, the speaker will need about five minutes per wine to discuss it, so you can adjust the number of wines according to how much time you want the whole presentation to last.

Glassware: Regular bowl-shaped wine glasses. One glass per person is still fine for this format if you're sitting on couches and chairs. If you're at a table, it's best to have one glass per wine for each person. That way the wines can be pre-poured, so the presentation isn't being constantly interrupted by the pouring of wine. It's good to have a piece of paper with circles on it for each wine glass, so the wines don't get confused. If you are not going from red to white wine anytime during your tasting, there is no need to rinse out the glass between samples.

Food: Skip the food during the tasting. Have some mild cheese and French bread available, and that's it.

Obtaining the wine: Depending on the jurisdiction, the speaker can buy and bring the wine and you pay him/her, or you'll have to get a list from the speaker and you will go out to buy the wine yourself.

FORMAT 6: BRING IN MARK PHILLIPS. (HEY, THAT'S ME.)

Focus: Learning about wine in a reception style format.

Best for: Any level of wine drinker.

How many people: Any number is fine.

Oh, I do the lectures also, but I list this one because I'm the only one who does this format. It's a blind tasting competition that is great for home wine tasting parties or work-related events. And I travel, so give me a call.

20

Tips to Enjoying Wine at Home

WHEN TO DRINK YOUR WINE

THEY SAY ONLY 2% of the wine made is meant to be aged. I'm not sure who "they" are. I haven't done the calculations myself and I don't know how long a wine has to be kept before it is considered "aging it." Regardless, I can say that most wine is meant to be consumed when it is released and on the shelf.

As the price goes up on a wine, the chance that it can age gets better. Wines under $20 are usually good to go right now. Above $20, I would still drink them soon, but you can decide. Be sure to read the chapter on "Why it's Stupid to Buy Expensive Wine." If you still decide you want to keep a wine for a few years, you should know how to age it.

Several factors can greatly affect the wine:

1. Temperature. The warmer the wine, the faster it will age. Usually when some expert recommends aging a wine, they are figuring on a storage temperature around 55°. For every 18° F you go above that (that would be 73°, which is room temperature for many), it ages the wine up to eight times faster! So if you keep the wine on a rack in your living room at 73° for one year, the wine will actually have aged almost eight years, and that's not good. What's worse is that the expert's recommendation on how long to age wine is just an educated (I hope it's educated) guess. I've heard lamentations from many a collector who waited too long to open a bottle, and it had gone over the hill.

2. Temperature variation. If the temperature varies more than 10 to 15 degrees daily, the wine will age even faster. That's why storing wine in the kitchen is the worst place to keep it because of the cooking that happens. If there is temperature variation and the wine is exposed to light, the wine will age up to 20 times faster! So now the wine you want to keep around for three months in the kitchen will really be five years old. It's a huge difference.

Not only does the variation of the temperature affect the aging of the wine, it affects it in the short term as well. If the temperature varies 20 degrees or so over a short period of time, it can ruin a wine in just a few days.

I learned my lesson regarding this several years ago. I bought about 12 cases of wine worth about $3,000 for a wine tasting event I was hosting in a couple of days. I didn't feel like unloading it all into my house, so I left it in back of my pickup truck, which had a cap over the bed and was parked in the shade. It was March, so the temperature was around 70 degrees in the day and close to 50 at night. In two days' time the wine was ruined. All of it. It wasn't corked, like many wines that are bad. Variation in temperature doesn't cause that. What it does do is make the wine insipid, no fruitiness to the wine at all. It doesn't taste bad, but it all tasted like water.

3. Humidity. Not really a big deal, unless you are going to keep your wine for decades — in which case, if the humidity is too low, usually under 60%, the cork may dry out and some air might get in. But a dry cork can maintain its integrity easily for five years, so for any length of time under five years, don't worry about the humidity.

Now you know: if you don't have the proper storage conditions, don't hold on to wine. Drink it. Wine refrigerators are sold all over now and are coming down in price, so you might want to consider getting one. If that doesn't work for you, find the coolest spot in your home that is dark and stays at a constant temperature, and that's where you should keep wine.

If all else fails, put the wine in the refrigerator, whether white or red. It meets all of the conditions needed for good storage. It's cool (too cool, but that won't hurt the wine). It's a constant temperature and I think it's dark, although I've never actually seen the light go off when I've closed the door.

Assuming you have the right storage conditions, I suggest following my 10 to 1 rule. For every $10 you pay for a wine in a store, age it for one year from the vintage date on the bottle. If you pay $20 for a wine, it should be ready to go in two years — two years from the vintage date, not the date you buy it. If you pay $50 for a wine, it should be ready to go five years after it was made, and so on up until $70. Almost any wine is ready to go in seven years; ten, for sure. That's when the components in the wine have integrated and the complexity has developed.

Just because most are ready to go in 7-10 years, that doesn't mean they can age longer. One a wine hits its maturity, it plateaus for years after that — not really getting much better, but not getting any worse. These guidelines are generalizations are there are plenty of exceptions. I've had red wines that are 20-50 years old and still good, so wines can go a long time, but those are against the odds. Think 7-10 years and you'll be safe.

The exceptions are vintage fortified wines and sweet wines. The earliest you want to drink those, to really experience what the wines have to offer, is at least 10 years after the vintage. And they can age indefinitely.

OPENING WINE

Thank god for screwtops. No more corkscrews needed. But since we'll never reach the point when all wines will be screwtop, a corkscrew is still needed. I prefer the Lever Pull from Le Creuset. However, since their patent ran out there have been many knockoffs.

The first knockoff that I was aware of was the Rabbit by Metrokane. I've tried one of the very first ones made, and it was bad; now, after trying dozens since, I can still say they're still bad. If someone gave me one, I'd throw it away. I have found metal ones at Bed, Bath and Beyond for around $10 that have worked well.

Whether you buy the original from Le Creuset or a knockoff, it should pull a natural cork out with ease. If you have to struggle at all, something is wrong. The lever type corkscrews aren't recommended for artificial corks. It seems the artificial corks wear out the Teflon on the cork-screw's worm too quickly. If I see an artificial cork, I use the Pocket Model from Le Creuset. (By the way, I don't get any compensation from Le Creuset for these plugs, nor have I ever gotten anything from them. I just like their products.) The pocket model seems to use the same worm as the lever model, but the Teflon on the pocket model doesn't seem to be affected by the artificial corks like the Lever Pull. What's nice about the pocket model is there is no pulling or struggling to get the cork out.

The traditional corkscrew, the waiter's tool, has gotten much better since they made the hinge jointed. It's still good to keep those around for problem corks.

There are several reasons to decant a wine. Traditionally, a wine needed to be decanted to let it breathe and/or separate the wine from sediment that formed in the bottle. You rarely will come across a wine with sediment if you are drinking wines 10 years old or younger. A wine usually will start to create sediment around 10 years old. The Traditionalists will say it "throws" sediment *(CJA – The Club member will use the word "throws" instead of "creates" just to sound cool)*. The sediment isn't harmful to you. I mean, you won't start having seizures, gagging, choking or breaking out in hives that require immediate hospitalization ... well, maybe you'll have the seizures, but they won't be bad. Kidding. But it's not good to serve a wine with sediment. The stuff can get into your teeth.

How do you know if the wine has sediment? Look. Hold the bottle up against a light and see if stuff is floating around in it. If so, you need to decant.

Club members decant per the Traditional Approach. First, you stand the bottle up for a few days. (Oh yeah, this takes advance work.) Then you light a candle. You pour the wine out slowly into a decanter, with the neck of the bottle between your eyes and the candle. Once sediment starts coming through the neck, you stop.

Too much work for me, AND there is too much wine left in the bottle. Since you are usually decanting expensive wine, that won't do. The way I do it is with a coffee filter. Put it in a strainer and hold it over a bowl

— a big bowl. I pour the wine into the strainer and it goes into the bowl through the coffee filter, catching all of the sediment. Presto! Fast, and not a drop of wine is wasted. Then I transfer the wine into a carafe or decanter, and away we go.

2. Decanting wine is a great way to serve inexpensive wine to guests. If you were to put a bottle of Yellow Tail on the table, your guests know how inexpensive that wine is (although there is nothing wrong with that). But why not decant it? Pour the Yellow Tail or box wine into a nice decanter and serve it. I guarantee you that serving a wine in a decanter will make the wine taste at least 3x more expensive. You can present the wine as a special "say the grape variety" from your collection. It's a great way to go. Whether you actually reveal the name of the wine is up to you.

2b A variation on the above theme. Now I'm moving into the realm of deception. (I do want to say that I'm not a dishonest person. In fact, I'm incapable of looking someone in the eye and lying. But the suggestions from this point on can be deceptive or used to teach people about wine. Up to you.)

Save the expensive bottles of wine once you finish them. When serving the Yellow Tail or whatever inexpensive wine in the decanter, place the empty expensive bottle down next to the decanter. Because your guests will rightly assume they are drinking a $50, $100 or $200 bottle of wine, listen to how they gush about the wine. The power of suggestion is so convincing in wine.

You might even ask the guests if the wine is worth it. Of course, it would be key for you to say first that the wine is okay, but you wonder to yourself if the wine is worth "whatever the expensive bottle that is sitting next to the decanter cost" just so they have the opening to say they agree. When given the opportunity to comment honestly, they will probably say it isn't worth THAT price, but maybe half that. Either way, I'll bet you dollars to donuts that the price they would pay for it is a lot more than the wine actually cost. And then after you all finish that bottle, you can tell them that the wine was just $6 a bottle — or don't tell them, and let them think you are serving very expensive wine to them.

For the record, I'm not condoning deception — unless it's just you and a date, and the fact that you're serving expensive wine would make a difference to the outcome of the evening.

2c. Take the deception one step further, and actually serve the Yellow Tail *in* the bottle of expensive wine.

3. Mix wine. As I am typing this, I am drinking a glass of fine red Cabernet, about $35 a bottle, mixed with Almaden box Cabernet. I promise. 50/50. It's great. I could probably even go 40/60 good Cab to box Cab, and it would be fine.

Well, let me state that box Cabernet isn't bad on its own. I did a tasting for a public television conference where I had Almaden box Cabernet in a carafe and a wine from the south of France that cost $35 and had been rated 91 pts by *Wine Spectator* in another carafe. I asked the guests to tell me which wine they preferred, and over 70% chose the box wine. There's some good box wine out there, and getting better. Australia is boxing better wine, which will be here soon.

So the box is okay on its own, but by mixing it with better wine, you can make the better wine last a lot longer and save money. You're just making your own blend, like they do at the winery.

I have even blended non alcoholic Cabernet with regular wine. Yes. It's true. I'm not quite sure why I did that, but you can cut the consumption of alcohol in half by doing that. If you plan to drive or have sex later, that might be a good way to go.

PROPER SERVING TEMPERATURE

The serving temperature of wine is key. Most folks drink the whites too cold and the reds too warm. White wines should be about 50 degrees. It's really a continuum between mid 40s and mid 50s.

A refrigerator is usually 40 degrees. That's too cold for most wine. Cold masks the flavor of wine. Not just wine, but cold masks the flavor of any beverage. A beverage at that temperature will have almost all bad flavors covered up by the cold. That's why you would serve Budweiser ice cold. Or really cheap wine. Because anything served at 40 degrees or cooler won't taste good or bad, just refreshing.

The less complex the wine, the cooler it should be served. If the wine is not good at all, serve it ice cold and it will taste okay. That's the way to unload wine you don't like on guests: serve it ice cold.

Decent, simple wine should be in the mid-40s. Wines that are around $8-$20 should be around 50. More expensive wines with more to offer should be in the mid 50s. The question that always comes up at my talks is, "How do you know how cold the wine is?" I'll get to that in a minute.

For red wines, the serving temperature should be in the mid-60s. Again, it's a continuum, the simpler the wine, the cooler it should be served and the more complex, the warmer. The range for reds is between high 50s to high 60s, but not over 70.

But what about the popular rule that red wine should be served at room temperature? That rule was written by the British a long time ago. Back then, and maybe still, room temperature there was a lot cooler than it is here. Room temperature here is often in the low to mid-70s, and that just doesn't cut it for reds. Reds that warm will taste out of balance, usually too alcoholic and less fruity.

So, back to the usual question about how to know if the wine is at the right temperature. Remember the 20-minute rule. If you keep your white in the fridge, pull it out 20 minutes ahead of time and it will be about 50 degrees. If you keep your red in your home at room temperature, put it in the fridge for 20 minutes and it will be in the mid- 60s. Easy, huh?

Are you anal? If so, here's a more exact formula. Wine warms up 16 degrees per half hour. It cools down 8 degrees per half hour, exactly half. Sooo, if your fridge is 40 degrees and you want to drink your better, more complex wine in the mid-50s, you would pull it out 30 minutes ahead of time.

Likewise for your reds. If your room temperature is 75 and you have a simple, guzzling wine such as Beaujolais Nouveau (which is basically grape juice with alcohol) that you want to drink at the high 50s, you might want to put that in the fridge for an hour ahead of time.

The whites won't taste much different following this rule but the reds, oh my God! The reds will taste SO much better! It will be an epiphany for you, especially with New World reds. Once you have experienced reds at the mid-60s, it will be impossible for you to have wines "warm" again. Reds that are too warm is one of my biggest peeves.

All right, here comes a tangent.

At restaurants, it's quite common to get red wine served too warm. One chain, the chain that rhymes with Norton's, serves its wine way too warm. Every time I've been to one and ordered red wine by the bottle, I thought they had put it in the microwave first before bringing it to the table. I wrote about that in an article once and the PR person for Morton's phoned me and said I must be mistaken. To prove it to me, she invited me to lunch at the Morton's in the Georgetown neighborhood in D.C.

We got there and had a white wine by the glass for starters. The wine list was given to me and I ordered a red wine by the bottle. The wine was brought out, and it was hot! I didn't get third degree burns from touching the bottle, but it was close. I asked her how this could happen, and she said that the wine closet was by the kitchen and quite warm. As Homer Simpson says, D'oh!

I COULDN'T BELIEVE IT. I'm sure that it would seem logical to anyone with at least half of a brain that she would call ahead and make sure that the reds would be at the right temperature. But no. What a mess.

But many other restaurants do the same thing. What do you do in that instance, when you know how good a red is in the mid-60s and you're getting it in the mid-70s, if not warmer? I ask for an ice bucket: ice with water, vs. one of those ceramic holders for chilled wines. I put the red wine in the ice water for a few minutes, and I'm golden. I'm okay with that.

It's getting a warm red wine by the glass that's tougher. You can't put the glass in an ice bucket. Oh, I guess you could, but it would be tough. When the warm red wine in a glass comes to me, I put ice cubes in the wine. Yep. I would rather have a watered down red wine that tastes good than a warm red that tastes like crap.

Speaking of manipulating wine, if you have red wine you don't finish in one evening and want to save it, put it in the fridge (more on that later). When I pour myself a glass of red wine that has been in the fridge at 40 degrees and I want to drink it in the mid-60's, it would take too long to let it warm up on its own, so I put it in the microwave for 15 seconds and it's the perfect temperature. I do. I'm not kidding. It's the best.

WINE AND SEX

Before 1990 when I had my first glass of wine, I'm not sure I really had experienced sex — I mean, romance. How does one have a romantic evening with a six-pack of Bud? Or a bottle of vodka and some mixers? I just don't get it. Oh, those things might have made it easy to get to the sex part of the evening, but I just can't imagine romance happening without wine, if alcohol is involved. (I had to add that last clause about alcohol to let you know that I don't think wine or alcohol is needed for romance. Certainly not. Romance can be had without wine, but it's hard to have wine without romance.)

I don't care what I'm doing: mowing the lawn with my Moscato d'Asti in the cup holder (actually it's usually in a cooler with ice, and when I need a swig, I just drink it from the bottle), doing laundry while grazing on a New World white or red, slugging back a few glasses of wine while shooting pool or throwing darts, sharing a luxury rosé Champagne with a wonderful gal, or just having a great bottle of wine by myself, it's all romantic. Wine just adds an emotional component, a pure sensual aspect to whatever you're doing. It is a bonding beverage. How many times have

you seen two people drunk on wine get into a fight?
Okay, a few times, but compared to drunks on beer or
hard liquor, it's nothing.

Wine is liquid romance. If the whole world drank
wine in moderation, there would be no wars — unless,
of course, the Traditionalists got riled up about folks
putting ice cubes in their wines.

And because wine and romance/sex are so closely
tied together, there are many analogies that work to
explain one or the other.

1. Long foreplay is the key to great sex. Foreplay
involves the appearance of someone, the aroma, and the
sense of taste. The longer it is drawn out, the better the
end result. The same for tasting wine. The appearance,
aroma and taste are all critical in tasting wine. The
longer those are drawn out, the better the experience
will be. I can remember the great wines I've had, and
I may take 5 to 10 minutes before I actually taste the
wine because the aroma is so confounding and sensual.
Every time I swirl the wine and smell it, it offers a new
component, a new tease. We can learn from foreplay
that it's important to draw it out as long as possible.
Anyone who doesn't draw out the tasting experience
probably hurries through sex, too.

2. Sometimes sex is just better alone. A few years
ago, a wine sales guy named Ron and I were on the
Armstrong Williams television show as guests, and
Armstrong asked us what was the best context to have
a great wine. Ron and I looked at each other, and we

both knew the answer: alone. Oh, I love sharing wine and the social element that comes along with that. But when it comes to an orgasmic wine, I would prefer to have it alone for two reasons.

First, if the wine is truly great and you're sharing it with others, everyone feels obligated to talk about it. That's exactly what screwed up my dinner at the Inn at Little Washington. The wine became the focus, and then it lost its luster because it was being beaten like a dead horse with analysis.

Second, an orgasmic wine makes one's brain go nuts. The wine is so complex and ethereal that it almost confounds the mind. It challenges me. Encourages me. Kids me. It's almost like I'm having an intimate moment with the wine. It's *our* experience. The wine and me. Hey, Ernest knows: "I drank a bottle of wine for company. It was Château Margaux. It was pleasant to be drinking slowly and to be tasting wine and to be drinking alone. A bottle of wine was good company." (Ernest Hemingway, *The Sun Also Rises*.)

3. Sex is more fun if you change things up every so often. If you're always in the bed, lights off and in the same position every time, sex will become boring after a while. Same with wine. You have to try different wines and keep expanding your parameters. Don't be a wine prude. You may not like every wine you try, but you'll learn more about your preferences from each one.

4. By adding soft lighting, candles and romantic music, sex can be so much better. Wine can also benefit

by adding the same things, and food that pairs well with it. The truly orgasmic wines can be enjoyed by themselves (which I would prefer), but food can make almost every wine taste better.

What wine is best for romance? Good question. Just as romance is subjective, so is wine. Romance is all based on creating a mood. When you want to put some romantic music on, you could choose any number of artists, but one common theme is that it won't be loud or a fast, heavy beat. It's usually soft, slow and gentle. Emotional. Wine that is chosen for romance should be the same way. A wine shouldn't be full-bodied, knocking you over the head with power. It shouldn't be overly oaky, overly acidic or overly tannic because those are a shot to the system. The wine should be smooth. Elegant. Sophisticated.

5. Sometimes romance and long foreplay are just not what you're in the mood for. Wild sex is. Wild sex. That's when it's fast and furious, when buttons are a hindrance and get ripped off to get the clothes off. It's animal passion. For romance, there could be any number of wines that you might choose, like there are any number of CDs you could choose for romantic music. It all depends on the mood.

But when it comes to wild sex, there's one wine that makes you like an animal. In fact, in the old-school books, they say to pair this wine with "well hung game." I thought that meant an animal with big private parts, but I embarrassingly realized later that the author meant like a rabbit or something hung up for a long time. Okay. Regardless, the wine goes with big, powerfully flavored foods like truffles and heavy stews.

It's a red wine made in the Piedmont region of Italy. Barolo is the answer. It's made from the Nebbiolo grape and many producers make it. Be careful of who you have the wine with, because something WILL happen. Many producers make Barolo, and it makes a difference on what kind you get. The trend is for many producers to make an international version, a more fruit-forward style, that loses the traditional robust flavors from the more traditional version (which I prefer). Some traditional producers to look for are Bruno Giacosa, Giacomo Conterno, Mascarello and Aldo Conterno. But just as important as finding the right producer is to make sure the wine is at least 10 years old. It takes that long for the "animal" characteristics of the wine to show. Don't worry about the wine being too old. Barolo can age for decades. They won't be inexpensive, but what a wild ride you'll have when you drink one. Make sure you're with the right person!

6. In sex, everyone has their own preferences. In wine, it's the same way, and no way is the right way for everyone. Don't be shy or embarrassed by what you like. You'll enjoy wine (and sex) more if you follow your heart and not worry about what anyone else thinks.

7. And last. Both wine and sex create stains. (Mark, you should've stopped at #6) Well, it's true. And maybe it's a reminder to be a little more careful, knowing the consequences.

Is there any way that wine and sex aren't the same? Yep, now that you mention it, there is a way. You *can* have too much wine.

GETTING WINE STAINS OUT

Spilling wine: I used to really hate spilling wine on myself, especially red wine. I used to have a half dozen pairs of khaki pants that were nearly new but unwearable because of red wine stains on the legs from over-zealously swirling wine or just plain clumsiness. The spilling of the wine really wasn't the problem I had. It was that I didn't notice it until a few days later so the stain had set. I would come home from a tasting, strip and throw my pants in a pile to take to the cleaners, and they might sit there a few days or longer before they got cleaned. Once a stain is set, you have an uphill battle to get it out.

I had some free time one day and thought I would do some research on ways to get out red wine. I've heard people swear by any number of methods to get out red wine: club soda, white wine, water and salt, etc., but I wanted to know for sure.

It turns out that almost any liquid will work pretty well if it is applied immediately after the spill. The trick to getting a stain out is diluting as soon as possible, so any clear liquid like club soda, water, etc. can keep the stain diluted until you have a chance to wash the clothing.

But on some occasions the immediate application of some clear liquid just doesn't cut it. Oftentimes that seems to happen on a carpet or a tablecloth.

I ran across a study done at University of California at Davis, where they examined every wine stain removing suggestion ever used, and the winning stain remover was one you can make at home. Mix hydrogen peroxide with Dawn dishwashing soap (really, any liquid soap will do), 50/50 and apply it to the stain. It performed the best of all homemade remedies as well as the commercial ones.

So I mixed up the 50/50 mixture, got my six khaki pants out and tried it out. No luck. Ugh! I continued my research, and finally discovered the answer. The best stain remover for red wine (and maybe all other stains) is sodium percarbonate. It's kind of a new chemical on the market, but it does wonders! I tried it on my six pants and the old stains all came out. Good as new.

That was pretty impressive, but the final test was a whopper. An open bottle of red wine fell over in my car and spilled on the carpet, a big spill like two feet in diameter. (I know you might be wondering what I was doing with an open bottle of wine in my car, but I was just transporting it.) Anyway, so the spill happened nearly two years ago, and nothing I tried could get it out. I put the sodium percarbonate on there, and it took it out completely! Unbelievable. It's the best.

I was so impressed by its performance that I bought a 50-pound bucket of sodium percarbonate, because besides being used as a wine stain remover, it can be used as laundry soap, a tub cleaner, etc. It can be used for anything! There is one product whose key ingredient is sodium percarbonate, and that's OxiClean.

Sodium percarbonate (or OxiClean) comes in a powder form. For stains, put some powder onto the stain, pour a little warm/hot water onto the powder to make a paste and rub the paste into the stain. Let it sit for an hour or two or longer. For my car's carpet, I let it sit overnight. Rinse it off with water, and the stain should be gone.

I opened this segment on stain removal by saying that I used to hate spilling wine on myself. I say USED to, because with sodium percarbonate, I don't care anymore about spills. I know I can always get them out.

WHAT TO DO WITH WINE LEFTOVERS

What's wrong with this question? Leftovers? Whadaya, a wimp? Listen, donut head, when a bottle is open, your number one goal is to finish the wine. If the wine spews out of your mouth involuntarily, take a break for a few minutes, clean up the mess and then come back and finish the wine.

All right, let's say you're home alone and it's the third bottle and you j-u-s-t can't do it. I can understand that. What do you do with a half empty bottle of wine — and you don't have dogs? Let's review the options.

First, the main thing you want to do is get the wine

away from air. Air is the enemy of wine. It may help if a wine has to breathe, but outside of that situation, air is the enemy and should be avoided at all costs. Recognizing that, companies have invented all types of gadgets or systems to keep wine fresh if it is not finished.

The rubber stopper that goes in the bottle and then you pump it up, supposedly creating a vacuum in the bottle, is a popular device. Bad news, though. *The Wall Street Journal* did a study was done some time ago, and then asked Professor David Roe of the Portland State University chemistry department to test it as well. The results were that after two hours, you lose 25 percent of the vacuum. Overnight — in 12 hours — the vacuum is totally gone. *Decanter* magazine (probably the snobbiest one in the world) also reviewed the different ways to preserve wine, and the rubber stopper didn't perform well.

Some folks try to use inert gas that is sprayed into the bottle, displacing the oxygen and thus protecting the wine. The professional systems used in restaurants and wine shops have gotten pretty good, but the canisters you buy for home use don't work quite as well. However, the canisters are significantly better than the rubber stopper and pump method.

The best is a way that doesn't require you to buy a thing. Get the wine away from air — physically, not with a gadget or a system. If you have a half empty bottle of wine, you want to transfer that wine into a container where the wine will fill it to the top, thus displacing all of the air. Half bottles of wine, once finished and washed, work great. Geez, with all of the small water bottles around, they work great too. Tupperware. Ziploc bags. I don't care. Just put the leftover wine in a container where the wine can fill it up, and you're set.

But you're not done yet. The temperature still can dink you. In fact, that's what is the killer at most restaurants. The open bottle sits behind the bar where the temperature is warm, which means the wine goes down the tubes much faster. Wine stored at room temperature ages 15 times faster than wine stored in a refrigerator, so store both red and white in the fridge. If your red is in the fridge and you want to have a quick glass before you leave for work in the morning, I'm with you. But the wine will be cold. Whenever I am ready to have a glass of leftover red wine stored in the refrigerator, I pour about six ounces into a glass and microwave it for 15 seconds, and it will be just the right temperature to enjoy. I'm serious! It won't hurt the wine, and you'll be enjoying it just like you're supposed to. Now depending on the amount you pour, the type of glass you use and the wattage of your microwave, you may have to adjust the time a hair. But it's a great way to get wine to the right temperature in a heartbeat.

All right, I have a feeling you don't buy the microwave advice. I guess I'll have to tell you a story to prove it. I was at a dinner where one of the honorees was the owner and winemaker of Chateau Lagrange, a well-respected winery in Bordeaux. Accompanying him was his PR person, a petite gal from NYC who was a bit high-strung. She and I were talking and somehow my microwave advice came up and she was appalled, even offended. She defiantly stated that no fine wine like Chateau Lagrange should ever be put in a microwave. I gave a polite rebuttal, saying that it didn't hurt the wine, and even Chateau Lagrange could be put in the microwave with no ill effects. She stormed off and went to the winemaker and tattled on me. He replied that he puts wine in the microwave frequently. When guests come by to taste wine and he has to pull one out of the cellar that is 55 degrees, he puts the bottle in the microwave to warm it up to drinking temperature. The PR girl came back to me with her tail between her legs and apologized.

How long DOES the wine last once it's stored in the fridge, you might ask? More times than not in my experience, a white might last a day or two and a red, maybe an extra day or two over that. The wines don't go "bad" like turning to vinegar for many months, but they change so much compared to what they were like when you first opened them that they just aren't enjoyable. Either they have an "off" taste or they just taste insipid, like a soda without any fizz.

In my house, I give a white wine one day and a red maybe two before I think they change enough that I just don't want to drink them. Again, they're not rotten, it's just that I'd rather open a fresh bottle vs. drink the crap that's been opened. Other folks might add a day or two on to what I say. Whatever works for you is fine.

I have a problem, though. May I lie down on a couch and share something with you? It's funny, because most wine experts get their knowledge from older wine experts who got their knowledge from even older wine experts and so on. There are so many bits of information about wine that are just passed down from one wine person to another. And how long a wine lasts is one of those bits. Most wine experts will say a wine will last just a few days. I think the reason they stick to that is because who wouldn't finish a half bottle of wine in a few days, anyway?

Well, I'm the skeptic. So I open wines and purposefully don't finish them and store them to see what the truth is. I've done it with the rubber stopper, the inert gas, etc. At the time I am writing this, 9:30pm, I have a bottle of Sauvignon Blanc that cost $6 in my fridge that is ¾ full with a cork in it, and it has been there for eight months. Every week or so, I grab the wine and take a swig from the bottle to see how it has "developed." What is the kookiest thing is that the wine still tastes good. What's up with that?

The trick is that the wine is ice cold. Ice cold wine never tastes bad. As I mentioned before, cold masks the flavor of wine. When I let that same wine warm up to 50 degrees or so, it tastes terrible.

Are you seated now? If not, sit down because I'm on a roll and I'm going over the line.

Let's say you have a party and have just a bunch of wine left over that you won't be able to finish in the

next few days, and you don't want to risk keeping it for
several months. The first thing I would do is "marry"
the wines. If I had a bottle of opened cab and Pinot
Noir, I'd blend them together in the same bottle. Yes,
it's true. You're better off to have a full bottle (thus
displacing the air) of a mixed wine than two wines
that will get dinked by air. Hey, they blend wines at
the winery, what's wrong with doing it at home? Really,
the "combined" wine will taste fine, albeit different —
maybe better.

Okay, let's say you still have too much wine open,
combined even, that you can't finish in the next few
days. Here's the big answer — and so cool, literally.
Take the leftover wine in a bottle and make sure that
the bottle is at least 25% empty (does that make any
sense? At least 5 oz. should be poured out of the bottle).
Put a cork in it and put the bottle in the freezer.

Yes. The wine WILL freeze. I've done it for six
months. I took the wine out. Let it defrost on the counter for six hours and tasted it. Perfect.

You can also put the wine into ice cube trays. When
you need some wine for cooking, instead of opening a
bottle of wine, just grab a few wine cubes.

Freezing wine has all kinds of benefits. The neighborhood kids love my popsicles. Just kidding!

Wow, so much to write about saving wine when I
could have spared myself carpal tunnel syndrome if everyone would just finish their wine when they open it.

COOKING WITH WINE

I love cooking with wine ... and sometimes I add it to the dish. Yuk yuk. Who's there? Stop it. Stop it who? No, I mean stop writing this silly stuff and get to cooking with wine.

I don't know what they actually put into the stuff called cooking wine that you buy in a supermarket, but it's nasty. I would never use that stuff in anything I cook. I'd rather go without than use it. The point to cooking with wine is to add flavor, and it would take just one drink of the cooking wine in the store to realize that isn't the flavor that should be added to any food. The rule of thumb is if you wouldn't drink it, don't cook with it. Remember that when you are thinking about using leftover wine that is no longer drinkable. Leftover wine CAN be used for marinating, because it still has the qualities that are key in a marinade.

So, as long as the wine is drinkable, it's good to cook with. You have two options:

1. Use box wine. It may not be what you would choose to drink, but it certainly is drinkable. And the bonus part of using box wine is that it stays fresh for a long time.

2. Use nicer wine. That doesn't make much sense, though, because the nuances that make a wine nicer than a box wine will be lost in the dish. The other drawback is that you are opening a whole bottle to use just a little to cook with. I'd have to assume you would

be drinking the root either while you're cooking or during the meal.

3. Try to match the wine to the dish, not just having nicer wine. Certain wines lend themselves to certain foods. If you have a buttery Chardonnay, it is great for a *beurre blanc*. A Zinfandel or Shiraz, with its real fruity berry character, works well for a fruit sauce.

Miscellaneous Hints:

1. Don't use a sweet wine when the recipe calls for a dry wine. A Cream Sherry, Marsala, Port, etc. is not a substitute for regular wine.

2. When you use wine to deglaze a pan, the alcohol burns off and the flavor of the wine gets concentrated. Whether the wine is fruity or sweet, the fruitiness or sweetness will be more concentrated as the wine is reduced. When you use the cooking wine you buy in the store with a ton of salt in it, the salt becomes more concentrated.

3. Wine is a great marinade because the acid in the wine breaks down the fibers of the food, making the food cook faster and more flavorful.

WHAT'S THE BEST CORKSCREW?

I've listed my favorite corkscrews in order of preference from top to bottom.

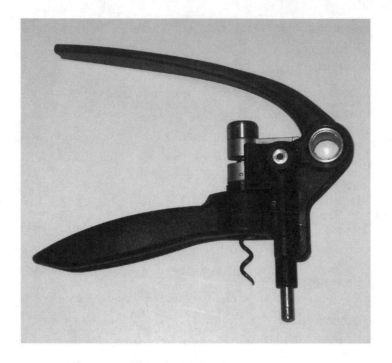

My favorite corkscrew is the Lever Pull, the one from Le
Creuset. They held the patent on it until 1999 and that's
when the Rabbit corkscrew from Metrokane was introduced, which I don't like at all. I don't think it works
well. However, there are a bunch of generic lever pulls
now. I bought one from Bed, Bath and Beyond for $12
that works great…but gave it away, as I like to use my
Le Creuset Lever Pull just because it's the original.

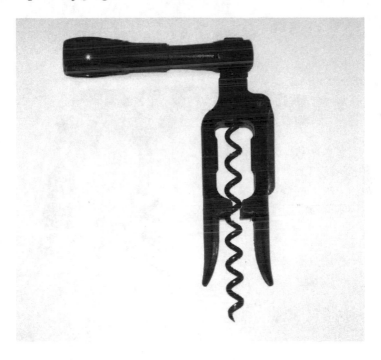

The two drawbacks to the Lever Pull is that it's not very portable because of its size and it doesn't work well on many artificial corks. It will remove them, but it's a bear to try to get the cork off of the worm. That's why I love the Pocket Model Screwpull from Le Creuset, (pictured at right) open, ready for action on the left and closed with the foil cutter knife extended. It makes opening a bottle effortless, as there is no lifting; the cork just comes right out. It works on all corks easily and it's portable. My vote for best all-around corkscrew in the world.

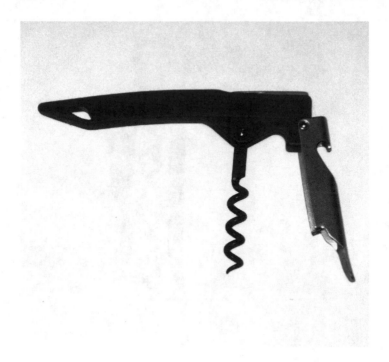

If you want something even more compact, the waiter's tool corkscrew is the best. The one to the right is called the Winner, and it's different than the traditional waiter's tool as the lever is offset so when you pull the cork out, the cork comes out straight vs. being pulled to one side with the traditional waiter's tool. Works great!

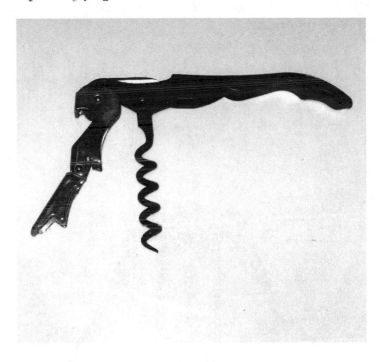

The double-hinged waiter's tool isn't too bad. The extra hinge in the lever allows you to pull the cork out a little and then place the second hinge on the bottle lip to pull the cork out the rest of the way ... straight vs. the traditional waiter's tool. The Winner still works better, I think.

Last (and least), the angel wine corkscrew. These drive me nuts. The worm isn't long enough, so corks often break. It doesn't pull the cork all the way out, so you have to pull the cork out the rest of the way. Ugh. But it's better than nothing.

HOW TO KEEP A WINE JOURNAL

My memory stinks for remembering names of wines. You'd think that being in the "business" I would develop an aptitude for that, but I can't. I'm a dummy. Whether or not you share my Achilles heel, keeping a record of what you tasted, at least for a while, will help you make sense of the world of wine. Everything will come together like the flavor profiles of each grape variety, the difference in wine depending on the region where it's made and the value of wines at certain price points.

To do this, you need to write the wines down in a journal. I think keeping a wine journal is a gas. Write down all of your thoughts about the experience. It can easily turn into a diary of the occasion, and that's fine. Interview the folks who shared the wine with you. Recount the funny things that happened. Try it a few times and you'll be hooked once you go back and read what you wrote. Visit www.winetasting.org to get a handy pocket wine journal.

It helps to keep the label as well, because the visual cues can trigger memories of the wine. Labels can be tough to get off, but here are a few methods (reprinted with permission from an article written by the famous Joel Mitchel of Beekman Wines & Liquors, at www.beekmanwine.com):

We all know how frustrating it can be trying to remove some labels from wine bottles. Removing labels used to be quite simple, but new glues have been developed to prevent labels from coming off in restaurant wine buckets. These glues make it difficult to remove the labels at all, but the following methods will almost always work.

Several different glues are used today and you can't tell which one was used by looking at the label. No single technique works every time on every label, but there are some relatively safe bets. First try to peel the label off starting in a corner. If you are lucky and the winery used the new "peel and stick" type of label, the label will come right off (However, it will immediately stick to anything it comes in contact with!). Most times you will not be so lucky.

The Soaking Method - this is becoming less effective as fewer water-soluble glues are being used.

Equipment: 1 tall Igloo water jug (the picnic kind), tall enough to hold a bottle, Ivory Detergent, paper towels, wax paper, a single edged razor blade, a heavy book, a cork, and a glass of wine.

1. Fill the jug with warm water and 2-3 drops of Ivory Detergent.

2. Fill the wine bottle itself with VERY hot water and immerse it in the jug.

3. After about 30 minutes, the label should either be floating in the jug or loosely clinging to the bottle. If not, continue the soak for 2 hours or overnight.

4. If the label still isn't off, take the bottle out of the jug and fill it again with very warm water. Cram an old cork into the top and dry the bottle well. Get the label as dry as possible.

5. Lay the bottle on a towel to steady it. Use the single-edged razor blade to scrape the label off. Start working from the left side of the label, following the curve of the bottle, to about the middle of the label. Then start from the right side of the label and cut back to the center. Work back and forth until the label is off.

6. Put the label between towels to blot off as much moisture as possible. Be careful! Some of the new glues are of the "peel and stick" variety and will stick to anything. If you find one of these, press the label down on some plain white paper and trim around the label.

7. Place the label on a piece of waxed paper with paper towels on top of it and weight it down with a heavy book until the label dries.

8. The glass of wine? You know what that's for!

The Blow-drier Method - Some of the new glues are unaffected by water, but will melt enough to slide the label off the bottle after "toasting" the label with a blow-drier for about 5 minutes. A heat gun will work faster. Try this if the soaking method doesn't work or if you don't like razor blades.

The Strapping Tape Method - This method separates the layer of the label with the image on it from the layer with the glue. Go to any office supply store and buy a roll of clear 3" wide strapping (packing) tape.

1. Cut off two strips of tape that are about 4" wider than the label.

2. Fill the bottle with VERY hot water (trying not to get the label wet). Wipe the bottle dry.

3. Put a strip of paper about 1/2" wide across the sticky side of both ends of the tape so the ends won't stick to the bottle.

4. Working from one side of the bottle to the other, attach the tape to the bottle so that it just extends (about 1/4") above the label. Bring the tape across the label, using some type of straight edge to smooth it out as you go.

5. Once you have the first strip in place, if it doesn't fully cover the label, attach the second strip right under the first.

6. Use the back of a spoon to rub hard all over the label.

7. Starting at one edge, slowly start to peel off the tape.

8. Once the label is removed, trim the edges with a scissors.

You can purchase a couple of products that supposedly work:

Wine Appeal Label Remover (I like the name) — http://wineappeal.com/Products/LabelRemovers/
2. Labeloff — www.iwawine.com

21

Miscellany

ARE SCREWTOPS BETTER?

I'M REALLY TORN ON MY preference. Something has to be said for the convenience of opening a wine with a quick twist of the cap. On the other hand, the ceremony of pulling a natural cork out of a bottle adds to the romance of wine.

Winemakers have three choices in closures, the term referring to what they use to close the bottle. For years it was natural cork. In the late '90s, the synthetic cork came on to the scene. And then, most recently, the screwtop (or Stelvin) was introduced. Let's look at the pros and cons of each one.

Natural Cork is made from the bark of a cork tree, which is in the oak tree family. Strips of cork are cut off the tree and then plugs are cut from the strips and cleansed with a chlorine solution. Something bad happens, though, if the chlorine isn't rinsed off of the corks. A chemical forms, called 2,4,6-trichloroanisole (thankfully, TCA for short). This is very potent and if enough of it gets into wine, it makes the wine smell like a moldy, musty basement. The term for a wine that has been infected with TCA is "corked." The occurrence of a corked wine was once thought to be as high as 10%. But now the cork industry has moved away from chlorine to using peroxide to cleanse the corks, which has reduced the occurrence frequency of TCA.

Pros: Corks naturally "breathe," letting minute amounts of air into a wine bottle, which helps a wine age and buffers the development of another flaw in wine, volatile sulfur compounds like hydrogen sulfide and mercaptan. Hang with me here, as I'm going to refer to these sulfur compounds later. These sulfur compounds are different than sulfur dioxide (SO2 or sulfites), which is a "good" sulfur that is added to most wines to keep them fresh and kill bacteria.

Cons: The occurrence of TCA, which can ruin the wine.

Artificial Cork is also referred to as plastic cork or synthetic cork. The use of artificial corks did not happen because of a shortage of natural cork. The reason artificial corks were invented was because of a whole bunch of pissed-off winemakers. They were making good wine that was ruined by faulty natural corks that were contaminated with TCA. The wine was being sent back by unhappy customers, and the winery had to pay for that. So they switched to using artificial corks that don't have TCA.

Pros: No TCA to ruin the wine.

Cons: There seems to be a belief that artificial corks do not last as long as natural corks, so they aren't meant to be used in wines that are meant to age. That's not a negative in itself, but you should be aware of that when holding on to a wine with an artificial cork ... like more than three years. Also, artificial corks can wreak havoc on the lever corkscrews that open a bottle really quickly. To save your lever corkscrew, don't use it on artificial corks.

Screwtops, also called *Stelvins*, bring back fond memories of my experience with Boone's Farm as a kid. And that's a problem for the screwtop: it's been associated with cheap wine. However, that seems to be waning as so many more wines (and very good wines, I might add) have screwtops. The screwtop is typically used for a wine that is meant to be drunk young and is very fruit-forward, a New World style wine. Screwtops breathe less, keeping oxygen from seeping into the bottle much better than either natural or artificial corks. In winemaking, non-oxidative processes are used to make really fruity wine. Lack of oxygen means fruitier, simple, easy-drinking wine. More oxygen in winemaking means less fruity wines but more complex wines. If a winemaker uses a non-oxidative process to make a fruity wine, he doesn't want to lose that fruitiness once the wine gets in the bottle by using a cork that lets air in. So he uses a screwtop. That's good for you to know because now when you see a screwtop wine, you'll have a pretty good idea it's a simple, fruity wine.

Pros: Well, clearly, no need for a corkscrew. Keeps a wine fresher because it doesn't let air seep into the bottle.

Cons: Still haunted by the perception that screwtop wines are cheap. Second, while the fact that screwtops don't let air get in is a good thing for freshness, it can be a bad thing, too. Those bad sulfur compounds seem to occur more often in a wine with a screwtop vs. with either type of cork. Oxygen keeps the sulfur compounds from forming and the air that gets into a bottle past the corks seems to be enough. But the screwtop does such a good job at keeping out air that it also allows the bad compounds to form. It is pretty difficult for most folks to notice the bad sulfur compounds that smell like rotten eggs, burning rubber, skunky, etc. unless they are very prevalent — which they aren't, more times than not.

CALORIES IN WINE

Will wine make me fat? You're darn tootin'. The calories in wine come from the alcohol. Many German wines are low in alcohol, so they are the least fattening. Reds are higher than whites and fortified wines, like Port, are loaded with calories. I went to Portugal a few years back for 10 days to tour the Port wine region. I had Port for breakfast, lunch and dinner, as well as visited wineries and did tastings there. (Okay, so I didn't spit very often. That's what did it.) Anyway, I gained 20 pounds in 10 days. I'm not kidding. I was so fat when I got home, I joined a health club and luckily was able to lose the weight in a month and a half.

To determine how many calories are in a glass of wine, you simply take the percentage of alcohol, multiply times the number of ounces you drink, and multiply that by 1.6. Simple. So a 15% alcohol wine, in a 5 oz serving, means 1.6 x 15 x 5 = 120 calories. There are 25 ounces in a bottle.

WHAT IS BAD WINE?

As you have learned from several examples I've given, it is hard to tell when a wine is bad, even for an expert at times. Disregarding that vagary and subjective nature of individual taste for right now, I'll explain the three categories of ways that a wine can be bad.

OUT OF BALANCE

A good wine is one that you like. Theoretically, it's good to you because you think it's balanced; the components fit together properly. Why do Club members ridicule certain wines like oaky Chardonnays, Merlot, white Zinfandel, etc.? Because they are out of balance   to them.

Take white Zinfandel. It's sweet, which to many folks is a negative. But there are some great sweet wines that are just as sweet that are revered by Club members, like German Rieslings or Sauternes. The difference between those and white Zinfandel is that they have acidity to balance out the sweetness and white Zinfandel doesn't. Is sugar water tasty? No. But add lemon to it (acidity) and you have lemonade, a winner. It's all about balance.

Merlot is derided by Club members named Miles because so many of the mass-market Merlots are made with no structure, lacking any character. Of course, not all Merlot is bad. One of the most famous wines in the world is Chateau Petrus, a winery in Bordeaux that is made from almost all Merlot and costs hundreds, if not thousands per bottle, but that has character.

And oaky Chardonnay? Well, just the reason that "oaky" is in front of "Chardonnay" reveals why Club members don't like it. All of the great Chardonnays in the world are put in oak barrels, so they are oaky. But when a wine has too much oak, it's out of balance.

Club members dislike wines that are out of balance — *their* balance. Many consumers like the wines that Club members dislike. Who's right? Well, we're back to the subjectivity of wine. A good wine is one that YOU like.

WINEMAKER MISTAKES

Most faults that are found in wine by professional judges are the result of winemaker's mistakes, things that could have been avoided. To identify the fault takes some training. Get a load of the following faults that wine judges should be able to identify:

1. Sulfur Compounds: Aroma of rotten eggs

2. Ethyl Mercaptan: Skunky aroma

3. Acetaldehyde: An acrid aroma

4. Secondary fermentation happening in the bottle: Yeasty or musty aroma and usually a bit of spritz in the wine

5. Ethyl Acetate: Aroma of nail polish remover (acetone)

6. 2,3 Hexadienoic Acid: Aroma of bubblegum

7. Too much Sulfites added: Burning sensation in the aroma, plus the smell of sulfur

I haven't even listed all the causes, as it gets much more technical, but you can see that there are a lot of ways a wine can be bad because of a winemaker's mistake. Very, very few people on this earth can consistently recognize these faults. And it's not that these faults are there or they're not. It's a continuum, and it's up to a taster to identify the faults in whatever concentration they appear in the wine.

The following faults are not the winemaker's fault, necessarily, but they can be prevented with proper oversight:

8. TCA: "Corked" wine. The result of using contaminated natural corks, but it can also occur from contaminated oak barrels or the addition of contaminated wood chips. Wood chips are thrown into the wine in the winemaking process as an inexpensive alternative to oak barrels to get the oakiness in wine without the expense of using oak barrels.

9. Brettanomyces (or Brett for short, thank God): This smells like a barnyard, the underarm of a college football lineman or a horsy aroma (which I take offense to, having owned a horse, — named Beaver — and I don't recall him ever smelling like Brett). Brett aroma is most noticeable in red Burgundy, and is considered a positive aroma within reason. In fact, I love it. It's caused by a surface yeast that forms on equipment, barrels, walls, whatever in moist environment due to lack of sterilization.

HANDLING ERRORS
Wine can go bad from mishandling in three ways.
1. Transporting – I was scheduled to do a wine tasting during the summer for a major hotel company and they said they would be happy to buy the wine for the tasting. Fine by me. One of the sales reps at the hotel was assigned to go buy the wine. On a sunny afternoon in Washington, D.C., temperature in the 90s, the

sales rep left the hotel on a mission that would take him to several wine shops, as all the wines couldn't be obtained at just one. He made the first stop and put the wine in his trunk. Visited the second store and did the same. On the way to the third store, he stopped to do an errand that took about 20 minutes. Got to the third store, bought the wine and went back to the hotel. Mission accomplished. The wine was brought into the hotel and the whites were chilled.

I arrived about 30 minutes before the tasting was to begin. The hotel staff brought out the wines and I noticed that the cork was sticking up a bit on each bottle. That's the worst thing you can see. I asked about how the wine was obtained and the guy who got the wine told me the story above.

A raised cork, even a little bit above the top of the bottle, means that the wine was heated, resulting in a maderized wine, a wine that has basically been cooked. But even worse in this case, the corks had moved up enough to break through the foil. Ouch. That's really bad. Sure enough, all the wine tasted like sherry. Rotten.

In the warmer months, you can't leave wine in the car, especially if the windows are shut or if the wine is in the trunk, two scenarios where you are creating an oven. It only takes about 30 minutes is those cases for a wine to become cooked. If you're going to buy wine in the summer, make the trip to the wine shop your last stop and head straight home.

2. Temperature Variation – I told you in a previous chapter of the story of buying the wine and leaving it in my pickup truck in springtime. Any time wine is left in a situation where the temperature varies over time, it makes the wine taste like water; not bad tasting, but completely bland.

3. Dead Wine – This is a term I made up to describe a wine that has been opened and then exposed to oxygen. It isn't really oxidized, as it shows no negative qualities. Rather, it's very similar to the result of Temperature Variation, as the wine lacks fruitiness. I experience this most often at restaurants in the wines poured by the glass. The bottle is opened the night before, and by the next day it's basically gone flat, lacking fruit and tasting insipid.

Although wine by the glass gives you many options without having to order a whole bottle, the downside is that you might be getting day-old wine. It's best to ask for a fresh bottle to be opened whenever you order wine by the glass.

So where does that leave you? You're not going to be able to identify most of the faults, and that's okay. You're not a wine judge. Oh, by the way, if you are a wine judge and you can't identify these, resign. And since 90% of the wine judges I've met can't identify these faults, the state of judging is a joke. It's true.

Anyway, it's impossible for people to recognize these faults. And then there are some wines that smell/taste really weird, but that's how they are supposed to be.

So when you don't like a wine, don't worry about whether it's a fault of the wine or not, just don't drink it. If you're in a restaurant and you don't like a wine, send it back.

One last point: you can see that most of the faults are identified in the aroma. That's why it's so important to swirl the wine in the glass to "open up" the aromas and take some time to smell it. It's all in the aroma ... the orgasmic qualities of wine as well as the faults.

WHY DO SOME WINES COST MORE THAN OTHERS?

There are two reasons a wine costs what it does. First, production costs. If the land and labor and grapes cost more, then the winery must price the wine higher to recoup their costs. Labor in California costs significantly more than, let's say, South America. But that doesn't make a huge difference in the cost of the wine compared to the cost of land.

In the Central Coast region of California, where the grapes for box wine are grown, an acre of land can cost as little as $10,000 per acre. In Napa Valley, one will easily pay $130,000 and up to $300,000 per acre, so the winery will have to charge a lot more for their wine to recoup their costs. In South America, you'll pay a fraction of the cost compared to Napa acreage and get high quality vineyards sites. And then there are vine density and yields that add to the equation, but that's more than we need to worry about here. I think you get the idea that prime vine-yard sites in Napa, Sonoma, Bordeaux, Burgundy and other prestigious growing areas in the world cost a mint.

So the places to look for values are parts of the world where land is less expensive: South America, parts of Spain and Italy, Australia, etc. Of course, there are still values in the more prestigious wine areas if the owners bought the land a long time ago, when the price was much lower. And if a winery is more interested in mak-ing great wine than building a fancy winery and tast-ing room, that will keep the price of their wine down.

But the most important reason a wine costs what it does is ego, especially for the more expensive wines ($30 and up). Typically, the retail price of the wine is twice what the winery sells it for. Less expensive wines work on a lower markup and the winery makes their profit on volume, while a low-production wine has to be sold at a higher profit per bottle to give the winery a profit.

But here's the catch. No wine that I know costs the winery more than $20 to make, even with low yields on expensive land. So when the winery is selling a wine for $50 to the distributor to be a $100 bottle of wine on the shelf, it's being done for the winery's status in the marketplace. A winery's rationale is that other wines made by their neighbors are selling for x, and their wine is just as good or better, then they should sell their wine for the same, or more. And the inflated pricing competition gets higher and higher.

Most of the really expensive wines, $100+ a bottle, don't offer that much better a tasting experience than wines half the price or less. The expensive wines are usually snatched up by investors hoping to resell them. There are wealthy folks who buy them to drink — but typically, just because they are expensive and/or have gotten a high rating. In my experience, in blind tastings, those same folks couldn't guess one of their expensive wines vs. a wine costing $30 or less. It's all about image.

Buying expensive wine is risky in so many ways, as explained in a previous chapter.

WINE AND ACTIVITIES

A long time ago I graduated from just thinking about having wine during a meal, as an aperitif or while mingling. I found that wine could go well with a variety of activities. Each wine has its own personality, its own unique way of making you feel. It's more than just the flavor or the components of the wine. Different wines seem to work better for certain occasions. Following are some activities when I might enjoy some wine. You can use my experiences as a springboard to see how wine can be incorporated into your own activities.

Laundry. This is my favorite time to have a Chardonnay: the coolness to offset the heat of the laundry room. Since there is no food around, I'd opt for a New World Chardonnay that has lower acidity.

Using Power Tools. Boy, there's nothing that thrills me more than revving the circular saw a few times, taking a sip of a Corbières and doing some cutting. The Corbières and other reds from the south of France have that rustic, man's man feeling to them.

Mowing the Lawn. I bought a riding mower last year, and the cup holder is perfect for wine. Oh, I know, mowing might be considered a beer activity, but give me a Moscato d'Asti, maybe two bottles, and the mowing seems to fly by. I love it so much, I often cruise the neighborhood for a while after I finish the mowing. Moscato is so refreshing on a hot summer day, and since it's low in alcohol, I keep my mowing lanes straight.

Gardening. A rustic wine is in order, but because it's hot, a rustic white. I like a white Rhône like one made from the grape Roussanne and/or Marsanne. It has a mineral component and it isn't that high in acidity, so it works out well for the garden.

Cleaning the House. I have a maid, but she comes once every two weeks. With two dogs and a doggy door, in two days the place can get messed up. Dead squirrels and birds get brought in along with lots of dirt/mud. When I look at a mixture of carcasses, animal blood and dirt on the floor, I need to have something perky to get me through the cleaning. I like sparkling wine for this. Typically I'll go with my house sparkling wine, Aria from Spain. Fresh, lively and peppy.

Washing the Car. I usually pay to get my car washed, but every so often I like to bond with my car. Washing, vacuuming and polishing the leather keeps our relationship alive. When it comes to bonding, I like a red. I will choose a South African wine because it reminds me of the time I drove all over the wine country and had a great time. That's the car link. The Goats do Roam is a red that goes down easy.

Golfing. Another activity that most associate with beer, but somehow the tranquility of a golf course makes me think, "wine." The temperature affects my choice. If it is really warm, I like a good German Riesling, low in alcohol, so my swing won't be affected too much. And the Riesling is very refreshing besides. For the cooler days, I'll go with a red. Most reds are high in alcohol, which may not help my game, but I don't play well in cooler weather, so if the alcohol makes my game go to the dogs, I don't care. Typically, I'll sneak a bottle of Australian Shiraz on the course. The Shiraz works with most food cart fare, and is appropriate to drink out of a plastic cup.

Shooting Pool. Okay, the odds are slim that wine is served in a pool hall. And even if it is, it might be a little suspect, so I usually go with beer. But there have been times when the pool hall had a Ravenswood Zinfandel or Rosemount Shiraz as an option, two wines that pair well with chicken fingers and potato skins. I've had the best times shooting pool in someone's home where you can have the best of both worlds – shooting pool without all of the smoke *and* great wine. I'm not sure I can be beaten in that setting.

Having Wine in Public Places. It's usually illegal to drink wine in public or to bring it into sporting events, symphony halls, movie theaters, etc., but sometimes you just have to do it. That's when a Gatorade bottle is handy. It's got to have the squirt lid, so you don't have to remove the cap to drink the wine. I buy the Berry Flavored Gatorade bottle, so the red wine will look like the berry Gatorade. No smell. No spills. Priceless.

Going to the Symphony. Since I'm in the Washington, D.C. area, I go to the Kennedy Center for my musical excursions. However, the wine they serve in the lobby doesn't do it for me, so I bring my own. A really nice wine while listening to live classical music can't be beat. I splurge and get a nicer wine that fits the occasion. Because there is no food, I like a New World wine, and an American Pinot Noir is the obvious choice. Classic. Elegant. Sensual.

It was at the Kennedy Center where I learned the benefit of Gatorade bottles. The first time I smuggled wine into the symphony, I actually brought a bottle in with plastic cups. We were seated in the orchestra seats on the main floor. I had opened the bottle in the car and stuffed the cork back in the bottle. When the lights went down, I poured a glass for my date and me and we sat back and enjoyed the music. Perfect.

Intermission came, and we put our cups under our seats. Sure enough, someone knocked over a cup. Red wine flowed down the sloping floor for rows. It was a disaster. The place reeked with the smell of wine. The folks around us picked up the scent, noticed the wine and called the ushers. We knew we would be busted if we didn't run for our lives. We headed to the back of the main floor and sat low in some empty seats. Just in the nick of time, because ushers came swarming around the spill and talking with the folks to get a description of us. It was a little scary, but we weren't caught. The idea of wine and music was good, but I learned then that one has to have a smell-proof and spill-proof system. Gatorade bottles with the squirt tops are perfect.

Going to the Theater. I like a wine that is expressive, like the arts. I think some of the blended wines from California are just the pick — and they usually have artistic labels, which may impress the usher when you get caught, which means you'll just get thrown out vs. thrown in jail. What better winery than Bonny Doon for great value reds with artistic labels?

Going to a Sporting Event. For sporting events, you have to have something with more aggressiveness. What's more in your face than big, powerful California red Zinfandel?

Going to the Movies. You want to choose a wine that goes with the movie. I'll leave this one up to you. When I go to a multiplex and I'm not sure what I'm going to see, I usually bring a wine that is all-purpose, like a New World sparkling wine. I get a cup of just ice and enjoy the Champagne on the rocks. You can hardly find a better match than popcorn or chips with Champagne. I'm serious. And Champagne goes well with action, comedy or romantic movies.

Going to the Doctor. For a standard checkup, I'll choose a half bottle of Port. It works well with any sweet treats that are in the bowl on the receptionist's desk. And because Port has high alcohol, I won't be bothered so much if the prognosis is grim or if I have to get stuck with a needle.

Grocery Shopping. This is just a gas — could be one of my favorite wine-drinking activities. If the store is one of those that offers sampling of foods to graze on, I'll choose a red Rhône, like a Côtes du Rhône, that is very versatile with food. If it is a non-food sampling store, I like New World red that is low in tannin and acidity so it won't make me want to eat.

Bike Riding. A leisurely bike ride is a perfect time to enjoy a bottle of wine. Since it's usually difficult to keep a white chilled, I go with a red. I want an easy-drinking red, but one that also feels like it should be consumed outdoors. Here's where I go French, I guess because of the Tour de France. An International Style wine from the south of France is a good choice because it's easy-drinking, not too high in alcohol and low in acidity, so it doesn't need food (but would still work with PowerBars).

Cuddling up with a Book. I don't do cuddling.

Reading a Book in my Recliner. Okay, that's more like it. I usually go for a red here. I often have some cheese and bread, so I prefer Old World. I like Italian, but without too much acidity. The new style Tuscan wines that are a blend of Sangiovese, Cabernet Sauvignon, etc. that are under $15 are tasty and a pleasant wine to graze on.

Doing Taxes. It's a once-a-year activity, so I want to go all out. It's usually a luxury Champagne. If my tax bill is high, then I'm celebrating the fact that I actually make enough that I have to pay a lot. If I'm paying just a little or getting a refund, then that's worth celebrating also.

Playing Games. I love games! Dominoes. Pictionary. Scattergories. Taboo. Cribbage. Monopoly. I can go on and on. Can't play enough games. This is the time I'll choose Australian because Australians are a gregarious bunch, and that's the kind of atmosphere I like for games.

Cooking. I like white wine because its coolness feels good in a hot kitchen. And besides, the lower alcohol in white keeps the knife cuts to a minimum. I prefer a Sancerre or Pouilly Fumé, both Sauvignon Blancs from the Loire Valley. Those wines are all about food, so what better place than to enjoy them while cooking?

Sunbathing. Am I naked, or do I have a swimsuit on? If I have a suit on, I'll go for a refreshing white wine like Pinot Grigio. Cheap. Ice cold and guzzle it. If I'm naked, it means I'm probably traveling and that's good, so sparkling wine is good. But I think a little fun should be added, so my choice is a sparkling wine drink, like a Mimosa or Bellini.

Meeting Someone for a Cup of Coffee. The whole coffee house atmosphere is kind of artsy. That reminds me of movies, and that reminds me of the movie *Sideways*, so I'll go with a Merlot, just to spite Miles (a Club member). This is a good opportunity to use one of your travel coffee mugs instead of a Gatorade bottle.

Watching TV. I usually have some munchies, so I'll choose Old World wines. I choose the wine to match the show. For "The Price is Right," I like an inexpensive white, like a low-end white Burgundy. And with the show "24," because of the fast action and suspense, I want a wine that keeps me on my edge, like a Chianti; just enough acidity to keep me sharp.

Walking my Dogs. Because there is movement happening and spillage is possible, I prefer white, so if I do spill, it won't be so noticeable. I might go with an American Sauvignon Blanc. I don't take long walks, so the white won't warm up in the time that I'm out.

Snow skiing. Red all the way. High alcohol to keep me warm. Tawny port is the answer, and the Aussie port is the best value. To complement the port, blue cheese and walnuts are great — and easy to carry in your pocket.

Any activity can be better with wine. Just remember to consider the following to make your experience perfect.

Temperature: If there is no way to keep the wine cool, a red would be best.

Spillage issues: If you have to be discreet or can't afford to have spillage, use the Gatorade bottle.

Food: If there's food, it's a nice chance to pair the food to an Old World wine. No food? Go New World.

Mood: Probably the most important factor. Drink a wine that you are in the mood to have, and you can't lose.

WINE QUOTES

"The discovery of a good wine is increasingly better for mankind than the discovery of a new star."

—Leonardo da Vinci

"Wine is inspiring and adds greatly to the joy of living."

—Napoleon 1

"There are no standards of taste in wine ... Each man's own taste is the standard, and a majority vote cannot decide for him or in any slightest degree affect the supremacy of his own standard."

—Mark Twain

"As you get older, you shouldn't waste time drinking bad wine."

—Julia Child

"Wine is the most healthful and the most hygienic of beverages."

—Louis Pasteur

"Wine - the intellectual part of the meal."

—Alexandre Dumas

"A bottle of wine contains more philosophy than all the books in the world"

—Louis Pasteur

"*In Vino Veritas* (In wine there is truth)."

—Pliny the Elder

"Wine is sunlight, held together by water."

—-Galileo

"Be careful to trust a person, who does not like wine."

—Karl Marx

"Wine makes daily living easier, less hurried, with fewer tensions and more tolerance."

—Benjamin Franklin

"Wine to me is passion. It's family and friends. It's warmth of heart and generosity of spirit. Wine is art. It's culture. It's the essence of civilization and the art of living."

—Robert Mondavi

"Wine is a constant proof that God loves us and wants us to be happy."

—Benjamin Franklin

"Too much of anything is bad, but too much Champagne is just right."

—Mark Twain

"Wine is bottled poetry."

—Robert Louis Stevenson

"A house where neither wine nor welcome is served to friends, soon will have none".

— Rob Hutchison

"God made only water, but man made wine."

—Victor Hugo

"Beer is made by men, Wine by God."

—Martin Luther

"Wine is the most civilized thing in the world."

— Ernest Hemingway

"Wine improves with age. The older I get, the better I like it."

— Anonymous

"Drinking good wine with good food in good company is one of life's most civilized pleasures."

— Michael Broadbent

"I cook with wine; sometimes I even add it to the food."

— W. C. Fields

"Nothing makes the future look so rosy as to contemplate it through a glass of Chambertin."

— Napoleon

"My only regret in life is that I did not drink more Champagne."

— John Maynard Keynes

"I have enjoyed great health at a great age because every day since I can remember, I have consumed a bottle of wine except when I have not felt well. Then I have consumed two bottles."

— Attributed to a Bishop of Seville

"Wine makes every meal an occasion, every table more elegant, every day more civilized."

— André Simon

Bessie Braddock, a well-known socialist in England, attended a dinner party at which she was seated next to Winston Churchill, who had had quite a bit to drink. She said to him, "Winston, you are drunk!" He replied, "Madame, I may be drunk, but you are ugly, and tomorrow I will be sober."

Before leaving home to serve a one-year jail sentence, a white-collar criminal was quoted as saying, "I'm not worried about the reds; they'll keep OK. But I am worried about the whites."

— Anonymous

"Wine cheers the sad, revives the old, inspires the young, makes weariness forget its toil."

— Lord Byron

"I feast on wine and bread, and feasts they are."

— Michelangelo

"Water separates the people of the world. Wine unites them."

— Anonymous

"There is no gladness without wine."

— Talmud

"A meal without wine is like a day without sunshine."

—Brillat-Savarin

"A glass of wine is a great refreshment after a hard day's work."

— Beethoven

"Wine moistens and tempers the spirits, and lulls the care of the mind to rest….it revives our joys."

—Socrates

"For wine to taste like wine, it should be drunk with a friend."

— Anonymous

"Eating without wine is like eating ants."

— Anonymous

"One day old bread, your uncle's wine and donkey meat, are killers."

— Anonymous

WINE TRIVIA

- The bag-in-box was first developed in 1967 by Thomas Angove, in Australia.
- Mark Phillips consumed 51 bottles of wine while typing this book.
- The dye used to stamp the grade on meat is edible. It's made from grape skins.
- The average number of grapes it takes to produce a

bottle of wine: 600 or 2.5 pounds
- One barrel of wine equals 60 gallons or 25 cases or 300 ea 750 ml bottles
- One ton of grapes equals approximately 700 bottles of wine
- A morbid, irrational fear of or aversion to wine is called *oenophobia*.
- The Aztec of Mexico used a "rabbit scale" to describe degrees of intoxication. It ranged from very mild intoxication (a few rabbits) to heavy drunkenness (400 rabbits).
- Far more Merlot than Cabernet Sauvignon (nearly a 2-to-1 ratio) is planted throughout Bordeaux, although we call Cabernet Sauvignon "the Bordeaux grape."
- Wine corks contain 40 million nitrogen-filled cells per cubic centimeter. A cork can be compressed to half its size and recover its original dimensions within hours.
- All the essential vitamins are found in a glass of wine.
- Ninety-five percent of all the wine made each year is consumed before the next harvest.
- Antarctica is the only continent on Earth on which wine is not produced.
- One barrel of wine produces 60 gallons, 25 cases or 300 ea 750 ml bottles
- One ton of grapes equalt approximately 700 bottles of wine

- The dimple in the bottom of a bottle is called a punt and it is to strengthen the bottle.
- Split - 187 milliliters or one quarter of a standard size bottle
- Half-Bottle - 375 milliliters or one half of the standard bottle size
- Bottle - 750 milliliters of wine, this is the standard size
- Magnum - 1.5 liters or two times the standard bottle size
- Double Magnum - 3.0 liters or twice the size of a magnum, equivalent of 4 bottles
- Jeroboam - There are two sizes of Jeroboams: Sparkling wine Jeroboam equals 4 regular bottles, or 3.0 liters, while red wine Jeroboam equals 6 regular bottles, or 4.5 liters. Some 5.0 liter Jeroboams exist.
- Rehoboam - 4.5 liters or the equivalent of 6 standard size bottles
- Imperial - 6.0 liters or 8 regular bottles
- Methuselah - Same size as an Imperial, but is usually used for sparkling wines and is Burgundy-shaped.
- Salmanazar - 9.0 liters. 12 regular bottles, or one case.
- Balthazar - 12.0 liters. 16 bottles. Usually used for sparkling wines.
- Nebuchadnezzar - 15.0 liters. 20 regular bottles. Usually used for sparkling wines.
- Sovereign - 50 liters or 67 regular bottles

22

My Arrest
For Selling Wine

NEWS FLASH: IT IS ILLEGAL for an individual to sell wine. Oh, now I know. But years ago, I thought wine was like any collectible. You buy it, let it appreciate and sell it. Boy, did I learn my lesson the hard way.

In 1999, I was arrested by Virginia Alcoholic Beverage Control (ABC) agents for selling alcohol without a license. I had bought some wine from a diplomat who was being transferred overseas. The guy had a great selection of Lafite-Rothschild (the bottle on the cover of the book), but was unable to take it with him. I took it off his hands for a fair price. I didn't have the right storage conditions for it at the time, so I offered the wine for sale through the Wine Tasting Association (WTA), a group I run in the D.C. area. I was able to sell if for about half of what any store could sell it for because I got such a great deal on it.

I had sold a few cases worth of wine and I was just about out when I got a call from someone asking if I had any of it left. I wanted to hold a case for myself of the better vintages, so all I had left was the 1991 vintage, which wasn't good. The woman on the phone said she would take a bottle of the 1991, so we agreed she would come to my house to pick it up. She arrived at my house and we made some small talk, she paid me in cash and was on her way.

One hour later, police cars converged on my house. A dozen or so armed agents and uniformed police officers jumped out and surrounded the house. I'm not kidding. I answered the door and the lead agent said I was under arrest for selling alcohol without a license and they had a search warrant. They placed my wife, my daughter and me under armed guard in our living room while they searched our house for evidence. They were going to seize all of my wine, about 200 bottles, which would then be placed outside in an un-air conditioned van on a 90-degree day and be ruined. I stated that I only was selling the Lafite and that the rest of my wine shouldn't be seized. After a couple of hours of begging, they finally agreed to take just the one case of Lafite. Luckily, they took the wine away in an air-conditioned car.

My court date was a month later. It's a Class 1 misdemeanor to sell wine, and punishable on conviction by up to one year in jail and a $2,500 fine. But since I had a clean record I thought I might get a slap on the wrist and I'd be on my way.

My story of my arrest got into *The Washington Post* and *Wine Spectator.* I got hundreds of calls and emails from people who were shocked that I would be arrested for such a thing. Many offers came in from law firms to represent me *pro bono*. But I hired an attorney instead, Bob Battle. He's the man.

Bob and I arrived at the Courthouse for my trial — which was to take place in traffic court, for God's sake. Couldn't I have a courtroom to myself? Anyway, Bob spoke with the Commonwealth Attorney to see if a deal could be worked out, like probation or something, but the prosecutor said no. The Alcohol Beverage Commission (ABC) folks wanted to go for the jugular and put me away for a year! I guess I was going to be made as the example to others that you can't just sell wine.

Things didn't look good, because I had sold the wine. I even had to call my wife to let her know I might not be coming home for a year — a little scary. (Of course, that might have been a bonus for her.)

Recognizing there would be no deal, Bob asked to review the evidence the ABC folks had. ("Discovery" isn't a given in this type of case, so Bob didn't have a chance to review the evidence prior to arriving.) He looked at the bottle of 1991 Lafite the agent had bought and the records they seized. Then he sat alone for about 30 minutes, preparing his strategy.

The trial began with the prosecution calling Agent Valerie Hayden to the stand. I knew Valerie well, because I had talked to her to get previous one-day permits to conduct wine tastings in Virginia. Agent Hayden had been the first agent to my door to serve the search warrant. She took the stand and the prosecutor asked her about the date and time of the raid. The prosecutor continued by asking what was found during the search, like receipts, etc.

All of a sudden, Bob objected, to everyone's surprise. Bob asked if I had been read my rights at the time of the raid and my arrest. Agent Hayden said no. Bam! The judge ruled that because they hadn't read me my rights, no evidence could be introduced from the raid. Wow!

The frustrated prosecutor excused Agent Hayden and called Agent Stone, the woman who had actually bought the wine from me. Again the prosecutor asked her for details of the date and time, to identify me and of the sale itself. He asked if she had the bottle she had bought with her in the courtroom. She said yes and showed it to the court to introduce as evidence.

Bob objected again, out of the blue. Bob said that the bottle read "12% vol" on the label, and according to Virginia law, a label must say "alcohol" on the label, such as: 12% alcohol/volume or alc/vol. Since this label didn't, Bob said one wouldn't know for sure if it was wine. The 12% could mean 12% grape juice, or anything, for that matter. The prosecutor argued vehemently that everyone knew it was wine and that I

represented it as wine for the sale, pleading to the judge
how ridiculous Bob's argument was.

Bob calmly repeated that according to Virginia law,
it must say "alcohol" on the label or it couldn't be considered an alcoholic beverage, and thus it wouldn't be
against the law to sell. The judge agreed, dismissed the
case and ordered the case of Lafite (valued at several
thousand dollars) to be returned to me.

The ABC agents were stunned! Everyone was. I
hung around after the decision, talked to reporters and
just tried to get a grip on myself.

I left the courthouse and drove to the ABC office
in Alexandria to pick up my wine. When I arrived,
I heard another ABC agent talking to the distraught
Agent Hayden in her office. He was offering her a way
to still dink me. He said that the ABC was supposed to
return the $90 it had paid for the wine that they had
confiscated in their search, but that I probably wouldn't
think of asking for it, so she shouldn't bring that up.
Even better, he suggested that Agent Hayden offer to
carry the case of Lafite out to my car. While carrying
she could trip over my foot and drop the case. I couldn't
believe what I was hearing.

When the two agents finished, Agent Hayden came
out to meet me, unaware that I had heard the whole
conversation. I asked for the $90. She was stunned, but
got it for me. Then she led me back to the closet where
my wine was being kept, and according to plan, she
offered to carry it to my car for me. I said that wouldn't

be necessary, but she insisted. I almost had to fight her for my wine. I got the case, made sure no one was behind me or near me, and carried it to my car. What an ordeal!

I owe my freedom to Bob Battle, who is enjoying a few choice bottles of Lafite.

23

Bum Wines

I RAN ACROSS THIS WEB SITE by Zeke and it cracked me up. Next time you stop to talk to a bum, you'll be able to talk about wine on their level. Reprinted with permission from www.bumwine.com, a website by Zeke Ragsdale.

Cisco - 18% alc. by vol.
Cisco is bottled by the nation's second largest wine company, Canandaigua Wine Co., in Canandaigua, NY and Naples, NY — the same company as Wild Irish Rosé.

Known as "liquid crack," for its reputation for wreaking more mental havoc than the cheapest tequila. Something in this syrupy hooch seems to have a synapse-blasting effect not unlike low-grade cocaine. The label insists that the ingredients are merely "citrus wine & grape wine with artificial flavor & artificial color," but anyone who has tried it knows better. Tales of Cisco-induced semi-psychotic fits are common. Often, people on a Cisco binge end up curled into a fetal ball, shuddering and muttering paranoid rants. Nudity and violence may well be involved too. Everyone who drinks this feels great at first, and claims, "It's not bad at all, I like it." But, you really do not want to mess around with this one, because they all sing a different tune a few minutes later. And by tune, I mean the psychotic ramblings of a raging naked bum.

In 1991, Cisco's tendency to cause a temporary form of inebriated insanity led the Federal Trade Commission to require its bottlers to print a warning on the label. The FTC also forced them to drop their marketing slogan, "Takes You by Surprise," even though it was entirely accurate. Since those days, Cisco is harder to find outside the slums, although the FTC's demonizing of the drink only bolstered its reputation for getting people trashed. Anyone who overlooks the warning and confuses this with a casual wine cooler is going to get more than they bargained for. Cisco will make a new man out of you. And he wants some too.

Our research shows that Cisco is actually the second best tasting of the five great bum wines, especially if you're having one of those hankerings for cheap vodka, Jello and Robitussin. We must also note that Cisco is the best of all five bum wines at putting the darkest and puffiest bags under your eyes. The nuclear-tinted color of "Cisco RED" is reminiscent of diesel fuel. Most

Cisco flavors are named by the fruit flavor that they are trying to emulate, but the one pictured is simply called "RED." This chemical disaster will get your head spinning in no time. A test subject reports, "Strawberry Cisco has a bouquet similar to that of Frankenberry cereal fermented in wine cooler with added sprinkle of brandy for presentation." The sticky, sickeningly sweet taste with a hint of antifreeze really comes through in the repellant taste of Cisco. Available in various flavors, 375 mL and 750 mL sizes. Down a whole 750 mL and you had better be ready to clear your calendar as you suffer through Cisco's legendary two-day hangover.

MD 20/20 - 18% OR 13% ALC. BY VOL.

As majestic as the cascading waters of a drainpipe, MD 20/20 is bottled by the 20/20 wine company in Westfield, New York. This is a good place to start for the street wine rookie, but beware; this dog has a bite to back up its bark. MD stands for Mogen David, and is affectionately called "Mad Dog 20/20." You'll find this beverage as often in a bum's nest as in the rock quarry where the high school kids sneak off to drink. This beverage is likely the most consumed by non-bums, but that doesn't stop any bums from drinking it! Our research indicates that MD 20/20 is the best of the bum wines at making you feel warm inside. Some test subjects report a slight numbing agent in MD 20/20, similar to the banana paste that the dentist puts in your mouth before injecting it with Novocain. Anyone that can afford a dentist should steer clear of this disaster. Available in various nauseating tropical flavors that coat your whole system like bathtub scum, but only the full "Red Grape Wine" flavor packs the 18% wallop.

Liquor stores are starting to be infiltrated by a 13% variety of MD 20/20 Red Grape. There is also a new "Blue Raspberry" flavor with "BLING BLING." Even the lowest functioning of bums will know not to get swindled out of 5%.

NIGHT TRAIN EXPRESS - 17.5% ALC. BY VOL.

Don't let the 0.5% less alcohol by volume fool you, the Night Train is all business when it pulls into the station. All aboard to nowhere – woo wooo! The night train runs only one route: sober to stupid with no roundtrip tickets available, and a strong likelihood of a train wreck along the way. This train yard favorite is vinted and bottled by E&J Gallo Winery, in Modesto, CA. Don't bother looking on their web page, because they dare not mention it there. As a clever disguise, the label says that it is made by "Night Train Limited." Some suspect that Night Train is really just Thunderbird with some Kool-Aid-like substance added to try to mask the Clorox flavor. Some of our researchers indicated that it gave them a NyQuil-like drowsiness, and perhaps this is why they put "night" in the name. Guaranteed to tickle your innards.

THUNDERBIRD - 17.5% ALC. BY VOL.

As pictured to the left, look for the pigeon feces and you'll find this old bird. As soon as you taste this swill, it will be obvious that its makers cut every corner possible in its production to make it cheap. Self-proclaimed as "The American Classic," Thunderbird is vinted and bottled by E&J Gallo Winery, in Modesto, CA. Disguised like Night Train, the label says that it is made by "Thunderbird, Ltd." Anyways, if your taste buds are shot, and you need to get trashed with a quickness, then "T-bird" is the drink for you. Or, if you like to smell your hand after pumping gas, look no further than Thunderbird. As you drink on, the bird soars higher while you sink lower. The undisputed leader of the five in foulness of flavor, we highly discourage drinking this ghastly mixture of unknown chemicals unless you really are a bum. A convenience store clerk in Show Low, AZ once told me that only the oldest of stumbling Indian drunks from the reservation buy Thunderbird. Available in 750 mL and a devastating 50 oz jug.

The history of Thunderbird is as interesting as the drunken effects the one experiences from the wine. When Prohibition ended, Ernest Gallo and his brothers Julio and Joe wanted to corner the young wine market. Earnest wanted the company to become "the Campbell Soup company of the wine industry," so he started selling Thunderbird in the ghettos around the country. Their radio ads featured a song that sang,

"What's the word? / Thunderbird / How's it sold? / Good and cold / What's the jive? / Bird's alive / What's the price? / Thirty twice." It is said that Ernest once drove through a tough, inner city neighborhood and pulled over when he saw a bum. When Gallo rolled down his window and called out, "What's the word?" the immediate answer from the bum was, "Thunderbird."

WARNING: This light yellow liquid turns your lips and mouth black! A mysterious chemical reaction similar to disappearing-reappearing ink makes you look like you've been chewing on hearty clumps of charcoal.

WILD IRISH ROSE - 18% ALC. BY VOL.

The thorn in your hangover is a wild rose from Ireland. Bottled by Canandaigua Wine in Canadaigua, NY, the same company as Cisco. Like its brother Cisco, "Wild I" definitely has some secret additives that go straight to the cranium. Another web page claims that this foul beverage is a conspiracy by the Republicans to kill the homeless. It's called "wild" for a good reason, and bystanders should beware. Wild Irish Rose is sure to light a fire of drunken rage in your soul. A guy named "Richard" is mentioned on the label. A helpful guy named Carl wrote an email that refers to "Richard's Wild Irish Rose (named after his son, Canandaigua's current president Richard Sands)." Carl also found a website that talks about a Neil Diamond song with a part about this beverage in it. Neil Diamond agrees that where Wild Irish Rose is concerned, only those willing to sacrifice their liver need apply. The "White Label" variety of this beverage is definitely a hard wine to come to terms with. "White Label" smells like rubbing alcohol, and has no added flavoring to mask its pungent taste and noxious odors. Available in 375 mL, 750 mL, and a 50 oz jug.

Field reporter "Greyham" brings us this report: "Here is Wild I's devastating new addition, 'Wild Fruit with Ginseng.' I'll be honest with you: the normal Wild I has turned into some sort of fierce energy drink gone wrong mixed with the original to create a bumworthy migraine-inducing concoction. I purchased a 750 mL which goes for 3.99 and a 375 mL which goes for 2.59 (at least here in FL). Word on the streets here is that the bums are wary of it. I talked to a couple that said they'd prefer to 'stick with what's tried and true.' Apparently they haven't accepted it yet as the real deal. As for me, I drank the 375 mL on a semi-full stomach and was just ruined by the stuff. The flavor retains its same potent Wild I nastiness but has a whole new bouquet of fruity flavor added as well (potentially aimed at bums of the female persuasion). Upon completion of the 375, I was thoroughly inebriated and found myself honestly wondering where my next fix of the stuff was going to come from. This scared me so I immediately started drinking water ... here's the best part. After that relatively small bottle, I didn't piss until the next evening despite drinking copious amounts of water. There is DEFINITELY something in this stuff that dehydrates

you ... possibly the "ginseng" or whatever it is that they added to this already foul stuff."
RANKINGS:

Worst taste:
Thunderbird
Wild Irish Rose
Night Train
Cisco
MD 20/20

Getting wasted:
Cisco
Thunderbird
Night Train
Wild Irish Rose
MD 20/20

Warmth:
MD 20/20
Thunderbird
Wild Irish Rose
Night Train
Cisco

Wine Glossary

Acetic Acid — All wines contain some acetic acid or vinegar. If it is at least .07%, it can be detected.

Acid — It's key to wine. A wine without enough acid will taste flat. The four major acids in wine are: tartaric, malic, lactic and citric. Wines high in acidity are usually described as sharp, crisp, zippy, etc.

Aeration — Same as "breathing." It's the process of letting air interact with the wine. Not much aeration happens when the wine is left in the bottle. The wine needs to be poured in a glass or a carafe to really aerate. Aeration is best for red wines high in tannin. Most other wines don't benefit from aeration that much. It is bad to aerate a very old wine because the wine is quite fragile.

Aftertaste – How long the flavor lasts in your mouth after
you swallow. A 15-second flavor is normal for an average
wine.

Albarino (al bah REE n'oh) – A white grape grown in the
Galacia region in the northwest part of Spain. It is very
aromatic with a honey, peachy smell.

Abruzzi (ah BRUT see) – a region in Italy where the red
wine Montepulciano d'Abruzzo is made.

Alcohol – Gotta have it. A wine without alcohol is something I prefer not to have. The range of alcohol in wine
ranges from 5% (almost like a beer) to over 22% for fortified wines, which is the equivalent to about four beers.

Aligote (al ih GOAT tay) – A white grape grown in
Burgundy.

Alsace (al zahss) – French wine region in the northeast
that borders Germany. Great food wines with high acidity.
Mostly white wine is made here.

Alvarhinho (al va REEN yo) – A white grape grown in
the Vinho Verde region in northern Portugal. Same as the
Albarino grape from Spain.

Amarone (am ah ROAN nay) – A powerful red wine made
from the Corvina grapes in the Veneto region of Italy. It
is made by drying out the grapes, which concentrates the
juice.

Appellation – A grape growing region.

Appellation D'Origine Contrôlée (AOC) (ah pel ay shun
dah ree jean cone troll lay) – The French system of defining growing areas. It sets guidelines for the alcoholic
strength, yields, ripeness, labeling, varieties used and methods allowed to make the wine. The system is the reason
that the French are losing market share in the world (in
my opinion), because it is so restrictive.

Arneis (ahr NAYZ) — A white wine grape grown in the Piedmont area of Italy.

Asti Spumante — A sweet sparkling wine produced in the Piedmont region in Italy.

Auslese (OWSS lay sah) – Level of ripeness in German wines. It means "selection."

Ausone, Château (oh zone) — A prestigious winery in Bordeaux from St. Emilion and a rival to Château Cheval Blanc. Damn expensive.

Australia – A place where kangaroos live.

Austria – No kangaroos here.

Bacchus – The Roman God of Wine.

Bad Kreuznach (bahd kroyz nacht) – The first city I visited in Germany. I slept in a tent in someone's backyard, and the kids threw rocks at my tent all night.

Balance – Both a good and a bad thing in wine. It's good to have it. A good wine must be balanced among all of its elements. It's bad when you don't have it, and fall down from drinking too much wine.

Bandol (bahn dole) – A wine region in southwestern France that is known for its red and rosé wines. Grenache and Cinsault are the predominant grapes.

Banyuls (bahn yulz) – A red French dessert wine made from the Grenache grape. The best wine with dark chocolate.

Barbaresco – A red wine made from the Nebbiolo grape in the Piedmont region of Italy. Expensive.

Barbera – A red grape also grown in the Piedmont region and makes a wine called Barbera that is high in acidity.

Barnyard – A positive term used for describing Old World

wines, usually from Burgundy. A synonym for barnyard is "sweaty horse."

Barolo – The king of Italian reds made from the Nebbiolo grape in the Piedmont region of Italy. THE wine for wild sex.

Barossa Valley – An Australian wine region that is known for its Shiraz.

Barrel Fermented – Refers to wine that has been fermented in casks, usually 55-gallon oak barrels.

Barrique – The French name for a 225-litre Bordeaux style barrel.

Barsac (bar zack) – Sub-region of Sauternes in Bordeaux, France, making generally less expensive, Sauternes-like sweet wines.

Bâtard-Montrachet – (bah tar mon rah shay) – Damn good and expensive white Burgundy.

Beaujolais – A red wine made from the Gamay grape. Often a pretty good value.

Beaujolais Nouveau – Released on the third Thursday of November each year. Always tastes terrible. One of the great marketing scams ever in wine to get people to buy, and even celebrate, a product that is so bad. Ya gotta give 'em credit for that.

Beaumes-de-Venise (bome da veh-nees) – A dessert wine made from the Muscat grape. A region in the Southern Rhône of France, best known for its delicious white dessert wine made from Muscat grapes.

Beaune (bone) – Small city in the heart of Burgundy. Great place. Great food. Great people. Can't get back there enough.

Beaver - the name I chose for my horse and two dogs. I've

been to therapist.

Beerenauslese (bare en ows lay zah) – It means "selected berry picking" and makes a very sweet German wine.

Bergerac (bear jeh rack) – A region in Bordeaux that has some good value wines.

Bin – The term used on Australian wine labels, which means absolutely nothing.

Blanc de Blancs (blahn deh blahn) – Can't say the "c" sound at the end of the word Blanc ... but I do anyway, and always get scolded by the French. A Champagne term meaning "white from white," meaning a white wine made from white grapes – Chardonnay, in Champagne's case.

Blanc de Noirs – "White from black," which means a Champagne made from the red grapes Pinot Noir and Pinot Meunier.

Bonarda – A red grape from Italy, getting famous for its use down in Argentina.

Bordeaux – I think they make wine here.

Botrytis Cinerea – Also called "the noble rot," it's a beneficial kind of mold or fungus that may appear on late-harvested grapes, causing them to shrink and dry so the natural sugars become highly concentrated.

Bouquet – Smell, duh. But to a wine geek, bouquet refers to the aroma developed over time.

Bourgogne (boar goan yeh) – French for "Burgundy."

Brachetto – A sparkling sweet red wine from Italy. I like it, but you don't see it much.

Brix – Measurement system for sugar content of grapes. Who cares?

Brunello di Montalcino (brew nehl oh dee mon toll chee

no) Expensive wine made in southern Tuscany from the Brunello grape (a relative of the Sangiovese grape). I love the wine, but it's hard to find one worth the money.

Brut – A French term used for Champagne to denote that it's dry.

Burgundy – The holy grail of wine. So good. So expensive. So difficult to find one that's worth it. But when you hit, it's orgasmic.

Butt – A big barrel, and I'll stop here.

Buttafuoco – Yep, just like Joey, but it is actually an Italian red wine made in the Lombardy region of Italy.

Burnt – Describes a wine that has an overdone, smoky, toasty or singed edge. Also used to describe overripe grapes.

Buttery – A smell and taste sensation found in better white wines, particularly oak-aged Chardonnay. Indicates a smell of melted butter or toasty oak. Can also be a reference to texture, as in a rich "buttery" Chardonnay.

Cabernet Franc (ca burr nay frahn) – Don't say that "c" at the end of Franc, like I do. I was giving a talk on a cruise ship and said "Franc" with a hard "c" at the end, and all the French folks let me have it. A French red wine grape used in a Bordeaux blend. Also the up-and-coming grape for Virginia, but I don't think it will make it. Makes the light red wine called Chinon in the Loire Valley. Guzzling wine.

Cabernet Sauvignon – A red grape grown all over the world.

Cadillac (cah dee yak) I love that pronunciation. I can't even say the car name Cadillac the normal way any-more. In wine, Cadillac is a semisweet wine made in the Premières Côtes de Bordeaux district.

Cahors (cah-or) – Wine region in Southwestern France, close to Bordeaux, that makes a dark red wine from the Malbec grape.

Carbonic maceration – A fermentation technique that takes place inside the skins of whole, uncrushed grapes in the absence of air, in a carbon dioxide atmosphere. Used to make a fruity, easy-drinking wine like Beaujolais.

Carignan (cah reen yahn) – Red grape planted in southern France.

Carmenere (car men air) – A red grape grown in Chile that Andrew Stover of Washington, D.C. loves and thinks is an undiscovered gem.

Carole Withanee   The name of my mannequin that co-starred with me in a DC TV show and on my video blogs.

Cava – Spanish sparkling wine produced by the traditional French *méthode champenoise*, of bottle-fermenting champagne. The word *cava* originated in Catalonia and means "cellar."

Cedar/Cedary – Refers to an element of cedar wood in the bouquet of Cabernet Sauvignon that has been aged in either American or French oak. Can also be present in Cabernet blends that are aged in the same way.

Cellared by – Means the wine was not produced at the winery where it was bottled.

Chablis – A jug wine from California made from the Thompson Seedless and other white grapes. But the REAL Chablis is a white wine from Burgundy, made from the Chardonnay grape. Chablis is an orgasmic match with oysters.

Chambourcin (sham boor sahn) – A red French-American hybrid wine grape grown in the Eastern USA. When I see a wine made from it, I run. A lot of folks (over 60 years old) like it, but I just haven't had one that I could even get down the hatch.

Champagne – If I could have only one wine if I were stranded on a dessert island, this would be it. But when that happens, do I get unlimited quantities? And how do I keep it cold?

Chambertin (shaum ber tan) – A Pinot Noir vineyard in Burgundy that is one of the most famous in the world. Sells for hundreds per bottle. I didn't urinate on this vineyard. (See, it's a tradition to urinate in famous vineyards.)

Chaptalization – The process of adding sugar to the fermenting wine to raise the final alcohol level. Because the sugar is converted to alcohol, it does not add sweetness to the finished wine. It is used mostly in regions where grapes don't ripen fully.

Charmat – The process of making sparkling wine where the second fermentation happens in big tanks, instead of in the bottle like Champagne is made.

Chassagne-Montrachet (sha sahn yah mon rah shay) – A wine-producing area in Burgundy, making both white and red, but mostly you see white. Good stuff.

Chasselas – White wine grape variety most common in dry Swiss white wines.

Châteauneuf-du-Pape (sha toe nuff doo pop) – A red wine made in the southern region of the Rhône Valley. It is always made from a blend of grapes. Grenache is almost always at least 50% of the wine followed by Syrah, Mourvedre and Cinsault.

Chenin Blanc – The white grape that makes Vouvray from the Loire Valley in France. It's also grown in California and other regions. In South Africa, it is known as Steen.

Cheval Blanc, Château – Damn expensive wine from

Bordeaux. I'm sorry to say I've never had it. A personalized autographed copy of my book and other gifts to anyone who serves me a Cheval Blanc.

Chevalier Montrachet (sha vah l'ay mon trah shay) – A top-notch white Burgundy. The first one I ever knowingly had. It was one of the orgasmic wines of my life. I think the first white Burgundy I had was at the Mansion at Turtle Creek the night I had wine for the first time, but I'm not sure of that.

Chianti – Made from the Sangiovese grape in Tuscany. High in acidity and needs to be consumed with food.

Chinon (shi nahn) – A red wine made from the Cabernet Franc grape in the Loire Valley. Guzzling wine.

Cinsault (sahn so) – a red grape grown in the Languedoc region of France.

Claret   An old British term for red Bordeaux.

Classico – An Italian term that denotes the central part of a region. Chianti Classico vineyards are in the inner region of the Chianti region and are presumed to be superior sites ... but that's not necessarily the case.

Clos – An old term often used in French wine names that means a walled vineyard, like Clos de Vougeot, a famous Burgundy vineyard. (I did urinate there.)

Closed – When a wine is meant to age and opened up before its maturity, sometimes it will be "closed," meaning there isn't much to it. Breathing can bring it to life, if you're lucky. If not, you're dinked.

Cloying – Refers to ultra-sweet or sugary wines that lack the balance provided by acid.

Cold Duck – A superior wine that I consumed in grade school.

Colheita — A vintage Tawny Port

Concord — A native American grape. Probably my first taste of wine at the church I attended, where they used Mogen David Concord wine for communion. Not bad.

Condrieu (cohn drew) — A white wine made from the Viognier grape in the northern Rhône Valley.

Corbieres (cor b'air) — The name of the red wine and the region from the Languedoc in southern France. Made from Carignane, Cinsault, Grenache and other varietals. A good value. I can buy a Corbieres without worrying about the producer; and more times than not, get a bottle I like.

Corked — Describes a bottle of wine that is "off" due to the chemical trichloranisole (TCA) that is on a natural cork. My experience says about 10% of the wines I open are corked, more so from Europe than anywhere else.

Cornas — Wine region in northern Rhône that produces a red wine from the Syrah grape.

Cortese — White wine grape grown in the Piedmont region of Italy that makes the wine called Gavi.

Cosecha — Spanish word for "vintage."

Côte de Nuits (coat duh n'wee) — Mecca for wine. The northern part of Burgundy where reds are made that are the holy grail for wine enthusiasts.

Côte Rôtie — Expensive red wine from the northern Rhône Valley made from Syrah.

Côtes-du-Rhône — The broadest term for wine from Rhône Valley. Often a good value.

Crémant — A French term for a sparkling wine with half the fizz as Champagne.

Crianza — Spanish term for aged in oak.

Crozes-Hermitage (croz erm mee tahj) – A red wine from the northern Rhône made from the Syrah grape. Usually not worth the money.

Cuvée – A blend of grapes for a specific wine. Also a French term for vat.

Dao – A Portuguese wine region that makes some very nice reds. Worth a try.

Demi-Sec – Means "half-dry," but when it pertains to Champagne, it means sweet.

DOC or Denominazione di Origine Controllata (de nah mee na see own deh oh ree jeen ay con troh lah tah) – An Italian wine law that controls the production of wine in designated areas.

DOCG or Denominazione di Origine Controllata e Garantita (...eh gar rahn tee tah) Stricter than DOC, this stamp of approval only goes to wines that have been tasted by an official panel to guarantee their authenticity. Does not have anything to do with quality.

Dionysus – The Greek god of wine.

Dolcetto – A red Italian grape variety grown in the Piedmont region of Italy that makes easy-drinking red guzzling wine.

Domaine – French term meaning "estate," most often used in Burgundy.

Dosage (doh saj) – The process of adding a mixture of wine and sugar to Champagne just prior to closure. The amount of sugar added will determine if it is a Brut, Extra Dry, etc.

Douro (door oh) – The region in Portugal where Port comes from.

Dumb – Me, for taking on this book project. But in wine it

means a wine that is closed, not showing its true potential. Usually a temporary condition.

Echézeaux (eh sheh zo) – A big time vineyard in Burgundy for red wine.

Egri Bikavér (eh gree bee kah vair) — Also called Bull's Blood, this red wine from Hungary got its name from the Hungarian soldiers defense of the Turks near the city of Eger. The Hungarian soldiers were supposedly loaded up on this wine.

Eiswein (icc vine) – The German term for wine made from frozen grapes.

Est! Est!! Est!!! di Montefiascone – A wimpy white from Italy. Catchy name, though. The name comes from the story of a German bishop on his way to Rome who sent ahead a scout to find some wine. The scout was told to write the word Est (Latin for it is) on the side of any bar where he found good wine. At one spot he wrote Est! Est!! Est!!!, and when the bishop arrived, he loved the wine so much he spent the rest of his life there.

Extra Dry – A sweetness level of Champagne that is actually sweeter than Brut.

Faugeres (fo jehr) – A red wine made in the south of France from Carignan, Grenache and Cinsault. Always a pretty good bet.

Fitou (fee too) – Another red from the south of France, made like Faugeres.

Fixin (fee san) – A red wine area in Burgundy that makes pretty good wine, certainly a lot less expensive that some of the bigger name Burgundies.

Free-Run Juice – The juice that comes out of a grape with no or minimal pressing. It's the best of all the juice. A great wine might be made from only free-run juice.

Frizzante (frih zahn tay) – Means fizzy. Half the bubbles of regular sparkling wine. Moscato d'Asti is *frizzante*.

Fumé Blanc – A term made up by Robert Mondavi in the late 1960s as an alternative to Sauvignon Blanc (which it is). I guess he thought Fumé Blanc would be easier to pronounce. Only in California is the term used, and it usually means a Sauvignon Blanc that has been put in oak barrels.

Furmint – A Hungarian white wine grape used to make Tokay.

Gamay – The red grape that makes Beaujolais.

Garnacha (gar nahtch ah) – A Spanish term for the Grenache red wine grape.

Gattinara (gat tin nahr ah) – A red wine made from the Nebbiolo grape from Piedmont Italy. Can be a decent wine and a savings vs. buying a Barolo.

Gavi (gah vee) – A white wine around the city of Gavi in the Piedmont region in Italy made from the Cortese grape.

Gevery-Chambertin (jev ree shaum ber ten) — A well-known sub-region of Burgundy.

Gewurztraminer (ge wurtz trah mih ner) — A white grape that makes a very floral smelling wine that is off-dry and spicy. It's one of those wines that either you really like or really hate.

Gigondas (jee gohn das) – A red wine region in the Rhône valley made from the typical Rhône blend of Grenache, Syrah, Cinsault, etc. Used to be a good value, but it's been getting a little pricy lately.

Givry (jiv ree) – A small sub region of Burgundy where the wine is often more competively priced compared to wines from other sub-regions. One wine that I see around pretty often is Marc Joblot's Givry. (Yep, his name is pronounced "joe blow," basically. Fun to say. My friend threw up in his home. He makes nice wine.)

Grappa – To me it tastes like lighter fluid. An Italian spirit distilled from the skins of grapes.

Gran Reserva – The Spanish term for a wine that must be aged a minimum of five years, two of which must be in wood barrels.

Grand Cru (grahn crew) – The French term for great growth, the top of the line in wine.

Graves – A sub-region of Bordeaux that can produce some killer whites and reds.

Grenache – The red wine grape that is grown in southern France. It is the primary grape in Châteauneuf-du-Pape.

Grüner Veltliner (grew ner velt lee ner) – A white grape grown in Austria that can be very tasty and a great value. I've never had a Grüner I didn't like.

Halbtrocken (halb troke kin) – A German wine label term that means "half dry."

Haut-Brion, Château (oh bree on) – One of the top wines of Bordeaux. Silly expensive, but always good.

Haut-Medoc – A sub-region within Bordeaux. A wine labeled Haut-Medoc means the grapes used to make it can come from anywhere in the region.

Hectare (heck tair) – The metric measure of land equivalent to 2.741 acres.

Hermitage (erm ih taj) – A famous wine region in the northern Rhône Valley. The red wine is made from 100% Syrah.

Johannisberg Riesling (jo han iss berg ree sling) – A name given to Rieslings to denote they are sweet Rieslings.

Joey - one of my dogs I got from the shelter. He's a cutie.

Kabinett — The German wine label term for the lowest ripeness grapes at picking.

La Tache (la tash) — The wine that I had at the Inn at Little Washington. This is a vineyard entirely owned by Domaine de la Romanée-Conti. I just did a quick price check on the 1990, for which I paid $500 for at the Inn. I found it for $2,500 per bottle. Looks like I got a deal.

Lacryma Christi del Vesuvio — Translated, "the tears of Christ." Still sold in stores here, but nowhere near as famous as years ago. It's a white wine that doesn't have much to it, but the name is catchy, like Est! Est!! Est!!!

Lambrusco — An Italian sparkling red wine from the Lambrusco grape.

Languedoc (lang gwa doc) — A region in the south of France that offers great value reds.

Lees — The sediment remaining in a barrel or tank after fermentation, which is generally composed of dead yeast cells and small grape particles.

Legs — Term used to describe the droplets left on the inside of the glass after swirling, that ease down the surface as tears or "legs." The legs give no indication of quality.

Liebfraumilch (leeb frow milsh) — A German white wine; when translated, means, "milk of the Blessed Mother."

Maceration — Soaking the grapes' skins in with the juice to extract color and tannin from the skins.

Macon — A large sub-region of Burgundy that is known for good, modest table wines.

Madeira — Portuguese island in the Atlantic, about 400 miles off the coast of Morocco that produces an interesting fortified wine of the same name.

Malbec – A red-wine grape used in making Bordeaux, which has become more famous for the wines it's making in Argentina.

Malolactic Fermentation – A secondary fermentation occurring in most bottled wines which converts malic acid into lactic acid and makes a wine smoother, less acidic.

Malvasia – One of the most ancient of Italy's white-wine grape varieties. It is said to be a member of the Muscat family, which is often blended with other grapes, including the traditional Chianti. Also seen as a 100 percent varietal.

Marc – A distilled spirit made in all parts of the world from pomace, generally consumed after dinner.

Margaux, Château – One of the great wines of Bordeaux.

Marsanne (mar sahn) – A white grape grown in the south of France.

Master of Wine – A title bestowed by the Institute of Masters of Wine, which is hard to get and lets folks know that you know a lot about wine. I've seen Masters of Wine who couldn't recognize a corked bottle. Go figure.

Meritage (mer ih tij) – Everyone always wants to say Meritahj, but it is supposed to rhyme with Heritage as it is a combination of merit and heritage. This term was invented by California wineries to describe a wine that uses the same grapes as are used in Bordeaux: Cabernet Sauvignon, Merlot, Cabernet Franc, Petite Verdot and Malbec.

Méthode Champenoise – French term for how Champagne is made, with the second fermentation happening in the bottle that is sold on the shelf.

Meursault (mehr so) – Typically a white wine from

Burgundy, which can be very good. Great match with lobster.

Minervois (min er vwah) – A red wine made in the Languedoc region in the south of France. It's almost a can't-lose wine, and at a low price too. I don't remember ever having a bad one.

Monastrell (mon as strel) – A red grape grown in Spain and, the wines made from this grape are becoming more visible on wine shops' shelves. Usually a good value.

Montepulciano d'Abruzzo (mon the pool chee ahn no dah broot zoh) – Fun to say once you get the hang of it. This is another red wine that is a sure winner. It's hard to find a bad one, and it's reasonably priced.

Montrachet (mon rah shay) — This vineyard in Burgundy is one of the most famous for great white wine. It has an arch right off the road that everyone urinates on as part of the tradition, myself included.

Mosel-Saar-Ruwer (mo zle sahr roo ver) — One of the major German wine regions.

Mourvedre (more vay dreh) — A red grape grown in the south of France that is part of the Rhône blend.

Muscadet (mus cah day) – A dry white wine high in acidity made in the Loire Valley that is a great wine with oysters on the half-shell.

Muscat – A white grape planted all over the world, which is used to make all types of wine from sparkling, dry table wine, dessert wine, etc.

Nahe (nah huh) – A major German wine region.

Nebbiolo – The grape grown in the Piedmont region of Italy that makes Barolo and Barbaresco wines as well as others.

Negoçiant (neh go see ahnt) — A French term used to describe wine merchants who buy grapes and vinify them, or buys wines and combines them with their own wines to bottle and sell under their own label. Most common in Burgundy.

Nuits-Saint-George (new ee san johrj) — A sub-region of Burgundy that makes some great red wines.

Oenophile (ee no file) — A wine lover.

Orvieto — The name of an ancient town in Umbria, Italy that produces a dry white wine.

Passito (pas see toe) — An Italian winemaking process whereby harvested grapes are dried before being pressed to concentrate the sugars prior to fermentation.

Pauillac (paw yack) — A town in Bordeaux whose boundaries encompass some of the greatest vineyards of Bordeaux.

Penedes (peh neh dez) — A Spanish wine district near Barcelona.

Petite Sirah — A red grape variety, most widely grown in California, not to be confused with the true Syrah of the Rhône Valley of France.

Petit Verdot — Red wine grape variety most often grown in Bordeaux and used for blending with Cabernet Sauvignon.

Pétrus, Château (peh troos) — The most famous vineyard of Pomerol, a sub-region of Bordeaux. Pétrus costs a mint.

Phylloxera (fil lox er ah) — An insect that attacks and kills wine roots. Tiny aphids or root lice that attack *Vitis vinifera* roots and can devastate entire vineyards.

Picpoul (peek pool) — A white grape grown in the south of France. The wine is a great value for a light-bodied everyday wine.

Pinot Blanc — A white grape variety when made in

America, tastes like a Chardonnay. I don't get it.

Pinot Gris/Pinot Grigio — Same grape.

Pinot Meunier (pce no mew nyay) — The "other" red grape blended with Pinot Noir and Chardonnay to make Champagne.

Pinot Noir — Made famous because of the movie *Sideways*. Pinot Noir makes wines that are the Holy Grail for wine lovers.

Pinotage (pee no tahj) — A red grape that is a cross between Pinot Noir and Cinsaut, grown mostly in South Africa.

Plonk — A British term for simple, "ordinary" wine. Only wine geeks use the term plonk.

Pomerol — A sub-region in Bordeaux where mostly Merlot-based wines are produced.

Porter - Another of my dogs I adopted. Born on the same day as Squiggy....same mother, different fathers. Pouilly-Fuissé (poo ee fwee say) — A white Burgundy made from the Chardonnay grape.

Pouilly-Fumé (poo ce fu may) — A white wine from the Loire Valley made from the Sauvignon Blanc grape.

Primitivo — An Italian red grape thought to be the father of Zinfandel, but that was proven incorrect.

Priorato — A Spanish wine region that makes big, powerful red wines from the Garnacha grape.

Prosecco   An Italian white grape and the name of the sparkling wine it makes.

Punt - The dimple on the bottom of the bottle.

Puttonyos (poo tun yos) — The Hungarian term for the baskets used during the harvest to pick the overripe grapes to make Tokay. The number of baskets of grapes in the vat determines how sweet the wine will be. On the label it will say 1-6 puttonyos, with six being the sweetest.

Quincy (keen say) – A type of wine made from the Sauvignon Blanc grape in the Loire Valley. Similar to Sancerre, but a little more lively and not as complex.

Recioto (reh chee oh toe) – An Italian term for spreading the grapes on trays after harvest to age for several months until they are shriveled, which concentrates the juice. The result is a very sweet wine called Recioto della Valpolicella.

Reserva – A Spanish term relating to a wine that was aged for at least three years, including one year in wood barrels, before being released.

Residual Sugar – The amount of sugar left in a wine after fermentation.

Retsina – A Greek white wine that is flavored with resin. Whose idea was that? "Hey Cletus, this wine doesn't taste very good. Let's add some pine resin so it tastes like turpentine." Oh yeah. That's much better.

Reuilly (roo ee) – Another Sauvigon Blanc from the Loire Valley.

Rheingau (rine gau) – A German wine region along the Rhine River.

Rheinhessen – Another German wine region.

Rheinpfalz (rine faltz) – And the last "R" German wine region.

Rhône – French wine region.

Ribera del Duero – A Spanish wine region that specializes in reds made from the Tempranillo and Garnacha grapes. Rivals Rioja. The most famous winery in Spain, Vega Sicilia, is based here. I was doing a TV show on a small cable channel in Washington, D.C. when I first started off in wine. The owners of Vega Sicilia came to town and I asked to interview them. I had never heard of Vega Sicilia. (Hey, I was new in the wine world.) I found out from the sales rep that it was the most expensive Spanish wine.

I met the owners in their hotel room. It was cable access, like "Wayne's World," so I didn't have a crew. I carried in my camcorder and tripod, a microphone and some lights I had picked up at Home Depot. They looked at each other as if I was a joke. Well, I was. I guess they were used to being interviewed by real reporters with real equipment. My first question was why their wine cost so much. They were so offended they called off the interview.

Riesling (rees ling) – A white grape that can make a dry, off-dry or dessert wine.

Rioja – Wine region of northern Spain. Rioja is made from the Tempranillo and Garnacha grapes.

Ripasso – An Italian winemaking process where fermented wine is put into tanks with old grape skins, giving the wine more body.

Riserva – Italian term that means the wine was aged at least three years.

Rosé – A blush wine usually made from red grapes. The clear juice is in contact with the skins for just a short time, just long enough to turn the clear juice to a pinkish color.

Rosso di Montalcino (ross oh deem on tal chee no) – Often considered a "baby" Brunello, as it's made from the same grape and in the same region, but it is isn't aged as long as a Brunello and can be sold a year after the harvest. Usually a pretty good deal.

Rousanne – White grape grown in the northern Rhône Valley of France, most often used for blending with the white wine grape Marsanne.

Rueda (roo ay dah) — A white wine made in Spain from the Verdejo and Viura grapes.

Rully (roo ee) – A small sub-region of Burgundy that produces both red and white.

Saint-Chinian (sahn shin nee ahn) – Wine region of the Languedoc area of southern France that are good values.

Saint-Emilion (san tee mee l'yon) – Bordeaux sub-region where the wines are made from mostly Merlot.

Saint-Estèphe – The northernmost Bordeaux sub-region that has a few big name wineries, including Châteaux Cos d'Estournel, Montrose, Calon-Ségur, etc. An area of northern Haut-Medoc in the Bordeaux region.

Saint-Joseph (sahn jo sef) – A sub-region of the northern Rhône that is made from 100% Syrah.

Sancerre (sahn sair) – A sub-region of the Loire where both white and red wines are made. The white is more famous than the red. The white is made from the Sauvignon Blanc grape and is a classic match with goat cheese. The red is made from the Pinot Noir grape.

Sangiovese (san jee oh vay zee) – The principal grape of Chianti, Vino Nobile di Montepulicano and Carmignano wines from Tuscany. Usually pretty high in acidity.

Sassicaia (sa sah ky ah) – One of the first "Super Tuscans." Made from mostly Cabernet Sauvignon.

Sauternes (saw turn) – A Bordeaux sub-region where a sweet wine by the same name is produced from the Sauvignon Blanc and Semillon grapes that have been infected with the noble rot.

Sauvignon Blanc – Noble, white grape variety grown in the Loire and Bordeaux regions of France, with plantings now in other regions, including, California, New Zealand, Australia. Usually blended with Semillon grapes, and varies in style, but generally speaking produces soft, assertive, herbaceous, sometimes complex wines.

Sekt – German term for sparkling wine that is usually produced by using the *charmat* process.

Seyval Blanc – A hybrid grape that is widely used in the eastern US.

Soave (swah vay) – A white wine made in Italy from the Garganega grape.

Sommelier (som mel yay) – A wine steward in a restaurant.

Spätlese (shpayt lay sah) – The German term meaning "late harvest, late picked," and referring to white wines made with sweeter, late-harvested grapes.

Spumante (spu mahn the) — Italian term meaning "foaming," and referring to sparkling wines.

Squiggy - A dog I adopted. 50 pounds but actually chased down a baby deer and killed it. He was so happy! Died from drinking antifreeze left out by a neighbor.

Steen – The South African name for the Chenin Blanc grape.

Sur Lie – French term meaning "on the lees" and referring to the technique/method of storing wine, prior to bottling, in the yeast sediment and grape particles (lees) from the fermentation, producing a more complex wine.

Sylvaner – German grape, generally of lesser quality than Riesling and usually planted as a blending grape.

Tannin – The compound from the skin of the grape that dries out your mouth. It also is the aging ingredient in red wine.

Tartaric Acid — The prominent natural acid in wine.

Tartrates — Harmless crystals that often form on a cork, or in a bottle or cask, that are composed of potassium bitartrate from the tartaric acid naturally present in wine.

Tastevin (taht van) — A small, shallow, usually polished silver cup used by wine stewards or sommeliers in a restaurant for tasting wine; originally used in the Burgundy region of France.

Tavel (tah vel) — The most famous rosé of France made from the Grenache grape.

Tawny Port — A port aged in small wood barrels, giving it a nutty taste.

Tears — see Legs.

Tempranillo (tem prah nee oh) — A red grape grown in Spain that plays a major role in many Spanish wines.

Terroir — A French term that describes the characteristics of a particular vineyard to include the climate, soil and location.

Tokay — Dessert wine from Hungary.

Trebbiano — An Italian white-wine grape.

Trocken (tro ken) — German label term meaning "dry."

Trockenbeerenauslese (tro ken bair en ows lay sah), or TBA — A monster word that combines *Auslese*, meaning "special selection;" *Beeren*, meaning left on the vine until the grapes shrivel up, and *Trocken*, which means dry (that the grapes are on the vine so long they are practically dry). TBAs are very sweet and expensive.

Ugni Blanc (oo nee blahn) — A white-wine grape grown in France generally producing crisp, fruity white wines. In Italy called Trebbiano.

Ullage – The empty space in a wine bottle between the bottom of the cork and the surface of the wine. When buying an older wine, one should see if the ullage has grown, which means that the wine probably is oxidized.

Vacqueyras (va keh rahss) – A sub-region of the Rhône that makes a red wine from the typical Rhône blend of grapes.

Valpolicella (val pole ih chell ah) – A red wine from northern Italy. It's usually pretty light bodied.

Vendange – French term for "vintage."

Vendimia – Spanish term for "vintage."

Veneto – Wine region in Northeastern Italy, in the area of both Venice and Verona.

Verdicchio (ver dick ee oh) – Italian white-wine grape from Central Italy, generally producing a light-bodied, somewhat crisp white wine.

Vermouth – A fortified wine, white or red, that has been flavored with the addition of aromatic herbs or spices and is most often used as an aperitif or in the mixing of cocktails.

Vernaccia di San Gimignano (ver nah chah dee san jee mee yahn no) – A dry white wine made in Tuscany.

Vidal Blanc (voe dal blan) – A hybrid grape grown mostly in the eastern US.

Vin Doux Naturel (van doo nah too rel) – A category of fortified wines mostly from the south of France.

Vin de Pays (vahn duh pay yee) – The lowest level of French wine by category. There are many *vin de pays* regions. The one you'll most often see is Vin de pays d'Oc, which is in the southern part of France.

Vin Doux Naturel – Sweet French wine that has been fortified by the addition of brandy.

Vin Santo (veen sahn toe) – An Italian dessert wine made from the Trebbiano and Malvasia grapes.

Vinho Verde – White or red wines from the northern part of Portugal that are meant to be consumed young. Literally means "green wine."

Vino Nobile di Montepulciano (vee no no bee lay dee mon teh pool chea no) — Fun to say, and it's a pretty good value red wine from Tuscany.

Viognier (vee oh n'yay) – A white grape that is grown in the Rhône, and now quite a bit in the US. It makes wine with an aroma of honey, apricot and peach.

Volnay (vohl nay) – A sub-region of Burgundy that makes some great red wines.

Vosne-Romanée (vone roh mah nee) – Another sub-region of Burgundy, and this too has some great red wines.

Vouvray (voov ray) – A white wine made in the Loire Valley. It can be made dry, sweet or bubbly. An underappreciated wine.

Weissburgunder (vice boor gun der) – The Austrian and German name for Pinot Blanc.

Welschriesling (velsh ree sling) – A white grape grown in Austria. Not related to Riesling.

D'Yquem, Château (dee kem) – The most famous Sauternes.

Zweigelt (ts'vite gelt) – An Austrian red grape that is a cross between Blaufränkish and St-Laurent.

Notes

Notes